The Imperial Japanese Navy

Frederick Thomas Jane

Nabu Public Domain Reprints:

You are holding a reproduction of an original work published before 1923 that is in the public domain in the United States of America, and possibly other countries. You may freely copy and distribute this work as no entity (individual or corporate) has a copyright on the body of the work. This book may contain prior copyright references, and library stamps (as most of these works were scanned from library copies). These have been scanned and retained as part of the historical artifact.

This book may have occasional imperfections such as missing or blurred pages, poor pictures, errant marks, etc. that were either part of the original artifact, or were introduced by the scanning process. We believe this work is culturally important, and despite the imperfections, have elected to bring it back into print as part of our continuing commitment to the preservation of printed works worldwide. We appreciate your understanding of the imperfections in the preservation process, and hope you enjoy this valuable book.

THE IMPERIAL JAPANESE NAVY

[Photo by favour of Commander Takarabé, I.J.N.

THE BATTLESHIP CHIN YEN.

(The principal capture in the Chino-Japanese War.) [Frontispiece.

THE IMPERIAL JAPANESE NAVY

BY

FRED. T. JANE

AUTHOR OF
"THE IMPERIAL RUSSIAN NAVY"
"ALL THE WORLD'S FIGHTING SHIPS" (NAVAL ANNUAL), ETC.
INVENTOR OF THE JANE NAVAL WAR GAME (NAVAL KRIEGSPIEL)
ETC., ETC.

ASSISTED BY OFFICERS OF THE JAPANESE NAVY

WITH OVER 80 ILLUSTRATIONS FROM SKETCHES AND DRAWINGS
BY JAPANESE ARTISTS AND FROM OFFICIAL PHOTOGRAPHS

London

W. THACKER & CO., 2, CREED LANE, E.C.
CALCUTTA AND SIMLA: THACKER, SPINK & CO.
1904

All rights reserved

VA 653
J33

TO
MANY FRIENDS
NOW SERVING IN THE JAPANESE
FLEET, AND TO THE MEMORY OF
OTHERS WHO HAVE
DIED DOING THEIR DUTY
THIS VOLUME IS
DEDICATED

PREFACE

THIS book is uniform with my similar book on the Russian Navy, and is designed to have an exactly similar scope; that is to say, it traces the Japanese Navy from the earliest period up to the time of the outbreak of the war with Russia in February, 1904. It then deals with the dockyards of Japan, the armament and equipment of her Fleet, with her *personnel*, both officers and men, and finally with all those side issues and semi-political questions which have brought the modern Japanese Fleet into existence and governed the Japanese building programme. In an Appendix, certain matters that may seem to demand detailed attention are dealt with separately.

In preparing this book for the press—a task that I began so long ago as the year 1900—I have received the most kind and willing assistance of a great many personal friends in the Fleet of "Britain's ally." To them I would express my most cordial thanks. Especially would I mention my indebtedness in various— I might say innumerable—ways to Admirals Yamamoto Gombey, Dewa, Kamimura, Ito, and Ijuin; Captains Yamada, Uchida, Kawashima, and Kashiwabara; Commanders Kuroi, Takarabé, Hirose, Takeshita,

Yamanaka; Lieut.-Commanders Nomaguchi, Hideshima, Sato, Horiuchi; Staff-Paymaster Minuma; Lieutenants Ishikawa, Yamamoto, Yamagi, Fukura, Matsui, Sasaki; Engineer-Lieutenant Kimura; Chief-Constructor Matsuo; Constructor Kondo; and a great many others—all personal friends, to whose suggestions it is due that I came to write this book at all.

I am neither pro-Japanese nor pro-Russian. As I write, disaster is thick upon the Russian Fleet, and to many close friends in it go those sympathies which, had things been the other way about, would have gone as surely to the Japanese Fleet. To write this book without bias has been my special aim; and in view of the enthusiastic admiration which the Japanese Fleet is now evoking in the Anglo-Saxon world, I have especially tried not to be blind to such defects as the Japanese Navy may exhibit. This, however, is obvious in the body of the book, and needs no mention here, any more than reference is required in this Preface to the courage and skill which Japanese sailors have shown.

Portions of some of the chapters have, in some form or other, appeared in the *Engineer*, *Daily Chronicle*, *Daily Mail*, *Fortnightly Review*, *Collier's Weekly*, or *Forum*. To the editors of these papers I desire to make the usual acknowledgments,

F. T. J.

PORTSMOUTH.
1904.

CONTENTS

	PAGE
PREFACE	ix
I. EARLY HISTORY	1
II. THE OPENING OF JAPAN	13
III. EARLY WARSHIPS AND THE CIVIL WAR	21
IV. THE IMPERIAL NAVY	36
V. THE WAR WITH CHINA	101
VI. THE BATTLE OF YALU	115
VII. WEI-HAI-WEI	156
VIII. AFTER THE WAR WITH CHINA	168
IX. THE NEW PROGRAMME	218
X. THE JAPANESE DOCKYARDS	234
1. Yokosuka . 234 4. Sassebo	238
2. Tokio . 236 5. Maitzuru	241
3. Kuré . 237	
XI. NAVAL HARBOURS	242
1. Nagasaki . 242 4. Kobé	246
2. Takeshiki . 244 5. Kuré	246
3. Ominato . 245	
XII. THE MERCANTILE MARINE	249
XIII. THE JAPANESE ADMIRALTY	252
XIV. ENTRY AND TRAINING OF OFFICERS	257
XV. ENTRY AND TRAINING OF MEN	265
XVI. PAY, ETC.	267
XVII. FLAGS	275
XVIII. UNIFORMS, ETC.	276
XIX. PERSONAL CHARACTERISTICS OF OFFICERS	278
XX. PERSONAL CHARACTERISTICS OF MEN	303
XXI. MESSING	309
XXII. THE ARMAMENT AND EQUIPMENT OF THE FLEET	313
1. Guns . 313 4. Armour	329
2. Gunnery Accessories . 322 5. Engines and Boilers	330
3. Torpedoes . 325	
XXIII. OTHER NAVIES AS SEEN BY THE JAPANESE	337
XXIV. THE WAR WITH RUSSIA	340

CONTENTS

	PAGE
APPENDICES—	
OFFICIAL REPORTS, CHINO-JAPANESE WAR	359
LIST OF JAPANESE WARSHIPS	394
JAPANESE SHIP-NAMES (MEANINGS)	398
HISTORICAL SHIP-NAMES	402
A JAPANESE "AT HOME"	403
INDEX TO SUBJECT-MATTER	407

LIST OF ILLUSTRATIONS

	PAGE
The Battleship Chin Yen (*photograph*)	*Frontispiece*
Map of Japan	3
The Tsukuba	20
The Fuji Yama	23
The Adsuma	27
Japanese Officers in 1866	30
The Moisshin	31
The Asama	33
Battle of Hakodate (*from a Japanese print*)	37
The Seiki	41
Japanese Fleet at Manœuvres (*photograph*)	45
The Chin Yen at Evolutions (*photograph*)	51
The Tsukushi (*photograph*)	55
The Esmeralda (now Idzumi) (*plan*)	58
The Naniwa (*photograph*)	61
The Naniwa (*plan*)	63
The Sai Yen (*photograph and plan*)	65
The Fuso at Sea (*photograph*)	69
The Unebi	75
The Tschichima	79
The Hashidate (*photograph*)	83
The Matsushima (*photograph*)	83
The Hei Yen (*photograph*)	87
The Chiyoda (*photograph*)	89
The Chiyoda (*plan*)	91
The Akitsushima (*photograph*)	93
The Akitsushima (*plan*)	95
The Yoshino (*plan*)	96

THE IMPERIAL JAPANESE NAVY

I

EARLY HISTORY

THE earliest Japanese history, like that of all other nations, is a mass of myths and legends. But out of this one solid fact has been evolved: the Japanese were a race who invaded the island kingdom by way of Korea, much as the Saxons and other Teutonic tribes invaded Britain. They therefore used the sea at a very early period of their history.

They found aboriginal tribes when they came, and of these the Ainu still exist in the north, a race as distinct as our Celts in the north of Scotland. The immigrant race are always spoken of and accepted as Mongolians, though in Japanese legend the invaders had, as in similar Western myths, a divine origin. Incidentally, it is interesting to note that a Japanese, with kindred tastes to those Western *savants* who have found the cradle of the human race in Lapland or in Central Africa, has built a theory by which ancient Egypt was the early home of the Japanese. To support this theory numerous small similarities were brought forward; but it does not seem to have made headway in Japan, or to be known in the Western world. It is, as regards plausibility, about on a par with the Anglo-Israelite theory that had once quite a vogue in this country, and is by no means without disciples to-day.

Whence they came, however, is a matter of no moment here. Japanese national history begins with the expedition led by the Emperor Jimmu, at a date which a loose chronology fixes at 660 B.C. This is the earliest over-sea operation unconnected with deities and myths.

Jimmu, who, according to the legends, was the grandson of the Sea Deity's daughter, led an expedition eastward from Mount Takachiho, and eventually found himself on the shores of the Inland Sea, and here built a fleet, by means of which he reached Naniwa (Osaka), and consolidated the empire.

For the next seven or eight centuries the nation was forming; but beyond a legend, suggestive of the story of Jonah, nothing is heard of ships or boats till 202 A.D., when the Empress Jingo equipped a great fleet for the invasion of Korea. As an early instance of the use of "sea-power," this expedition has laid great hold on Japanese imagination; but since the transportation of the flagship by legions of fishes, with which the Empress has made an alliance, is the central point of the story, its nautical details can hardly be seriously considered. What is of more moment is the undoubted fact that the expedition took place, that it was a complete success for Japan, and laid the

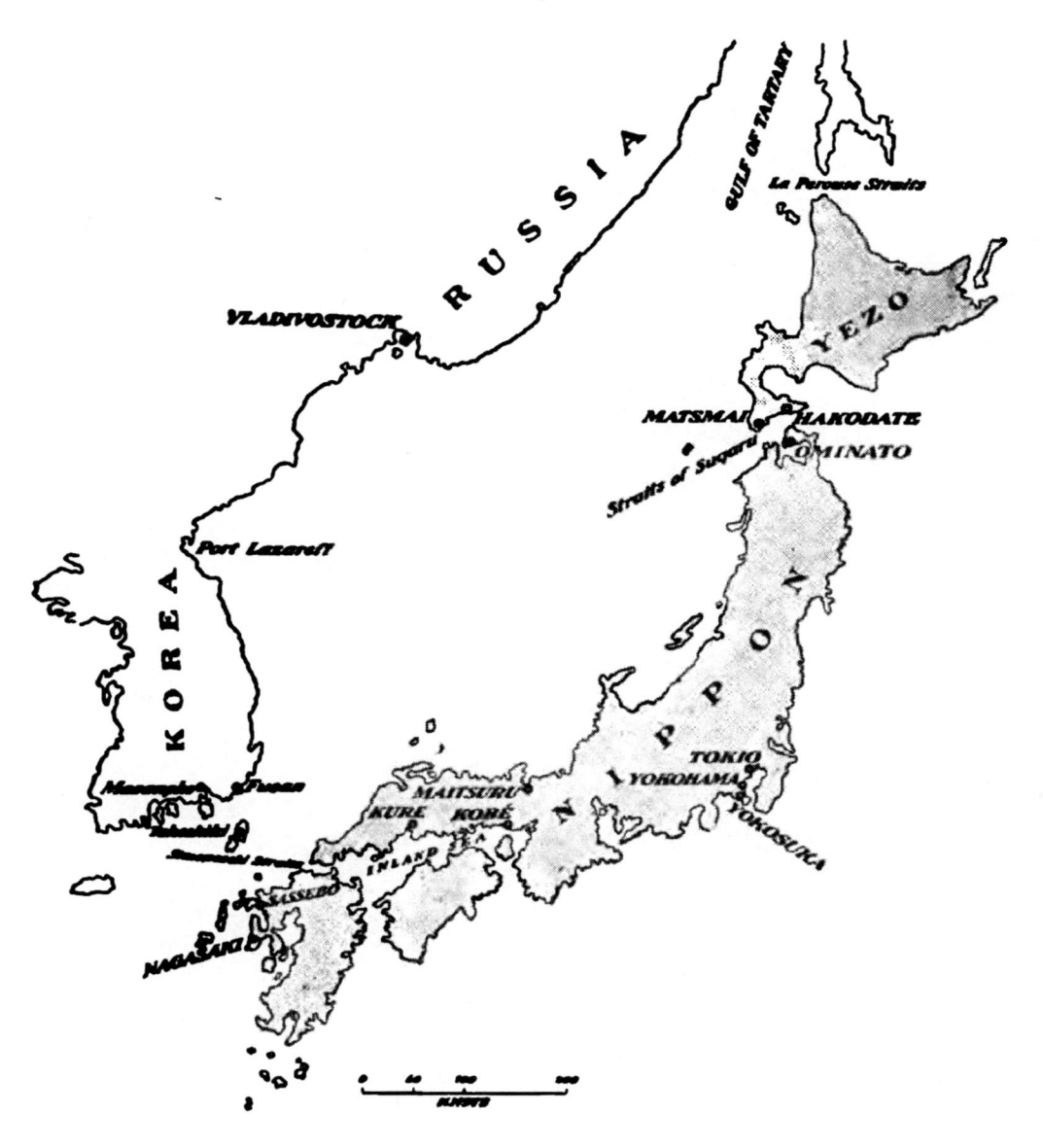

MAP OF JAPAN.

foundations of that Japanese interest in Korea which is to-day so potent a factor in the Far Eastern problem.

Korea paid tribute without question for some three hundred years. About the year 520, however, the Emperor Keitai Tenno collected a fleet, and conducted some operations against the Koreans that served to tighten Japan's hold on her over-sea possessions. From this time onward for the next two or three hundred years Japan grew as a trading nation, and intercourse with both Korea and China became common. As in those days every merchant ship became a warship when required, Japan must have ranked as a considerable naval power.

As for the ships, these may have been either mere boats or small coasting junks, probably differing very little from the boats and junks of the present day.

About the year 650 Japanese garrisons were driven out of Korea by hostile tribes, assisted by the Chinese, and with the expelled Japanese came many Koreans, an immigration that continued for some considerable period.

In the middle of the ninth century the Samaurii, or military caste, whose descendants to-day provide the bulk of naval officers, first began to arise. The Shoguns, afterwards to become such a power, were originally generals, there being one in command of each of the four military districts into which the Emperor Sujin had divided Japan. A Shogun with any special powers did not arise till the year 1200 or so, when Yoshinaka made himself *Sei-i-Shogun* (Chief Shogun).

As he was driven to suicide soon afterwards in the civil war then desolating the empire, the post did not convey any great advantage to him; but Yorimoto, whose troops had defeated him, became after a time *Sei-i-tai-Shogun* (great barbarian compelling Shogun). This civil war—between the Taira and the Minamoto clans—culminated in a naval battle. The former are credited with 500 junks, which, in addition to the soldiers, were crowded with women and children and the fugitive emperor. At Dan-no-ura, on the Inland Sea, these were overtaken by the Minamoto with 700 vessels, and the smaller fleet was annihilated. This decisive action ended the civil war, but it created the system of Shogun rule, whereby all the governing of the country was in the hands of Yoritomo, the Emperor being a mere figure-head and puppet in his hands.

The descendants of Yorimoto, as Shoguns *de jure*, did not exercise much power *de facto*, for regents (the Hojo) acted for them. In time, too, tutors came to act for the regents, and under this condition of government, plunged into a species of anarchy, Japan faced the great Chinese invasion of 1281.

Having resolved on the capture of Japan, the Chinese sent envoys demanding its surrender. These, after being sent from pillar to post in a search for the real governing power, were eventually killed by the populace. The Chinese then prepared a fleet of 300 of their own and Korean ships, added the Japanese sun to the consuming dragon on the Chinese flag, and invaded to consummate the capture. On the water they encountered no opposition, but on landing they were met and defeated by the Japanese, united in the presence of a common danger. A great storm at the same time destroyed the hostile fleet, and the invasion was at an end.

It was followed by more internal strife, till in 1333 the Hojo were finally put down. Shortly afterwards the chief power came into the hands of the Shoguns.

Despite the civil warfare, Japan still made headway as a maritime State. Trade and piracy were conducted not only with Korea and China, but Japanese vessels sailed regularly to the distant shores of Siam.

In 1542 the Portuguese first came into touch with Japan. Three cannon were presented to the Shogun, and a little later Pinto arrived on the scene, and taught the manufacture of gunpowder. Jesuits followed, and made such headway that in the next civil war the Christian Japanese, to the number of 600,000 or more, were a strong political factor.

In 1587 Hideyoshi the *Taikio*, the *de facto* ruler of Japan, issued an edict against the Christians, many missionaries were expelled, and the ports open to foreign vessels were finally limited to one only, Nagasaki, as at that time the suspicion first began that soldiers would presently follow the missionaries.

About the same period Hideyoshi, who had designs upon China and Korea, began to prepare warships.

He also endeavoured to create a fleet of European-built ships, but the traders whom he approached on the matter refused to sell their vessels. He had, therefore, to content himself with a junk navy, which was raised much as fleets were raised in England at the same period, by levies upon the coast districts. The princes of these districts were required to furnish sailors to man the ships that they provided.

The invasion of Korea was carried out by two divisions, the first of which, under Konishi, reached Fusan on April 13, 1592. The town, which had for some two hundred years been used as a Japanese trading port, was easily captured, and the army then marched to the capital. The fleet lay inactive at Fusan for some time, but Konishi, in the midst of a victorious career on land, presently conceived the idea of using his fleet also. It was, therefore, sent round to the westward, where it met a Korean fleet.

The Koreans, whose ships were constructionally superior, made out to sea, and the Japanese following, sustained a defeat that caused them to retire to Fusan again.

After this Chinese troops appeared in large numbers, and, though the invaders won a few battles, they were checked, and compelled to fall back.

Peace negotiations were opened in 1596, but these fell through, and in 1597 130,000 fresh Japanese troops were sent to Korea.

In the latter part of this same year the Korean fleet attempted to force the harbour of Fusan, but was signally defeated by the Japanese vessels. Most of the attacking fleet were destroyed. No headway was, however, made by the Japanese land force, and in 1598 the expedition withdrew.

In the year 1600 William Adams, an Englishman, reached Japan, and, though for a time imprisoned at the instigation of the Jesuits, he eventually gained liberty and consideration from Ieyasu, the Shogun. He built for the Shogun, first a small 18-tonner, and then, in 1609, a ship of 120 tons. In this ship some Spaniards who had been wrecked on the east coast of Japan were sent to Acapulco. They appear to have navigated themselves, and the vessel was kept, but a much larger ship was sent to the Shogun as a present in return for his kindness.

In 1611, owing to Adams's partiality for the Dutch, these secured from the Shogun permission to trade with any port in the country. A little later the British East India Company secured the same advantages, but, owing to the outbreak of war between England and Holland, a good deal of isolated fighting took place between the traders, till it ended in the withdrawal or destruction of the English.

In 1614 the Japanese ruler began to be thoroughly alarmed at the progress of Christianity, and the expected advent of Portuguese soldiers to take possession of the land. All foreign Christians were ordered to leave the country, all native ones to renounce their creed. In 1616 the majority of Christians who still held to their faith were disposed of by the same means that in Europe were used to ensure conversion to Christianity.

In 1637 a revolution broke out amongst some of the Samaurai, or soldier class, who had been compelled to become farmers. Such Christians as had survived the massacres joined these.

After some defeats, the rebels were shut up in a large deserted castle at Hara, where 160,000 men besieged them. A tremendous defence was made, and the besiegers, failing to make much headway, applied for and secured aid from the Dutch factory at Hivado. Guns were lent, and finally a Dutch warship, the de Ryp, 20 guns, bombarded the castle from the bay, without, however, effecting its reduction. Eventually the castle was taken, and practically the whole garrison executed.

In 1640 the rivalry between the Dutch and Portuguese, of which the Dutch assistance against the rebellious Jesuit converts was probably an incident, came to a head. It ended in the expulsion of the Portuguese, and the establishment of the Dutch at Nagasaki as the sole Western nation having dealings with Japan.

Here for two hundred years the Dutch traded unmolested. The civil commotion quieted down, and with her seclusion from the outside world Japan entered upon an era of domestic peace. There were no more great civil wars, and, save for the conflicts of the Samaurai against each other, the nation grew ignorant of the art of war.

As these Samaurai were the ancestors of modern Japanese naval officers, some account of their methods of training may be worthy of study, for to them it is undoubtedly due that Japan exists as one of the great Powers to-day. Otherwise she would assuredly have sunk to the Chinese level of an ultra-high civilisation in which courage has no place, and in which the military profession is lower than the meanest civil calling. From all this the Samaurai saved Japan.

The country was then under a feudal system. The Emperor, the nominal head of the State, was a mere figure-head, too sacred to concern himself with mundane affairs—a condition of mind which generations of clever tutelage at the hands of various Shoguns had produced. More often than not the Shogun's rule was of a similar nature, a regent being the real head of the State. Under the Shogun or his regent were the governors of provinces; under these the great feudal lords, each of whom maintained his Samaurai, or fighting men. The soldier-ant is the nearest natural equivalent to these Samaurai, who only very partially resembled our knights of the Middle Ages. Below the Samaurai, and cordially despised by them, were the lower classes, engaged in trade and agriculture. The exact social equivalent of the Samaurai in our society system does not exist, but probably the old "squireens," a now almost extinct class of small country gentry, would most nearly occupy the same social status. The Samaurai might be richer or poorer than the working class, but in all cases they cordially despised them, and were in turn respected or feared.

These Samaurai lived in a constant state of killing and being killed. If one of them left his house, he took his life in his hand from that moment. Duels were frequent, murders common, and the fearful form of suicide known as hari-kari was performed by them without a shudder at the slightest hint of an insult that could not be avenged. Vendettas, too, were everlasting, so that altogether the Samaurai were by heredity inured to a callous disregard of life and suffering. In all their crimes and vices they cultivated the grand Spartan virtues, and Japan will yet, perhaps, reap the benefit of those centuries of training.

II

THE OPENING OF JAPAN

THE knowledge of the Dutch hold upon Japan inspired other nations with a desire to secure similar benefits. Russia, in particular, strove to secure a footing, but all her attempts were unavailing. British and Americans met with a like fate; there was no Government that would deal with them, the law of isolation had gone forth, and isolated Japan remained. So greatly, too, did the nation esteem its state, that a law long existed whereby the building of a ship of any size was a crime punishable by death.

At last, in 1848, the United States, which had deep interests in the whale fisheries in Far Eastern waters, and was also concerned in establishing a line of steamers between California and the recently opened free ports in China, took official instead of merely individual measures to open up communication with Japan. A coaling station in Japan was an absolute necessity if the projected line of steamers was to be realised; but the reaching of any governing body with power to grant such a station was the difficulty.

However, in 1852, Commodore Perry was sent with a squadron to Japan, and reached the Bay of Yeddo in July, 1853, bearing a friendly letter from the President of the United States to the Emperor of Japan.[1] The commodore had orders to use force, if necessary, as a last resort;[2] but the thousands of troops that were gathered to meet him made no attack. Having managed to deliver his message and impress the authorities with the fact that an answer would be required, the commodore left.

So soon as he had gone the Shogun's Government found itself on the horns of a dilemma. If a treaty were made with the foreigners, internal trouble from a people already permeated with a desire to restore to power the real Emperor might be expected to a certainty; if they refused, the American show of force convinced them that grave trouble would lie ahead, trouble which the Japanese, with their old-fashioned fighting methods, could never successfully combat.

The most prominent personage in Japan at that moment was the Daimio of Mito. He advocated absolute refusal of the American demands, and the exclusion of all foreigners by force of arms, if necessary. He recalled the famous wars of the past, and nearly every Daimio in the country followed his lead. Forts were erected on the shore, the bells of temples melted

---

[1] The message was to the Shogun, whom all foreigners regarded as the Emperor.

[2] "Official Narrative of the Japan Expedition."

and made into cannon, and as many Samaurai as possible were drilled with the most modern fire-arms procurable. They got these through the Dutch at Nagasaki.

In the midst of this a Russian squadron appeared, also demanding a treaty and the opening up of the country, but again no force was used. Seven months after his first visit, Commodore Perry returned for his answer, and the war fever having evaporated to some extent, a treaty was actually signed on March 31, 1854.

This treaty provided for peace and goodwill between the United States and Japan, the opening of Shimoda as a treaty port, and the similar opening of Hakodate after an interval, the Americans agreeing that their ships should visit no other ports except from necessity. The other articles dealt with the care of shipwrecked mariners and the like, and "the most favoured nation" clause. England, Russia, and Holland soon secured similar treaties, Russia having the same ports as America, England and Holland having Nagasaki instead of Shimoda.

All this split Japan into two hostile parties, the *Jo-i* and the *Kai-koku*. The former, under the leadership of the Daimio of Mito, were bitterly anti-foreign, and also desirous of restoring the Emperor. The *Kai-koku*, on the other hand, supported the Shogun action, and had as their watchword the words spoken by one of them at the debate over Commodore Perry's demands: "As we are not the equals of the foreigners in the mechanical arts, let us have intercourse with foreign lands, let us learn their drill and tactics. Then, when we shall have made our nation united as one family, we shall be able to go abroad, and give lands in foreign countries to those who have distinguished themselves in battle."

For a time this party had the upper hand. Commercial treaties were made, and by 1860 Ni-igata, Hyogo, and Yokohama had been opened, with the Consuls of most nations established there. Ii-Kamon-no-kami, head of the *Kai-koku* party, imprisoned the Daimio of Mito, and executed several Samurai who had killed his adherents. Then, in 1860, on March 23, Ii-Kamon-no-kami was assassinated, and his party, no longer with a powerful head, made isolated preparations for civil war. Ships were purchased and manned by the retainers of the local governors of provinces, and troops raised. Meanwhile the foreign Legations were attacked, an American secretary was murdered, and other foreigners injured. Other murders, notably that of an English merchant named Richardson, followed, and an indemnity was refused. This led to the arrival of Admiral Kuper with seven ships at Kagoshima, August 11, 1863. He bombarded the forts and city, and also sank or burned three steamers belonging to the Daimio of Satsuma, whose men had committed the murder. After this the indemnity was forthcoming, but the Daimio promptly ordered more warships, and sent many of his naval officers to Holland to learn European methods.

THE OPENING OF JAPAN

In this same year the Daimio of Choshu, a member of the Jo-i, who had also secured a small fleet for himself, fired upon an American steamer, and afterwards upon the French gunboat Kienchang, which latter he damaged severely. The Dutch frigate Medusa was also roughly handled by his shore batteries at Shimonoseki, but replying, silenced them.

Both these acts led to reprisals. The United States warship Wyoming at once proceeded to Shimonoseki, where she blew up one Japanese steam warship, and sank a second, a small brig. The French warships Sémiramis and Tancrède followed, and subjected Shimonoseki to a bombardment that did considerable damage.

An indemnity was demanded and paid by the Shogun's Government for these attacks of foreign shipping, while the suppression of the Daimio of Choshu at Shimonoseki was also promised. This, however, was a task beyond the power of the Government, and finally the Powers interested decided to take action. A combined fleet, consisting of nine British, four Dutch, three French, and one hired United States steamer, went to Shimonoseki to reduce this bar to passage on the Inland Sea.

The attacking vessels were :—

British . . . Tartar (screw corvette), 20 guns.
Barrosa (screw corvette), 22 guns.
Leopard (paddle frigate), 18 guns.
Conqueror (two-decker), 101 guns.
Euryalus (screw frigate), 51 guns.
Perseus, 4 guns.

British	. . .	Bouncer (screw gunboat), 4 guns.
		Coquette (screw gunboat), 4 guns.
		Argus (paddle sloop), 6 guns.
French	. . .	Dupleix (screw corvette), 24 guns.
		Sémiramis (frigate), 36 guns.
		Tancrède (gunboat), 4 guns.
Dutch	. . .	Amsterdam.
		Djambi.
		Metal Cruyis.
		Medusa (frigate), 36 guns.
United States	. .	Takiang, no guns.

The United States ship was merely chartered to indicate American interest; all American vessels were then busy sinking each other in the civil war.

This fleet left Yokohama on August 28, 1864, and from September 5th to 9th it bombarded all the new forts that the Daimio had erected. At the end of that time Shimonoseki surrendered unconditionally, and an indemnity of three million dollars was claimed from the Shogun, and eventually paid.

For the next two years the Shogun's Government was busy trying conclusions with the Daimio, but as he had raised a large force of the common people, and drilled these in Western fashion, he easily held his own. British and French troops meanwhile were permanently stationed at Yokohama to guard foreign interests. Friction between these and the *Jo-i* party was common, and more than one assassination took place, but no naval demonstrations followed.

THE FIRST SHIP OF THE JAPANESE NAVY, THE TSUKUBA.

[*By a Japanese artist.*

III

EARLY WARSHIPS AND THE CIVIL WAR

AS already recounted, the sight of foreign ships had gradually put ideas of sea-power into the minds of the various governors of Japanese provinces. One of the first, if not the first, ships to be acquired was the Tsukuba, which still survives as a hulk. Her first name was the Malacca, and she was launched in the United States in 1851. She was, in her time, a fine-looking screw frigate of 1950 tons, carrying 20 guns, and able to steam at the then satisfactory speed of 8 knots.

The Riaden, a small screw yacht of 370 tons, and the Chiyoda-nata (Chiyoda type), of less than 140 tons, both schooner rigged, were enrolled about the same time, and then followed by the Kásuga, a two-funnelled, three-masted paddler, originally the Kiang-tse. She carried six guns, and for some time served as the Shogun's yacht.

Following this, the Fuji Yama, a full-rigged ship—a sailing frigate of about 1010 tons and 24 guns—and the 523-ton barque-rigged sailing-ship Ken-ho were purchased.

To learn how to work this naval militia, Japan imported instructors of various kinds from the Western world. In response to applications, the present Admiral Tracy was sent out by the British Government, and with him a small host of other Westerners. With their natural aptitude, the Japanese rapidly acquired the rudiments of sea service, while on shore the beginnings of a shipbuilding yard were made at Yokosuka. The British naval uniform was adopted with some slight differences. Officers were sent to Europe—chiefly to Holland—to study the principles of naval warfare, and at once a desire to possess ironclads arose.

Out of this came the purchase of Japan's first ironclad, the Adsuma.

The dimensions, etc., of the Adsuma were as follows:—

Displacement	1387 tons.
Material of hull	Iron.
Length	157 ft.
Beam	30 ft.
Draught (maximum)	$13\frac{1}{4}$ ft.
Armament	One 9-in. $12\frac{1}{2}$ M.L. Armstrong. Four $6\frac{1}{2}$-in. Parrot M.L. rifled.
Horse-power (nominal)	700.
Screws	Two.
Speed	9 knots.

The armour was $4\frac{1}{2}$ to $4\frac{3}{4}$ ins. thick, and distributed on a complete water-line belt and over both of the raised batteries. Though a very famous vessel as the Stonewall Jackson, her war services under that name were not extensive. She was built in France, and at

FUJI YAMA.

the end of 1864, when ready for sea, carried one large 13-in. 300-pounder (smooth bore) in the bow, and the two 70-pounders (rifled) in the main battery. No ship like her had ever been constructed before, and the Confederates, to whom she then belonged, spread alarming reports as to her power. Putting to sea, she reached Corunna in February, 1865, and was there blockaded by the unarmoured Federal ships Niagara and Sacramento. The former was a famous vessel in her way, of 5013 tons, 345 ft. long, 12-knot speed, and armed with twelve 11-in. smooth bores, throwing a 135-lb. shell each. These guns were not able to fire shot apparently, and the Sacramento was a weaker vessel. The Stonewall Jackson challenged these two to a duel *à la* Kearsarge and Alabama, but Craven, the Federal commodore, declined—wisely enough, for he could not have done anything against the ironclad with his few heavy pieces, while the ironclad would certainly have disabled and then rammed him.[1] Consequently, the Stonewall Jackson did not smell powder on that occasion, and the war ended very soon afterwards.

In 1866 a mysterious Japanese deputation came to America. Its object was long unknown, but the curiosity it excited was sufficient to cause telegraphic reports of its movements, and surmises as to its intentions, to appear in the London *Times* every now and again. Finally came the news that "the Japanese deputation have come to buy ironclads"—a statement at first treated as a joke.

[1] He was, however, court-martialled and punished for refusing to fight.

The Japanese do not, however, appear to have been large bidders for the forty odd ironclads that America then had to dispose of. Few of these "on sale" craft were fit for a sea voyage—they were merely hastily constructed monitors intended more often than not for river service. The Stonewall Jackson, however, being a sea-going ship, was purchased for the Shogun, and re-named Adsuma.

A gunboat or two changed hands at this period, and altogether the various Japanese governors collected between them a small, heterogeneous fleet, the very existence of which was scarcely known outside their own country. Indeed, twenty years later comparatively few people knew, and still fewer cared, that Japan possessed a navy at all.

The Adsuma has long been removed from the effective list and relegated to hulk duty. On account of her enormous ram, she was somewhat of a curio to naval visitors for many years, and the most vivid memory retained by some of our people of the harbour in which the Adsuma lay was the fashion in which the Japanese sailors used her ram. They walked down over it into the water when bathing.

Of the smaller vessels previously referred to the following may be mentioned:—

No. 1 Tébo was a swan-bow, three-masted, schooner-rigged screw steamer of 250 tons only. Two or three other ships like her existed.

The Unyo, built at Amsterdam, was little larger—295 tons only. She was a brig-rigged and ram-bowed

THE ADSUMA (ex STONEWALL JACKSON). *[By a Japanese artist.*

screw steamer, carrying three pivot guns (Krupp's), disposed in the centre line, as were the three big guns in the French Baudin and Formidable till these ships were reconstructed. The Unyo was wrecked many years ago.

The Moisshin, screw gunboat of 357 tons, is worthy of more attention, as she was the first ship ever built in Japan since the days of Adams. She was an enlarged edition of No. 1 Tébo, and exactly like her in appearance. Between the funnel and foremast a single Long Tom was carried. She was launched somewhere about the year 1865. Her construction was not, of course, purely Japanese—she was a craft upon which the Islanders practised and learnt construction with important material.

The Setsu, 935 tons, 8 guns, a sailing frigate, and the Chio-bin, a barque of 650 tons, originally used for trading purposes, also belong to this early period.

So also does a ship with more history, the Asama, a composite sailing-ship of 1445 tons and 14 guns. Her exact early history is shrouded in some mystery, but just previous to her entry into the Japanese fleet she was the property of a too-confiding pirate, who went into a Japanese harbour to refit, and had his ship taken possession of by the Japanese in consequence. The ship still exists as a gunnery hulk, and carries, or did till recently, eight 7-in. breech-loaders and four $4\frac{1}{2}$-in. muzzle-loaders.

With these ships, built and building, Japan found herself engaged in that civil war of which the Mikasa,

Asama, and other ships of to-day are the direct outcome. The officers had had some years of Western training, chiefly in Holland and Denmark. The accompanying illustration, from a Japanese photograph, indicates the uniform of the period. There were in the Navy in those days two schools—the party of progress and those opposed to change—by no means necessarily identical with the same political parties. Indeed, of

the two, the *Jo-i* seem to have chiefly availed themselves of the war-training to be secured from the foreigners whose expulsion was one of their political tenets. This, perhaps, was due in part or in great measure to the other factor in the dispute—the question as to whether the Emperor or the Shogun and his representatives should be ruler of the country. This became eventually the sole question.

In 1867 the Emperor Kōmei died, and was

THE MOISHIN.

succeeded by his son, the present Emperor, Mutsohito, then a boy. His advisers had by now concluded that the anti-foreign agitation was a mistake, and thenceforward it was only carried on by a few isolated Daimaios. The real problem was one of ruling, and this culminated in 1867 by the Shogun resigning his power, and becoming a species of minister.

The adherents of neither party were favourably disposed towards this middle course; and ultimately civil war, in which the ex-Shogun's party were continually defeated, resulted.

The ironclad Adsuma was in the hands of the Imperialists, as also were most of the other warships; but the ex-Shogun had owned seven ships, mounting between them 83 guns, and these Yenomoto, his admiral (one of the Dutch-trained officers) absolutely refused to surrender. Chased by Nahamoto, the Imperial admiral, he took refuge in Hakodate, where the remnants of the rebels had collected. A naval action resulted disastrously for Yenomoto. In July, 1869, the rebels finally surrendered, and Japan entered upon a new era, in which much of the power hitherto wielded by the Diamios passed into the hands of the Samaurai, whose descendants now supply the bulk of naval and military officers, retaining all the courage of their fierce ancestors, and more of their exclusiveness than is generally supposed. But further particulars under this head will be found in a later chapter.[1]

[1] See Personal Characteristics.

IV

THE IMPERIAL NAVY

WITH the sea fight off Hakodate the civil war ended. The feudal fleets were abolished, and all ships were enrolled in an Imperial Navy—a proceeding that, of course, increased its strength. Some reorganisation of *personnel* was also effected, bringing the Navy more into line with the Western model.

Naval advisers came and went. They included, during the period 1865–1885, the present British admirals Tracy and Hopkins, the eminent French naval architect M. Bertin, and finally Captain Ingles, R.N., of whom more will be found in the Appendix.

The same year in which the Adsuma was launched the Riu Jo[1] was set afloat at Aberdeen. She, too, was possibly originally destined to fly the Confederate flag, but about this details are hard to procure. Particulars are :—

Displacement	2530 tons.
Material	Composite.
Length	213 ft.

[1] Pronounced "Dĕĕn-Jho," but the exact sound cannot be rendered.

Fleet of Nakamoto, Adsuma leading.

Fleet of Yenomoto

BATTLE OF HAKODATE.

[*By a Japanese artist.*]

Beam . . . . 41 ft.
Draught (extreme) . . 19 ft.
Armament . . . One 6¼-in. Krupp.
Six 70-pdrs.

The horse-power was 975 nominal, the speed 9 knots. She was single-screwed, and carried 350 tons of coal. Like all the early sea-going ironclads, she had a 4½-in. iron armour-belt, and 4 inches over the amidship battery. The heaviest gun was carried in the bow on a pivot. The ship still exists as a hulk. She did not reach Japan till the Civil War was over.

The Ho-sho, launched in England in 1867, is also retained as a gunnery tender at the present day. She is a small gunboat of 320 tons, carrying one 7-in. Armstrong M.L. and one 5½-in. Krupp B.L.

Some other early Japanese ships may now be referred to.

The Nisshin was built at Amsterdam, and ordered, probably, previously to the Civil War.

Tonnage . . . . 1470.
Material of hull . . Wood.
Armament . . . One 7-in. M.L.
Six smaller M.L.
Speed on trial . . . 11 knots.
Single screw, swan-bow, barque-rigged corvette.

The Amagi of the same period was built in Japan. Particulars of her are :—

Tonnage . . . . 526.
Material of hull . . Wood.
Armament . . . One 6-in. 2¼-ton Krupp.
Four 4¾-in. Krupp.

Horse-power (nominal)	720.
Speed	11 knots.
Screws	One.

In appearance she more or less resembles the foregoing.

She was followed by the Seiki, also built in Japan, and famous in her way, because she was the first Japanese ship to make a voyage to England. Particulars :—

Tonnage	857.
Material of hull	Wood.
Length	200 ft.
Beam	30 ft.
Draught	13 ft.
Armament	One 6-in. 2¼-ton Krupp. Four 4¾-in. Krupp.
Horse-power	1270
Speed	11 knots.

Save that her stern was sharper, she was, to look at, much like the Amagi. She is now removed from the Japanese Navy list.

A sailing training brig of 153 tons, the Ishikawa, and a larger brig, the Tateyama, of 543 tons, were built or acquired prior to 1877.

The Banjo was built by the Japanese on the same model as the Amagi. Particulars are :—

Displacement	667 tons.
Material of hull	Wood.
Length	154 ft.
Beam	25 ft.
Draught (mean)	12 ft.

THE AKIKI. [*By a Japanese artist.*

Armament	One 6-in. 2½-ton Krupp.
	Two 4¾-in. Krupp.
I.H.P.	590.
Speed	10·5 knots.
Screws	One.
Coal supply	107 tons.

She is swan-bow, barque-rigged, and has one funnel.

This ended this particular period of Japanese shipbuilding.

In the year 1875, or thereabouts, the Japanese finally decided to embark upon a war navy, and laid the foundations of that fleet which some twenty years later was to vindicate its existence at Yalu and Wei-hei-wei. In that year a then modern ironclad, up-to-date ironclad, and two armoured cruisers, on what was then the best accepted model, were ordered.

Of these the Fu-So,[1] designed by Sir E. J. Reed, and launched at Samuda's Yard, Poplar, England, in 1877, was then a powerful second-class battleship. In design she resembles the French Rédoutable, though of only half her size. Particulars are:—

Material of hull	Iron.
Displacement	3718.
Length	220 ft.
Beam	48 ft.
Draught	18⅓ ft.
Original armament	Four 9·4-in. Krupps in the main-deck, central-armoured battery.
	Two 6·6-in. Krupps in unarmoured barbettes above the armoured battery.

---

[1] Pronounced Föö-Só.

Horse-power	3500.
Nominal speed	13 knots.
Screws	Two.
Coal	360 tons.
Nominal radius	3500 miles at 10 knots.

The armour is distributed in a complete belt of iron from 9 to 4 ins. in thickness. The battery armour is 8 ins., with 7-in. bulkheads forming a redoubt. The engines, by Penn, are horizontal compound trunk. She was then barque-rigged, with a single funnel. She carried no torpedo tubes, but these were added later. Just previous to the war with China the Japanese reconstructed and re-armed her, removing the mainmast, and fitting military tops to the fore and mizzen; 6-in. Q.F. were mounted in the barbettes in place of the old 6·6-in. Either immediately before or directly after the war, two additional 6-in. Q.F. (as shown in the photograph of her at sea) were mounted, one on the forecastle and one on the poop behind shields; and subsequently four further 6-in. Q.F. replaced the old guns in the battery, these having been found well-nigh useless for modern warfare. This by no means exhausts the history of the Fu-So, but her subsequent adventures will be found on a later page.[1]

Russia with the General Admiral would appear to have inspired the idea of the Hi-Yei[2] and Kon-go. The former of these was launched early in 1878 at Milford Haven, the latter at Hull towards the end of 1877. The ships are sisters. Details are:—

---

[1] See Chino-Japanese War.   [2] Pronounced "Hēē-Yey."

Chin Yen. Chiyoda.

THE JAPANESE FLEET IN LINE ABREAST. NAVAL MANŒUVRES.

[*Official photograph.*

Material of hull	Composite.
Displacement	2250 tons.
Length	231 ft.
Beam	40¾ ft.
Draught	17⅓ ft.
Armament	Three 6·6-in. Krupp.
	Six 6-in. 2¼-ton Krupp.
	Four Nordenfelts.
	Two torpedo tubes.
Horse-power	Hi-Yei, 2270.
	Kon-go, 2035.
Screws	One.
Speed (nominal)	Hi-Yei, 13 knots.
	Kon-go, 13·7 knots.
Engines (by Earle)	Horizontal compound.

The armour is a mere iron strip on the water-line, varying from 4½ to 3 ins. in thickness.

In 1876 a new Imperial yacht, the Jin-Jei, was launched. She is a paddler, with swan bow, two funnels, and two high pole masts—a pretty-looking vessel.

Displacement	1464 tons.
Material of hull	Wood.
Length	249 ft.
Beam	32 ft.
Draught	14¼ ft.
Armament	Two 4¾-in. Krupp.
Horse-power	1430.
Speed	12 knots.

In 1879 began what later events constituted the supplementary Japanese shipbuilding programme. In 1879 Elswick built for China those once famous "alphabetical gunboats," a series of "flat-irons" of the Rendel type, to carry one gun. Like a good many other Chinese vessels, they were destined to fly the Japanese flag at a later period of their existence. Altogether there were eleven of these craft, named after letters of the Greek alphabet, but re-named by the Chinese. They were named Lung-shang (Alpha), Ho-wei (Beta), Fei-ting (Gamma), Tche-tien (Delta), the first two of 340 tons, the other two of 420 tons, and which the Chinese still own. The remainder are a little larger, four, Chen-tung (Epsilon), Chen-Sei (Zeta), Chen-nan (Eta), Chen-pei (Theta), of 490 tons, and Chin-pen (Kappa), Hai-chang-ching (Lambda), and Chen-chung (Iota) of 500 tons. Japan now owns all of this last batch, except the Hai-chang-ching.

Gamma and Delta carry a 38-ton Armstrong M.L.; all the others are armed with the 11-in. 25-ton gun. Horse-power varies from 235 in the smaller craft to 472 in the larger. There are slight differences in dimensions, but the largest only runs to 125 ft. long by 29 ft. broad. Two other rather smaller gunboats once existed, but these the French sunk at Foochow in the early eighties. The development of small guns has long since rendered this type of gunboat useless; but, apart from that, the bad care taken of them by the Chinese would have made them of no service.

China in 1881 was making some considerable efforts towards being a naval power, efforts that continued till 1889, when they suddenly died out, or resolved themselves into the building of small craft by Chinamen. A Chino-Japanese war was a possibility in 1881 as much as in 1890. Neither side was, however, ready for the conflict, and in the early eighties Japan's energies were concentrated on training *personnel*, China's on acquiring *materiel*. In 1881 the latter had launched for her the big ironclad Ting Yuen at Stettin, followed a little later by the Chin Yuen, now in the Japanese service. From the time China first had them, Japan coveted these ironclads; by the irony of fate, she did not secure them (or rather the one that was left) till far superior ships of her own were on the stocks.

The Tung Yuen sank at Wei-hai-wei during the war; the Chen Yuen, her sister, was taken at the same time. Her details are:—

Displacement	7350 tons.
Material of hull	Steel.
Length	308 ft.
Beam	59 ft.
Draught	23 ft.
Armament (originally)	Four 12-in. 20 cals. Krupp.
	Two 6-in. Krupp.
	Eight machine guns.
	One torpedo tube in the stern; one on each beam forward of barbettes.
Horse-power	6200.
Screws	Two.
Speed (on first trials)	14·5 knots.
Engines	Two sets, three-cylinder horizontal compound.
Coal	1000 tons.

The arrangement of the heavy armament is upon the system that in 1880 was held to be the system of the future—four big guns able to fire end-on or on the broadside. The ideal warship of those days was to fight in line abreast. The advantages of that disposition were seen, while its disadvantages were ignored. It was not realised how easily an enemy could get round upon either flank and mask the fire of nearly all the units in this cumbersome formation, the advantages of which lie only in going into action against an enemy right ahead.

When the Chin Yen was the Chinese Chen Yuen she carried thin shields over her big guns. The 6-in. pieces were in the extreme bow and stern, each in a 3-in. turret. The big gun shields were removed before the war. The Japanese captured these with Port Arthur, and have since replaced them. They have also mounted a 6-in. Q.F. in the bow turret, substituted a 6-in. Q.F. behind a shield for the after turret, and mounted two additional Q.F.'s upon sponsons specially built near the mainmast. Two 6-pounder Q.F. and a number of 3- or 2½-pounders have also been added on the upper deck. The photograph shows the ship as she now is.

The armour of the Chin Yen is distributed as follows: Amidships for 150 ft. is a 14-in. compound belt. Under-water and at the end of it this belt thins to 10 ins. Forward and aft of it is a protective deck 3 ins. thick. The ends of the belt are joined by flat bulkheads of 14 ins. Rising from this redoubt are the barbettes, 12 ins. compound. The starboard one is forward, the port somewhat aft of it.[1] The

---

[1] In the plans generally published of these ships this order is, in error, reversed.

Chin Yen. [*Official photo.*
THE CHIN YEN AT EVOLUTIONS WITH THE JAPANESE FLEET. 1902.

big gun hoods are quite thin, 4 ins. or less; between the big guns in the conning tower, 8 ins. in thickness.

The ship, it will be seen, is of the British Ajax or Colossus type—very much a "soft ender." She is, however, given a good deal of protection in the way of specially arranged watertight compartments, and there is also a species of cofferdam.

In 1881 Elswick set afloat the Arturo Prat, a small cruiser originally intended for Chili, but subsequently purchased by Japan and re-named Tsukushi. China had two sisters built at the same time, the Tchao Yong and Yang-wei, both of which were sunk at Yalu. Particulars of the Tsukushi are as follows:—

Displacement	1350 tons.
Material of hull	Steel.
Length	210 ft.
Beam	32 ft.
Draught (maximum)	16½ ft.
Armament	Two 10-in. 32 cals. Elswick.
	Four 4·7 in. Q.F.[1]
	Four 1-pdr. Q.F.
	Two torpedo tubes.
Horse-power	2887.
Screws	Two.
Speed on trial	16·4 knots.
Sea speed	(*circa*) 12 knots.
Coal	250 tons.
Engines (by Hawthorn Leslie)	Horizontal compound.

The ship has no armour deck, or protection of any sort.

In 1882 the construction of wooden ships was

---

[1] These replaced four non-quickfiring guns.

still proceeding in Japan. In that year they launched at Yokosuka the Kaimon, of which the measurements are :—

Displacement	1367 tons.
Material of hull	Wood.
Length	211 ft.
Beam	32 ft.
Draught (mean)	16½ ft.
Armament	Eight 4¾-in. Krupp.
	Two 3-pdr. Q.F.
Horse-power	1125.
Trial speed	12 knots.
Screws	One.
Coal	180 tons.
Complement	230.

The engines were constructed in Japan at the Yokosuka Dockyard, and are of the horizontal compound type. This was the first ship put together by them of which they constructed the engines also.

The following year they launched the Tenriu at Yokosuka. Details are :—

Displacement	1547 tons.
Material of hull	Wood.
Length	212 ft.
Beam	32½ ft.
Draught (mean)	16½ ft.
Armament	Eight 4¾-in. Krupp.
	Two Nordenfelts.
Horse-power	1165.
Trial speed	12 knots.
Screws	One.
Coal	256 tons.
Complement	214.

The ship is practically a sister to the Kaimon.

Tsukushi.　　　Naniwa.　　　Tsukushima.

JAPANESE CRUISER TSUKUSHI AT SEA.

[*Official photo.*

The engines of both were made at Yokosuka, and are of the same type. Both ships have swan bows, one funnel, and are barque-rigged. The sterns are rather square.

In 1884 Elswick suddenly sprang the deck-protected cruiser on the world. In that year was launched the famous Esmeralda. She was, like the Arturo Prat, built for Chili, and as a Chilian cruiser bore a share in the Chilian revolution. When the Chino-Japanese war broke out Japan made overtures for this ship, and in 1895 purchased her through the agency of Ecuador. The war was over before the cruiser could be employed, but she was probably purchased against possible eventualities with Russia, France, and Germany. Being now obsolete, she has not proved a valuable acquisition, and the Japanese speak of her as a very bad sea boat. Particulars of this once famous vessel are:—

Displacement	3000 tons.
Material of hull	Steel.
Length	270 ft.
Beam	42 ft.
Draught (maximum)	19½ ft.
Armament (originally)	Two 10-in. 32 cals.
	Six 6-in. 32 cals.
	Two 6-pdr. Q.F.
	Five 1-pdr. Q.F.
	Two Gardners.
	Three torpedo tubes, one of them in the bow.

The six 6-in. B.L. have been removed by the Japanese, and six 4·7-in. Q.F. of 40 calibres substituted.

When new the Esmeralda was one of the swiftest ships afloat. Her I.H.P. natural draught was 6500, with an 18·5-knot speed on her trials in 1885. She carries 400 tons of coal, with provision for 200 tons more.

Protection is afforded by a steel deck 1 in. thick on the slopes and ½ in. on the flat. Over the loading stations of the big guns a 1-in. steel skin is carried.

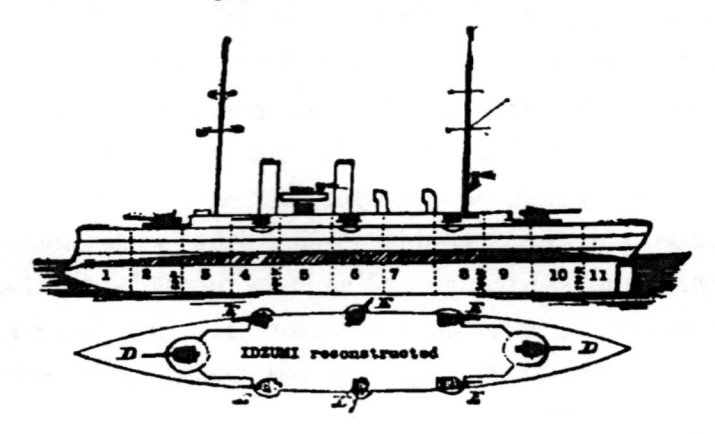

ESMERALDA, NOW IDZUMI.

News of the Esmeralda's fame soon reached Japan, and two glorified editions of her, the Naniwa and Takachiho, were promptly ordered. Japanese home construction was not, however, affected, and three composite vessels, Yamato, Katsuragi, and Mushashi, were put in hand, and launched in 1885–86. Details of these are as follows :—

Displacement	1502 tons.
Material of hull	Composite.
Length	207 ft.
Beam	36 ft.

Draught (mean)	15 ft.
Armament	Two 6·6-in. Krupp.
	Six 4¾-in. Krupp.
	Four Nordenfelts.
	Two torpedo tubes.
Horse-power	1600.
Trial speed	18·5 knots.
Complement	231.

As before, Yokosuka made the horizontal compound engines, and in the Katsuragi twin screws were attempted for the first time. These ships are now employed for training squadron duties. They have clipper bows, and are, generally speaking, small editions of the British Raleigh. They are all three barque-rigged. The Mushashi is distinguished by a red band, the Katsuragi a yellow one.

The "warship Naniwa-kan," as she used to be called in England, in defiance to all explanations to the effect that the affix "kan" simply meant "warship," attained a good deal of celebrity while under construction. The British Navy had then no ships like her, and the Mersey class, then building, though more heavily gunned on about the same displacement, were popularly considered very poor substitutes, since their biggest guns were 8-in. pieces only, against the Naniwa's 10-in. The big gun had at that time a very great hold on popular imagination.

Details of the Naniwa, and her sister, the Takachiho, are as follows:—

Displacement	3700 tons.
Material of hull	Steel.

Length	300 ft.
Beam	46 ft.
Draught	20 ft.
Armament	Two 10-in. 32 cals. Krupp.
	Six 6-in. B.L. Krupp.
	Two 6-pdr. Q.F.
	Fourteen smaller Q.F. and machine.
	Four torpedo tubes.

(Elswick 6-in. Q.F. have lately been substituted for the old 6-in. B.L.).

The big guns are generally described as Elswick pieces, but they are not, although Elswick built the ships.

Engines (Hawthorn, Leslie & Co.)	Horizontal compound.
Horse-power	7120.
Speed on trial	18·7 knots
Sea speed	(*circa*) 15 knots.
Screws	Two.
Coal (normal)	350 tons.
,, (maximum)	800 tons.
Radius with full bunkers	(*circa*) 5000 miles.
Complement	357.
Search-lights	Four.

Protection is afforded by a steel deck 3 ins. on the slopes, 2 ins. on the flat. The engine hatches have a 3-in. glacis. The conning tower is $1\frac{1}{2}$-in. steel, and the loading stations of the big guns have a similar protection.

As originally rigged, the Naniwa and Takachiho carried a top on each mast. After the war, in which they did not exhibit the best of sea-keeping qualities, these tops were lowered, and light platforms erected

THE NANIWA (present rig).

(*This is the cruiser that sunk the Kowshing.*)

NOTE.—The sinking of the Kowshing will be found described in the chapter on the Chino-Japanese war. Special interest attaches to the Naniwa on account of the fact that during this war she was commanded by the present Admiral Togo.

THE IMPERIAL NAVY

where they used to be, as in the illustration. The old rig, which is tolerably familiar, will be noticed in the illustrations dealing with the war. The Naniwa and Takachiho both took part in the first engagement at Asan; the Naniwa subsequently made her name familiar to the world over the Kowshing affair. Both ships participated at Yalu and Wei-hai-wei. The Naniwa was launched on March 18, 1885, at Elswick, the Takachiho on May 16th in the same year. In appear-

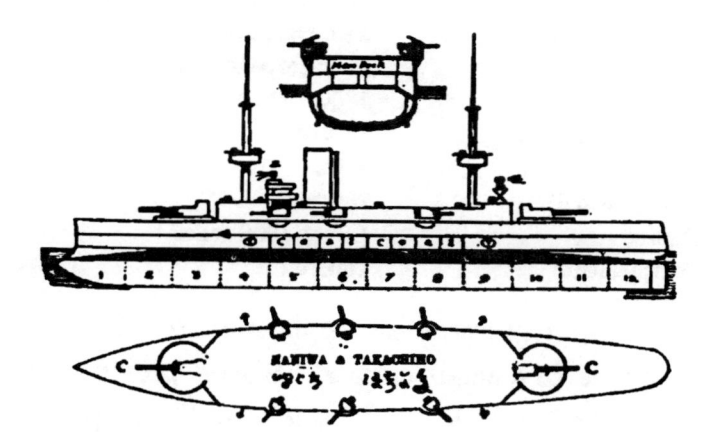

ance the two craft are almost absolutely identical; for convenience, and to enable their own officers to distinguish them, the Takachiho has a red band round her instead of the orthodox black one. As a further guide, she carries a couple of signal yards on the main, in place of the single yard carried there by the Naniwa.

Meanwhile China continued to have ships built in England and Germany, and in 1886 there was launched at Stettin a small cruiser, the Tche-Yuen (Tsi-Yuen is a more familiar spelling), which was destined to be taken over by the Japanese at Wei-hai-wei in 1895. Her details are:—

Displacement	2300 tons.
Material of hull	Steel.
Length	246 ft.
Beam	33 ft.
Draught (maximum)	18 ft.
Armament	Two 8·2-in. Krupp, forward in an armoured turret.
	One 6-in. Krupp aft.
	Four 4-pdr. Gruson Q.F.
	Two Gatlings.
	Four torpedo tubes.
Horse-power	2800.
Speed on trial	15 knots.
Screws	Two.
Coal (normal)	230 tons.
Radius	(*circa*) 1000 miles.
Complement	180.

This ship represents an application of the Italian Lepanto idea to a small cruiser. She is provided with a steel protective deck, 3 ins. thick on the slopes; the hull is otherwise unprotected, but the fore turret, containing the 8-in. guns, is heavily armoured with 10-in. compound, thus rendering it proof against any of the 10-in. guns afloat in the Japanese Fleet at the time she was built. Indeed, at Yalu there were only three guns present in the Japanese Fleet against which the Tche-Yuen's turret armour was not proof. However, the possession of a little impenetrable armour is of small service to a warship—the odds being always against any one particular spot being hit. At Asan, in which the Tche-Yuen suffered rather severely, none of the

SAI YEN (ex TCHE-YUEN).

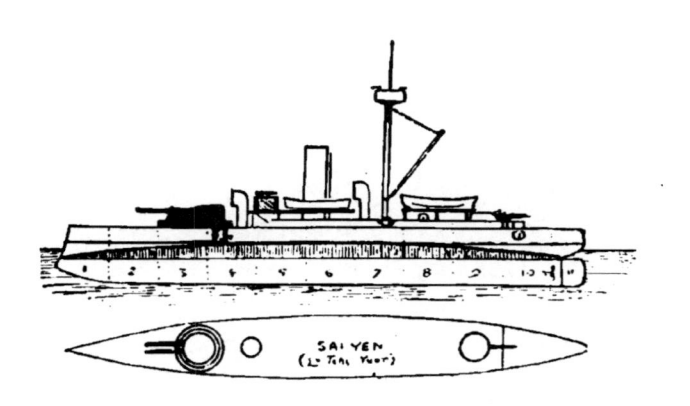

Japanese guns against her were able to pierce this forward turret.

In 1879 Japan had already had four torpedo boats built for her at Yarrow's. These craft displaced only 40 tons. In 1886, however, Yarrow's built the first-class twin-screw torpedo boat Kotaka. This boat is remarkable as the first armoured torpedo boat ever constructed. She has 1-in. steel plating all over her machinery compartment, and the subdivision of the hull is, for a torpedo boat, singularly complete. In her way the Kotaka was the forerunner of the destroyers, being larger than the run of torpedo boats even now. Full details of her are:—

Displacement	190 tons.
Material of hull	Steel.
Length	170 ft.
Beam	19½ ft.
Draught	5 feet.
Horse-power	1400.
Speed on trial	19 knots.
Screws	Two.
Coal carried	50 tons.
Torpedo tubes	Six.
Armament	Four machine guns.

The torpedo tubes are thus disposed: two forward, firing right ahead, a pair amidships, and another pair a little abaft of them. The Kotaka made a name for herself in the war, and previously to that was a successful craft. However, for some reason Japan had no more boats from Yarrow, or, indeed, from England, for the next ten years, the next, a batch of fourteen, being ordered from Creusot. These were launched in 1889.

The Kotaka, after being built, was sent out to Japan in sections, and there put together again. The Creusot boats were sent out in similar fashion, while a further seven were put together entirely at Kobe, in Japan. All these boats were small ones of 56 tons, $114\frac{1}{2}$ ft. long, $10\frac{1}{2}$ ft. beam, and 6 ft. draught. With 525 I.H.P., they made 20 knots on trial. They have two torpedo tubes, carry two 1-pounder Q.F., a complement of 16 men, and are single screw. One of them was lost off the Pescadores in December, 1895, and a couple at Wei-hai-wei in February of the same year.

Japan still continued the construction of other craft, having launched the Maya[1] at Onohama in 1886, the Akagi[2] at the same yard in 1887, the Atago[3] at Yokosuka in 1887, and the Chiokai[4] at Tokio in the same year. The Maya and Chiokai were, as before, composite, but the other two are noteworthy as being constructed entirely of steel. A large proportion of the material for them was imported, and the building was rather a case of merely putting together.

The dimensions, etc., of all are identical, and are as follows:—

Displacement	622 tons.
Length	$154\frac{1}{4}$ ft.
Beam	27 ft.
Draught (mean)	$9\frac{1}{4}$ ft.
Horse-power	700.
Trial speed	(*circa*) 12 knots.
Screws	Two.

[1] Pronounced Maï'yà. [2] Ak-à-gĕĕ. [3] At-à-go. [4] Tchio'ka'i.

JAPANESE FLEET AT SEA. FUSO LEADING.

[*Official photo.*

THE IMPERIAL NAVY

Coal supply . . . 60 tons.
Complement . . . 104.

In appearance and armament they vary much. The Maya carries a couple of 6-in. Krupp's, with two 3-pounder Q.F. and a couple of machine guns; the Chiokai and Atago are armed with one 8-in. Krupp and one 4·7-in. gun and two machine guns; the Akagi carries two special French guns of about 4·7-in. calibre. These guns are the only ones of the kind in the world, and singularly powerful pieces—Hebrieu guns. The objection to them is that their lives are short. They proved too powerful for the little Akagi, and shook her up badly on trial. They were afterwards fired with reduced charges, except at Yalu, where they proved very useful, owing to their power.

The Ahagi has a raised forecastle, the other three have not. All used to be schooner-rigged, but just before the war a fighting-top was fitted to the Akagi's foremast, and a crow's-nest to her main. To distinguish them, the Maya has a black band, the Chiokai a red one, the Atago yellow. The Akagi's band is black, but her forecastle and fighting-top distinguish her. In addition, she has a rather elaborate green scrollwork on the bow. She has also sponsons for her machine guns. At Yalu this ship lost her mainmast, and the damage was left unrepaired for a long time in deference to naval sentiment; it has, however, been replaced lately.

Reference has already been made to the transfer of

torpedo-boat building from British to French firms. M. Bertin was at that time naval adviser to the Japanese Government, consequently French design for large ships secured a similar victory in the year 1887-8. With such ships as she now had, Japan was beginning to be able to stand alone, many English instructors were dispensed with; but she was yet some distance from her present independence. French enterprise saw its chance and took it; all the foreign-built ships of the new programme came from France.

These were the Itsukushima, Matsushima, and Hashidate (this last put together in Japan), the Unebi, Tschishima, and some smaller ships (laid down in Japanese yards), Yayeyama, Oshima, and Takao.

The ships built in Japan during the Bertin *régime*, 1887 to 1890, are distinctly French in design and appearance. The first to take the water was the Takao, launched at Yokosuka in 1888. Particulars are:—

Displacement	1778 tons.
Material of hull	Steel.
Length	229 ft.
Beam	34 ft.
Draught	14 ft.
Armament	Four 6-in.
	One 4·7-in. Q.F.
	Two torpedo tubes.
Horse-power	2300.
Speed on trial	15 knots.
Sea speed	(*circa*) 12 knots.
Screws	Two.
Coal supply	300 tons.

Boilers . . . . Two cylindrical.
Engines (made at Yokosuka) Two sets horizontal compound.
Complement . . . 220.

She is fitted with military and searchlight tops on both masts. The four 6-in. guns are in sponsons in the waist, the 4·7-in. is carried right aft. There is no protection of any sort to the machinery. She was the first steel ship built in Japan.

TAKAO.

About 1887 Japan definitely decided to draw all her Q.F. guns, 6-in. or 4·7-in., from Elswick, and all heavy guns from Canet. Krupp's pieces were discarded. This resolution was adhered to till 1902–03, so far as Elswick was concerned, but Canet guns were given up some years ago. Elswick guns were, in 1890, shipped to France for the Itsukushima and her sister· At present (1904) new guns are on the Vickers model.

Following the Takao, Yokosuka launched the

despatch vessel Yayeyama in 1899. She was designed by M. Bertin. Her dimensions, etc., are:—

Displacement	1605 tons.
Material of hull	Steel.
Length	315 ft.
Beam	$34\frac{1}{2}$ ft.
Draught	15 ft.
Armament	Three 4·7-in. Q.F.
	Six machine guns.
	Two torpedo tubes.
Horse-power (forced draught)	5630.
Speed on trial	20·7 knots.
Screws	Two.

The engines were provided by Messrs. Hawthorn, Leslie & Co. of England, and, instead of the horizontal compound previously fitted in Japanese-built ships, are horizontal, direct-acting, triple expansion. The boilers are of steel; there are six of these—cylindrical.

Over the engines and boilers a $\frac{1}{2}$-in. steel deck is carried, affording, in conjunction with the bunkers, some slight protection.

The Onohama Yard laid down a vessel in this year, the Oshima. She was launched in 1890. Particulars:—

Displacement	640 tons.
Material of hull	Steel.
Length	233 ft.
Beam	$25\frac{1}{2}$ ft.
Draught	$15\frac{3}{4}$ ft.
Armament	Four 4·7-in. Q.F.
	Eight 3-pdr. Q.F.
Horse-power (forced draught)	1200.
Speed on trial	16 knots.
Screws	One.

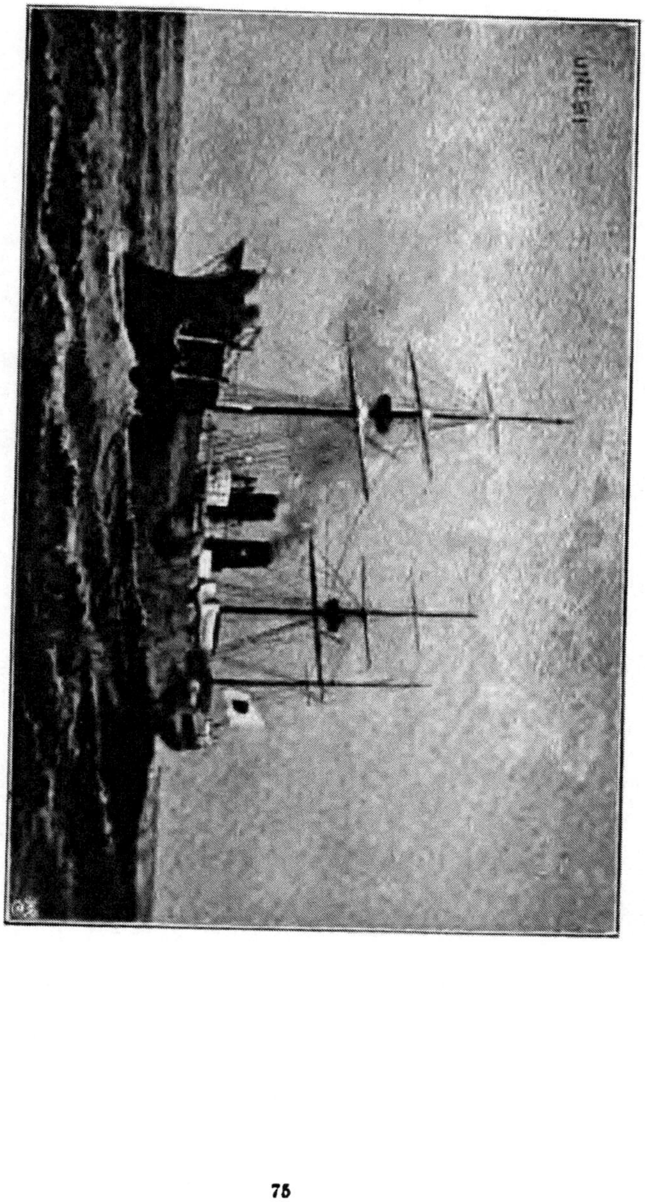

THE IMPERIAL NAVY

There is no protection to the machinery. The engines were built at Yokosuka.

Meanwhile, shipbuilding abroad had been proceeding apace, but disaster attended both the earlier vessels. The first, the Unebi, a cruiser of 3650 tons, with four 6-in. Q.F. as her principal armament, mysteriously disappeared while on her way out to Japan [1] and still in the contractors' hands. Her loss was officially attributed to instability, and seems to have inspired the Japanese authorities with a profound distrust for French shipbuilding; at any rate, the Chiyoda, a vessel generally resembling the lost Unebi, was given to Thomson Yard at Clydebank for construction. She will be described in due course later on.

The second French-built ship, upon the same general plan as the French Milan and Japanese Yayeyama, was the Tschishima, of 750 tons displacement. In appearance she was nearly identical to the French Milan. She met with disaster in the Inland Sea almost immediately after the Japanese took her over (1892), and all her crew were drowned. The Tatsuta was ordered from Elswick to replace her.

The Itsukushima, the first of the "Bertin cruisers," so-called after their designer, was launched at La Seyne in 1889. Captain Ingles, R.N., naval adviser to the

[1] It was currently reported, and for a long time believed in Japan, that the Unebi had been captured by the Chinese and taken into one of their harbours. Another report was to the effect that the Chinese had waylaid and destroyed her—a not impossible incident. A typhoon is, however, a more likely cause. It may be remembered that our gunboat Wasp mysteriously disappeared in Far Eastern waters, and nothing was ever heard as to how she perished.'

Japanese, had strongly persuaded them against ironclads; they had been advised against the big gun also. However, they were bent on mounting a gun able to pierce any armour in the Chinese Navy or in foreign warships likely to come to the Far East. By the irony of fate, these big guns contributed nothing to the victory of the Yalu; however, the decision of the Japanese to have them cannot be condemned, in view of the fact that naval construction everywhere in '88

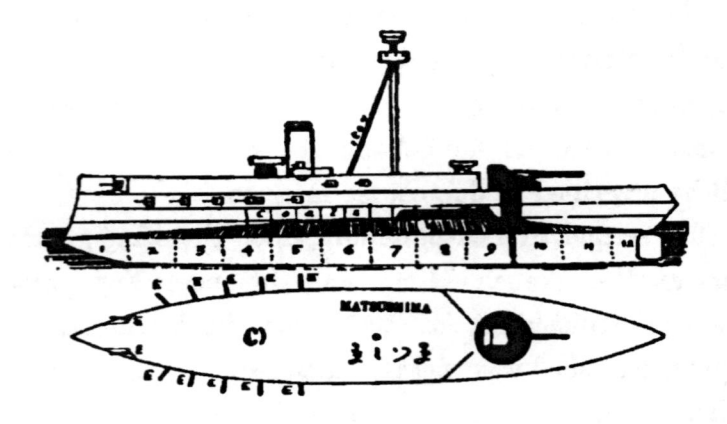

was based upon the big gun. Having a full idea of their requirements, the Japanese settled upon the Italian Lepanto as embodying the most useful type of ship for them, and the Itsukushimas were ordered on that principle.

Particulars of the Itsukushima are as follows:—

Displacement	4278 tons.
Material of hull	Steel.
Length	295 ft.
Beam	50½ ft.
Draught (maximum)	21¼ ft.

TORPEDO GUNBOAT TSCHICHIMA—LOST BY CAPSIZING IN THE INLAND SEA.

Armament[1].	One 12·8-in. Canet.
	Eleven 4·7-in. Q.F. Elswick of 32 cals.
	Five 6-pdr. Q.F.
	Eleven 3-pdr. Q.F.
	Six machine guns.
	Six torpedo tubes (bow, stern, and four on the broadsides).
Horse-power (natural draught)	3400.
Trial speed (natural draught)	15·7 knots.
Horse-power (forced draught)	5400.
Trial speed (forced draught)	16·5 knots.
Screws	Two.
Engines	Triple expansion.
Boilers	Six cylindrical.[1]
Furnaces	18.
Coal supply	400 tons.
Complement	360.

For protection there is a steel deck 1½ ins. thick on the slopes. With this is associated a cellulose belt and coal protection. The total protection, so far as penetration is concerned, is not, however, more than equivalent to what a 6-in. belt of old iron armour would afford, and it would keep out nothing above a 4·7-in. shot, and that only at long ranges. Over the engine hatches is a patch of thick steel armour.

The heavy gun barbette is a strip of 12-in. Creusot steel, with a 4-in. steel shield over the breech of the gun. There is an armoured hoist that affords some support, but, speaking generally, the gun is more or less at the mercy of shell bursting underneath it.

The Hashidate was built from the same designs at

---

[1] Now Belleville.

Yokosuka, and is practically identical with the Itsukushima, save that the battery guns aft are in small unarmoured sponsons, and obtain thereby a slightly greater angle of fire. She is further distinguished by a red band; the Itsukushima, being the first of the class, has, of course, a black band.

Grave doubts were soon entertained as to the seaworthiness of these two ships, and the Matsushima being a little more behindhand than the others, her design was altered. She carries the big gun aft, which makes her a better sea boat. The battery is shifted forward in the main deck. In place of the single 4·7-in. that her companions carry in the stern, the raised fok's'le of the Matsushima contains two of these pieces, firing through recessed port.

Her small quickfiring armament is also different, there being sixteen 3-pounders.

All three ships have a single tripod mast abaft the funnel, with a couple of tops on it. Each now carries three signal yards.

The Itsukushima was launched on July 11, 1889, and commissioned in Japan in 1891. The Matsushima, launched on January 22, 1890, went out in 1892. The Hashidate was not launched till March 24, 1891, but early in 1893 she was in commission.

It had been hoped that these ships would attain speeds of 17·5 knots; none of them, however, ever reached it.

HASHIDATE. [*Official photo.*

MATSUSHIMA.

Torpedo Boats. 1891.

In 1891 Japan had built for her by Normand at Le Havre a 75-ton torpedo boat, 118 ft. long, two tubes, and a trial speed of 23 knots. She is a twin-screw boat.

Two other boats, 90-tonners, were also launched in Germany at Elbing. Length, 128 ft.; trial speed, 23 knots; one screw; armament, three tubes and three 1-pounder Q.F.

China in 1890 launched a home-built diminutive of the Itsukushima, the Ping Yuen. The Japanese took her at Wei-hai-wei, but she has never been of any use to them, and she now does duty as a gunnery hulk. Particulars of this craft are:—

Displacement	2600 tons.
Material of hull	Steel.
Length	200 ft.
Beam	40 ft.
Draught	19 ft.
Armament (originally)	One 10·2-in. Krupp, 25 cals.
	Two 6-in. Krupp.
	Eight 3-pdr. Q.F.
	One 1-pdr. Q.F. (in the top).
	Four torpedo tubes.

The old 6-in. Krupp are now replaced by a couple of 45-calibre Elswick 6-in. Q.F. for drill purposes. The old 10-in. gun remains, and, being always cocked up in the air at an extreme elevation, is the most noticeable and characteristic feature of this ship, which every Japanese regards as a standing joke. An enormous dragon adorns each broadside. Japanese officers who come to Portsmouth always, by the way, christen our Hero "the British Ping Yen."

The Ping Yuen was begun as a 16-knot, 2850-ton ship, a copy in fine of the Stettin-built King Yuen. In an early stage of construction, however, her length was much reduced, *for economical reasons*. She appears to have had much the same machinery as the King Yuen originally. This, however, was tinkered in fitting, and some of her boilers were stolen, or otherwise dispensed with! On trial she made 10·5 knots for a short period, but, after being taken care of by the Chinese, soon sank below that modest speed. It is doubtful whether she made as much as 6 knots at Yalu.

There is a 2-in. steel protective deck in places; amidships and under water there is a small patch of 8-in. compound armour. The barbette is a 5-in. strip of armour; the conning-tower has the same thickness. A thin shield—removed during the war—covers the big gun.

On June 3, 1890, the third-class cruiser Chiyoda, built to replace the lost Unebi, took the water at Clydebank. Particulars of her are as follows:—

Displacement	2450 tons.
Material of hull	Steel.
Length	308 ft.
Beam	43 ft.
Draught (maximum)	17 feet.
Armament	Ten 4·7-in. Q.F. 40 cals.
	Fourteen 3-pdr. Q.F.
	Three Gatlings.
	Three torpedo tubes (of which one is fixed in the bow).

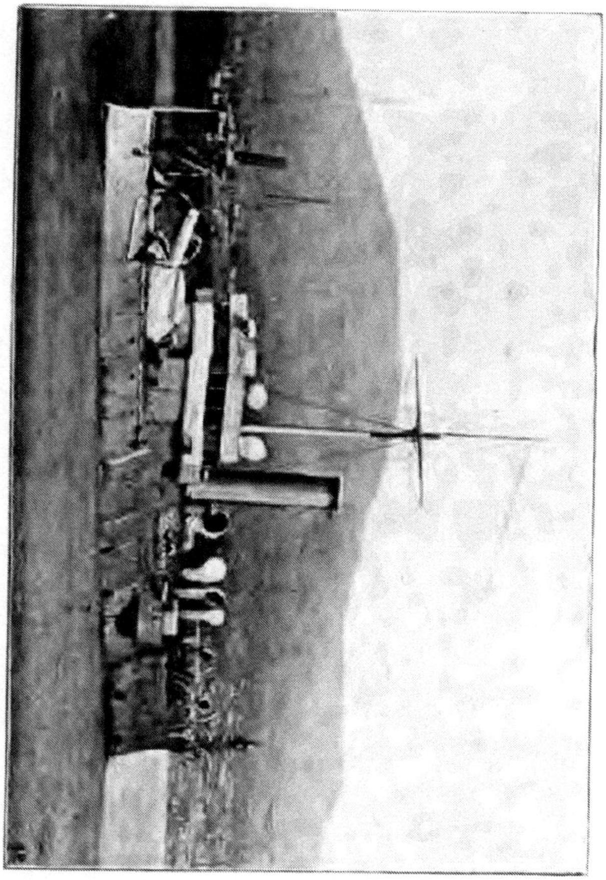

THE IMPERIAL NAVY

```
Horse-power      . . .  5600.
Trial speed      . . .  19 knots.
Engines          . . .  Two sets, triple expansion.
Boilers          . . .  Belleville.
Complement       . . .  350.
Coal supply      . . .  420 tons.
```

She was the first ship in any navy to be fitted with water-tube boilers, which were barely coming into existence in those days. Hers are of the Belleville type.

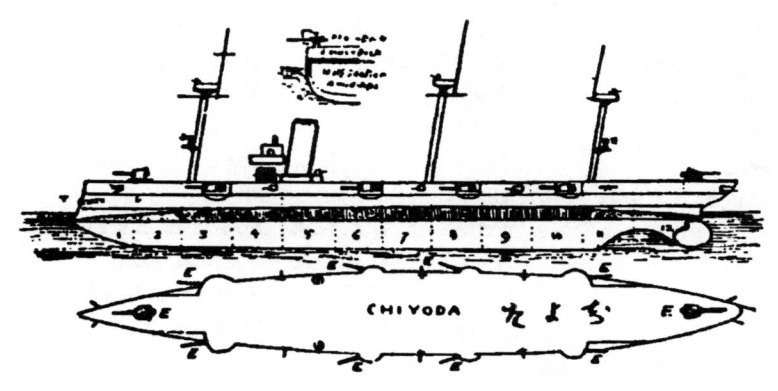

For protection she depends on a 4¼-in. chrome steel armour belt, 200 ft. long, amidships. Forward and aft of this is a protective deck 1½ ins. thick on the slopes. Throughout the entire water-line is a cellulose belt, and she is divided into 84 watertight compartments. The guns have no protection beyond the ordinary shields. They are, however, very well disposed.

In 1898 she was practically reboilered, the old tubes being replaced by some specially large ones, in order to enable her to burn Japanese coal, which sooted the ordinary tubes.

In 1890 the Akitsushima was laid down at Yokosuka.

It was at first supposed that she was a sister to the Matsushima. The Yoshino was contracted for at Elswick towards the end of this year. Both were launched in 1892, and commissioned just before the war with China.

The Akitsushima was the last ship to be built in Japan with imported material. She is practically a small copy of the U.S.S. Baltimore. Details of the two, for comparison, are as follows:—

	AKITSUSHIMA.	BALTIMORE.
Displacement	3150 tons.	4600 tons.
Material of hull	Steel.	Steel.
Length	302 ft.	328 ft.
Beam	43 ft.	$48\frac{1}{4}$ ft.
Draught	$18\frac{1}{2}$ ft.	23 ft.
Armament	Four 6-in. Q.F. (D).	Four 8-in. 25 cals. (C).
	Six 4·7-in. Q.F. (E).	Six 6-in. (D.)
	Ten 3-pdr. Q.F.	Eight small Q.F.
	Four torpedo tubes.	Five torpedo tubes.
Horse-power (forced draught)	8400.	10,060.
Speed on trial	19 knots.	20·1 knots.
Engines	Vertical triple expansion.	Horizontal triple expansion.
Boilers	Cylindrical.	Four double-ended Scotch.
Screws	Two.	Two.
Coal (normal)	500.	400.
„ (bunker capacity)	800.	900.
Armour deck on slopes	3-in. (*e*).	4-in. (*d*).
Other protection		Cellulose belt and cofferdam.
Complement	330.	395.

The Akitsushima mounts 6-in. guns in the foremost and aftermost sponsons; four 4·7-in. are carried

[Photo by favour of Commander Kurri, I.J.N.

AKITSUSHIMA.

amidships, the fifth on the forecastle, and the sixth astern. She has thus a broadside fire of two 6-in. and four 4·7-in., against two 8-in. and three 6-in. in the Baltimore. Assuming that ship's guns to be now

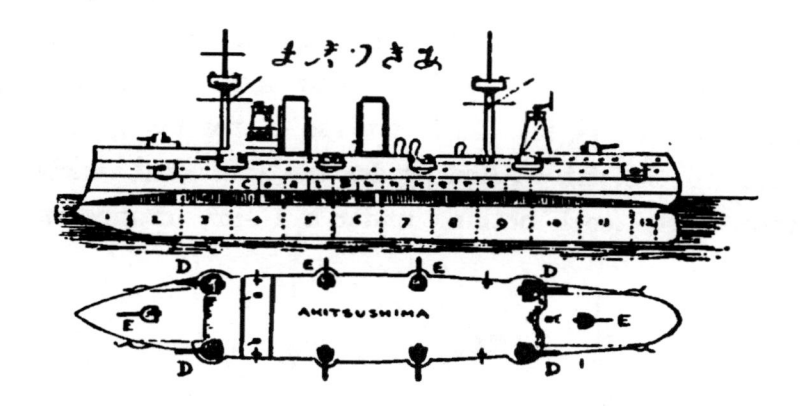

replaced by Q.F., the Akitsushima would bring the equivalent of a 6-in. gun less.

The Yoshino, when new, was the swiftest cruiser in the world, and very few ships are equal to her yet. Particulars of her are:—

Displacement	4150 tons.
Material of hull	Steel.
Length	350 ft.
Beam	46 ft.
Draught (maximum)	19 ft.
Armament	Four 6-in. Q.F.
	Eight 4·7-in. Q.F.
	Twenty-two 3-pdr. Q.F.
	Five torpedo tubes (one of them fixed in the bow).
Horse-power (forced draught)	15,000.
Trial speed ,, ,,	23·031 knots.
Engines (Humphrys, Tennant & Co.)	Vertical triple expansion.

96 THE IMPERIAL JAPANESE NAVY

Boilers	Cylindrical.
Screws	Two.
Coal (maximum bunker capacity)	1000 tons.
Complement	360.

The normal coal supply, at 4150 tons displacement, is about 400 tons. Bunkers are disposed amidships in the usual fashion above the armour deck. Amidships this deck is $4\frac{1}{2}$ ins. thick on the slopes ($= c$) and 2 ins. on the flat. Allowing for the additional resistance of the coal, nothing under a 10-in., or modern 9·2 or 9·4-in., could penetrate to the engine-room, and then only with solid shot. The watertight compartments are exceptionally numerous. With natural draught the ship has made 21·6 knots.

The 6-in. guns are thus distributed: one on the forecastle, one on the poop, the other two in the foremost sponsons. The other broadside guns are 4·7-in. and 3-pounders. The bow and stern chasers have an arc of fire of 270 degrees, the 6-in. guns in sponsons fire 3 degrees across the bow and 60 degrees abaft it.

Photo by Sir W. G. Armstrong, Mitchell & Co., Ltd., Elswick.

YOSHINO.

The aftermost 4·7-in. fire 3 degrees across the stern and 60 degrees before it. The broadside guns have an arc of about 120 degrees. Each of the fighting-tops carries a couple of 3-pounder Q.F., four on each bridge, two under the forecastle forward, two under the poop well aft, the remaining six between the guns amidships.

Towards the end of 1893 a violent agitation against the Navy filled the Japanese newspapers. The existing types of ships—particularly the Chiyoda and Itsuku-shima class—were unfavourably criticised. The *personnel* was not free from these attacks; it was in some quarters demonstrated useless and inefficient. In the midst of these attacks the war with China loomed and broke out. After that war nothing further was heard on the subject of the *personnel's* "defects."

The primary result of the agitation was a new ship-building programme. The only ships actually under construction at that time were the Suma, building at Yokosuka, and laid down in March, 1893, and the Tatsuta, ordered to replace the lost Tschishima, building at Elswick. The new programme embodied "two first-class battleships of the most powerful type," a cruiser at Yokosuka of the Suma type, and a sloop Miyako, laid down at Kuré in 1894. This programme was also a subject of attack in a portion of the Japanese press.

Before, however, anything could be done, the battle of Asan and the affair of the Kowshing precipitated the war with China. Consequently, on the outbreak of war, the Tatsuta, launched at Elswick on April 6, 1894, and hastily completed in August of the same year, was stopped as contraband on her way out at Aden.

The Tatsuta is a torpedo gunboat. Particulars as follows :—

Displacement	875 tons.
Material of hull	Steel.
Length	240 ft.
Beam	27½ ft.
Draught (mean)	9½ ft.
Armament	Two 4·7-in. Q.F.
	Four 3-pdr. Q.F.
	Five torpedo tubes (one fixed in bow, the others in pairs—a pair on each quarter).
Horse-power (forced draught)	5500.
Trial speed	21 knots.
Engines (Hawthorn, Leslie & Co.)	Vertical triple expansion.
Screws	Two.
Coal supply (normal)	188 tons.
,, ,, (maximum capacity)	200 tons.
Complement	100 men.

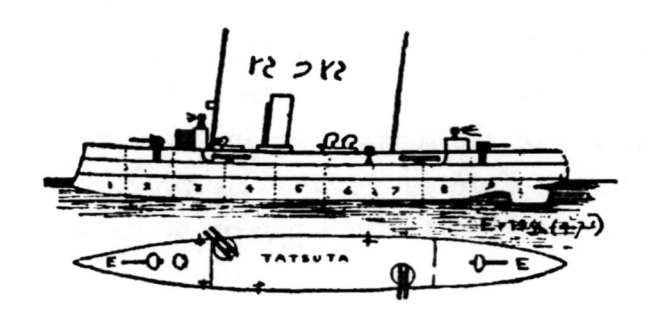

CHAPTER V

THE WAR WITH CHINA

JAPAN was not long in finding uses for her navy. The massacre of some shipwrecked Japanese in Formosa led to the despatch of a punitive expedition, the expense of which was paid by China, the suzerain, without any too much good-will.

In 1875 Koreans gave trouble, by attacking a Japanese steamer that had visited one of their ports for coal and provisions, and in the midst of wild excitement a fleet was despatched, which, however, accomplished its object without bloodshed. A commercial treaty was concluded, and Japanese influences once more begun to gain ground in the Hermit Kingdom.

Mention has already been made of the Satsuma clan, whose anti-foreign sentiments had brought them into conflict with the British ten years before. A large portion of this clan were still violently conservative, and Saigo, the then head, having retired from Tokio, set up military schools, which something like 20,000 young Samurai entered. Owing to his known reactionary ideas, Saigo was naturally viewed with some suspicion, but it is questionable whether he was at first imbued with anything but a strong imperialism. Amongst other things, he advocated the seizure of Korea, which, at that time, could have been done without much opposition, if any, from Russia, then busy over her war with Turkey. The Russian danger crusade was not, however, taken seriously by the people at large, and Saigo, in preaching war with Russia, was regarded as a visionary, crying "wolf" where no wolf was to be found.

On the other hand, war with China was a foregone conclusion for a long time before it occurred. Both China and Japan wanted Korea, and while China claimed a suzerainty over Korea, Japan insisted that it was an independent State. On account of this, strained relations were continual.

In the spring of 1894 an insurrection broke out in Korea, and China, to indicate her suzerainty, despatched troops to quell it. At the same time she sent a Note to the Japanese Government, notifying her intentions, using the term "tributary State" for Korea.

Japan replied by a Note, refusing to accept the "tributary State" expression, and a little later announced her intention of sending 4000 troops to Korea—claiming this as her right under the Chemulpo Convention—which specified that if China sent troops to Korea, Japan might do the like.

China protested, and, after the exchange of many Notes, despatched ten transports full of troops from Taku between July 21 and July 23. She also sent to Asan in Korea the small cruiser Tche Yuen and the gunboat Kuang-ki.

THE BATTLE OF ASAN (PHUNG-DO).

ON July 25th the Chinese warships Tche Yuen (Tsi Yuen)[1] and Kwang-Yi (Kuang King), coming from Asan in Korea, with awnings up, and generally unprepared for action, encountered off the island of Phung-do a portion of the Japanese flying squadron, consisting of the Naniwa (Captain Togo),[2] Yoshino (Captain Kawara), and Akitsushima (Captain Kamimura), the Yoshino flying the flag of Rear-Admiral Tsuboi.

Many accounts of this action have been written. The one I give here differs in many details from the narrative currently accepted; however, it is based on the personal narratives to me of officers of the Japanese ships engaged, and appears to me to afford by far the most reasonable explanation as to how the fight came about.

The Tche Yuen was never a good steering ship, and her steering-gear, which had been for some time in a state of neglect, broke down just about the time the Japanese ships were sighted.

This caused her to alter her course, and she bore down upon the Japanese, coming nearer and nearer. The idea went round that she purposed torpedoing.

---

[1] Now the Sai-Yen.
[2] Admiral in command of the main fleet in February, 1904.

Every gun in the Japanese fleet was thereupon laid upon the Tche Yuen's conning-tower, red flags hoisted, and the Chinese ships ordered to keep off. This the leading vessel, Tche Yuen (Captain Fong), was unable to do, and she pressed so closely on the Naniwa that Captain Togo turned and headed towards her.

The Tche Yuen hoisted a white flag, but still continued to approach. Thereupon the Naniwa opened fire, the other ships following suit. The Japanese version, that the Tche Yuen fired a torpedo first of all, while under the white flag, generally credited, is, on the evidence of Japanese officers, quite incorrect. No torpedo was fired; they expected one—that is all.

The conning-tower of the Tche Yuen was hit five times at the first discharge, the first lieutenant and a sub-lieutenant, who were inside, being killed, though the captain, who stood beside them, was unhurt. He vacated the tower, and gave orders to clear for action. In the circumstances he made a very passable fight for it, despite the subsequent Chinese allegations of cowardice. Caught unprepared, his fighting did not amount to much; but that was a natural sequel to his unpreparedness.

Long before the Chinese could reply, the Japanese, at 3000 yards, had practically put the ship *hors de combat*. A large shell hit the armour-deck, and glancing up, struck the fore-turret, disabling one of the 8-in. guns. All men on deck were killed, wounded, or driven away, and in a little while the fore-turret was again hit and the gun's crews killed. A shell burst in the funnel base, killing or wounding men in the stokehold, and all the upper works were riddled.

At about this stage the Tche Yuen did what she should have done long before, got the hand-steering wheel going, and, this done, she made off for Wei-hai-wei, keeping up a mild fire on the Japanese ships from her after 6-in. gun. This retreat was the only thing she could do; to remain would have been madness.

The Japanese attempted no pursuit, despite Chinese stories to the contrary. They believed that the Chinese battle-fleet was near by, and were chary accordingly. The only hit obtained by the Tche Yuen was on the Yoshino's bridge, and this did little harm. On the other hand, the Tche Yuen, though she lost three officers and thirteen men killed, and twenty-five wounded, was not seriously damaged structurally, for within a week she was repaired. She, however, looked a fearful wreck; and an idea obtains that the Japanese thought that the sight of her would have a strong moral effect on the Chinese, which to some extent it did. If so, it was no unwise move; the ship, sound or damaged, could never be a serious enemy to them.

While this was going on the Kuang-Yi, disregarding orders to retire, attempted to charge and torpedo the enemy.[1] In this, of course, she failed, and, being on fire, most of her crew killed or wounded, she ran ashore. What was left of her crew—eighteen men all told—reached the land. The Naniwa, which had engaged the gunboat, continued to pound her, till a

[1] See Appendix for Chinese version of this affair.

JAPANESE FLEET IN LINE ABREAST OFF CHEMULPO DURING THE WAR.

[*Official photo.*

torpedo in the stern-tube blew up, and practically destroyed her completely.

This battle, save that it began the war, was a quite unimportant event, and has never been regarded in the Japanese Navy for more than it is worth. It is chiefly interesting on account of the pluck exhibited by the Chinese captain of the Kuang-Yi, and for the fact that in it Togo of the Naniwa first came to the front.

SINKING OF THE KOWSHING

THE Battle of Asan began at 7.5 a.m. on July 25, 1894. It was well over when, at 8.30 a.m., the British-owned transport Kowshing was sighted in the distance, and at 9.15 a.m. the Naniwa fired two blank charges at her and signalled to her to stop.

The Kowshing was perfectly well known to the Japanese, Lieutenant Kuroi, of the Intelligence Department, having informed his Government on July 14th that she was chartered as a transport for Chinese troops. She was commanded by Captain Galsworthy of the British mercantile marine, and had on board, besides her officers and crew of 64 men, 1100 Chinese soldiers and the German Von Hannacken, who was in the Chinese service.

The Naniwa ordered the Kowshing to follow her, and to this capture the captain assented, but the Chinese on board insisted on returning to Taku instead. Four hours were spent in negotiations, at the end of which time Captain Togo advised the Europeans in the Kowshing to leave. Before this was complied with the Chinese were in a state of mutiny, and Togo, dreading the arrival of the Chinese battle-fleet, gave the order to open fire on the transport. At 1.10 p.m. he fired a torpedo, which missed, and a broadside that hit the Kowshing in the engine-room. Five minutes later she began to sink, and at 1.46 went under.

Most of the European officers jumped overboard, and the majority were rescued by the Naniwa's boats. The Chinese on board the sinking ship opened a heavy rifle-fire on everything and everybody. The story that the Japanese fired on the men in the water does not appear to have any foundation in fact. The statement that they did so rests on the authority of the German Von Hannacken, who was hardly in a position to observe the exact facts as he swam to safety. It is probable, and, indeed, to be presumed, that the men on the Naniwa's tops fired at the Kowshing, in order to keep down the fire which the Chinese soldiers directed at the Japanese boats sent to pick up the European survivors.

About half the Chinese were picked up by a French gunboat or escaped to the islands; no attempt to save any was made by the Japanese. For this they have received stronger condemnation than they merit. To risk being killed by one lot of the enemy in order to save another lot is not a necessary act in war ethics. This was Captain Togo's view, situated as he was in a position of considerable danger, owing to the supposed propinquity of the Chinese fleet. From panic, or the idea that the Japanese would give no quarter, the Chinese had to all intents and purposes gone mad *en masse*; and whatever theories armchair critics may evolve, the amount of blame actually due to Captain Togo is of a trifling nature. He had to choose between two evils, and chose the least.

The legality of the attack on the Kowshing was hotly contested; but in the end it was established that

Japan was inside her legal rights. As to the ethics of the matter—well, the moralist who objects is apt to fail to realise that the Kowshing carried 1100 of the best soldiers China could put in the field, and they had been destined to fight the Naniwa's countrymen. To allow them to proceed would have been a splendid exhibition of legal-mindedness, but it would also have been a criminally stupid act from the patriotic standpoint.

SUBSEQUENT OPERATIONS

AFTER this there was a lull. The Chinese battle-fleet, led by Admiral Ting in the Ting Yuen, put to sea searching for the Japanese. Ting was anxious to fight, and his *personnel* was in a good state of efficiency; his *materiel* was otherwise. Still, at this early stage, had he encountered the Japanese fleet, he was far more likely to have destroyed it than he was later on.

He had, however, to reckon with Li Hung Chang and Loh Feng Lo. These presently ordered him not to cruise east of Wei-hai-wei and the Yalu river; and this order practically put the Chinese fleet out of the operations. It has been stated many times that Li Hung Chang was bribed by the Japanese to give this order, and it is possible that he was. It is more probable, however, that for the Chinese to be defeated was a part of his own peculiar policy.

For some time, therefore, nothing happened. The Japanese feinted at Wei-hai-wei and Port Arthur, but for a good six weeks they spent most of their time in sea work—drilling and preparing for battle. The Chinese ships, on the other hand, lay inactive, steadily deteriorating morally, as inactive ships must.

It was stated in Japan that British cruisers at this time acted as Chinese scouts, giving information as to Japanese movements. It is a difficult matter to authenticate or even to refer to. I have seen Chinese official reports (translated ones) in which two cruisers are specifically mentioned, but a Chinese official report is not necessarily confirmation. There is no question whatever but that the Chinese spread the rumour of British sympathy and benevolent neutrality; it is fairly clear, too, that now and again they obtained information as to Japanese whereabouts from British men-of-war. But it is not proved that this was anything more than in the course of ordinary conversation, and there is no reason whatever to believe that the British Government had a hand in the matter.

VI

THE BATTLE OF YALU (HAI YANG)

JAPAN, having been as good as presented with the command of the sea, swiftly moved an army into Korea. This went on till, in September, China began to realise that if she wished to hold that country she must use the sea as transport. At Ping Yang her land forces had suffered a severe defeat; reinforcements were urgently required. Ting was, therefore, ordered to convey these to the Yalu River.

On Sunday, September 1st, at 1 a.m., Ting sailed from Talien Bay, having with him the Ting Yuen (flag), Chen Yuen, Lai Yuen, King Yuen, Ping Yuen, battleships;[1] and the cruisers Chin Yuen, Chih Yuen, Tche Yuen, Tchao Yong, and Yang Wei; two gunboats, Kuang Kai and Kuang Ping; four "flat-iron" Rendel gunboats; four torpedo boats; and five transports, carrying a thousand men each.

Reaching the mouth of the Yalu on the same evening, he sent the transports, under convoy of the Ping Yuen, Kuang Ping, and torpedo boats, up the Yalu River, anchoring twelve miles out with his main fleet.

---

[1] Except in the case of the first two, only by courtesy so called.

Early next morning the smoke of the Japanese, burning Takashima coal, was observed on the horizon.

It has never been clearly demonstrated whether the meeting was accidental or designed. The balance of evidence, to my mind, is in favour of the theory that Admiral Ito calculated that the Chinese would, after Ping Yang, send ships to the mouth of the Yalu, conveying troops. That certainly was Admiral Ito's theory.

The Chinese lay with banked fires. On seeing the Japanese smoke, they got up anchor, and adopted the prearranged battle-formation—line abreast *en échelon*, the centre strong, the wings weak. Line abreast was the best formation for the Chinese fleet, which was best in bow fire, but the weak ends of the wings were a serious error. In addition, the Yang Wei and Tcho Yong were slow at getting up anchor.

The Japanese came along in line ahead, the flying squadron leading the main astern of it.

The rival squadrons were as follows:—

Japan: 8 cruisers, 1 old battleship, 1 old "belted cruiser," 1 gunboat, and 1 armed liner.

China: 4 battleships, 3 cruisers, 3 gunboats, with (coming from the Yalu) 1 battleship, 1 gunboat, and 2 torpedo boats.

The Japanese fleet fought by signals throughout; the Chinese fought without signals, on a prearranged plan. In *materiel*, so far as ships went, the fleets were about on a par in fighting value. Actually, the Japanese were superior—in part from the possession

ADMIRAL ITO.

JAPANESE FLEET.

	Ship.	Tons.	Captain.	Armament.	Speed in 1894.
					Knots.
Flying squadron.	Yoshino [1]	4150	Kawara	Four 6-in. Q.F., eight 4·7-in. Q.F.	20
	Takachiho	3650	Nomura	Two 10-in. Krupp, six 6-in.	15
	Naniwa	3650	Togo	Ditto	16
	Akitsushima	3150	Kamimura	Four 6-in. Q.F., six 4·7-in. Q.F.	16
Main fleet.	Matsushima [2]	4277	{Omoto, Dewa}	One 12·6-in. Canet, twelve 4·7-in. Q.F.	14
	Chiyoda	2450	Uchida	Ten 4·7-in. Q.F.	?
	Itsukushima	4277	Yoko-o	One 12·6-in. Canet, eleven 4·7-in. Q.F.	14
	Hashidate	4277	Hidaka	Ditto	14
	Fuso	3718	Arai	Four 9·4-in. Krupp, two 6-in. Krupp	11
	Hi Yei	2200	Sakurai	Nine old 6-in.	9
Out of line.	Akagi	615	Sakamoto	Two 4·7-in. Q.F.	8
	Saikio-maru [3]	2913	Kano	Two light guns and some small Q.F.	10

[1] Rear-Admiral Tsuboi.   [2] Vice-Admiral Ito.   [3] Vice-Admiral Count Kabayama.

	Ship.	Tons.	Captain.	Armament.	Speed in 1894.
Battle-line.	Yang Wei	1350	—	Two 10·2-in., four 4·7-in. Krupp	Knots. 6
	Tchao Yung	1350	—	Ditto	6
	Ching Yuen	2300	—	Three 8·2-in., two 6-in. Elswick	14
	Lai Yuen	2850	—	Two 8·2-in., two 6-in. Krupp	10
	Chen Yuen	7430	Lin	Four 12-in., two 6-in. Krupp	12
	Ting Yuen[1]	7430	Lin-Poo-Chin	Ditto	12
	King Yuen	2850	—	Two 8·2-in., two 6-in. Krupp	10
	Chih Yuen	2300	Tang	Three 8·2-in., two 6-in. Krupp	15
	Kuang Chi	1290	—	Three 4·7-in. Krupp	10¾
	Tsi Yuen	2355	Fong	Two 8·2-in., one 6-in. Krupp	12⅔
Inshore.	Ping Yuen	2100	—	One 10·2-in., two 6-in. Krupp	6 or 7
	Kwang Ping	1000	—	Three 4·7-in. Krupp	10
	One torpedo boat	128	—	Three tubes	15
	,, ,, ,,	69	—	Ditto	16

[1] Admiral Ting.

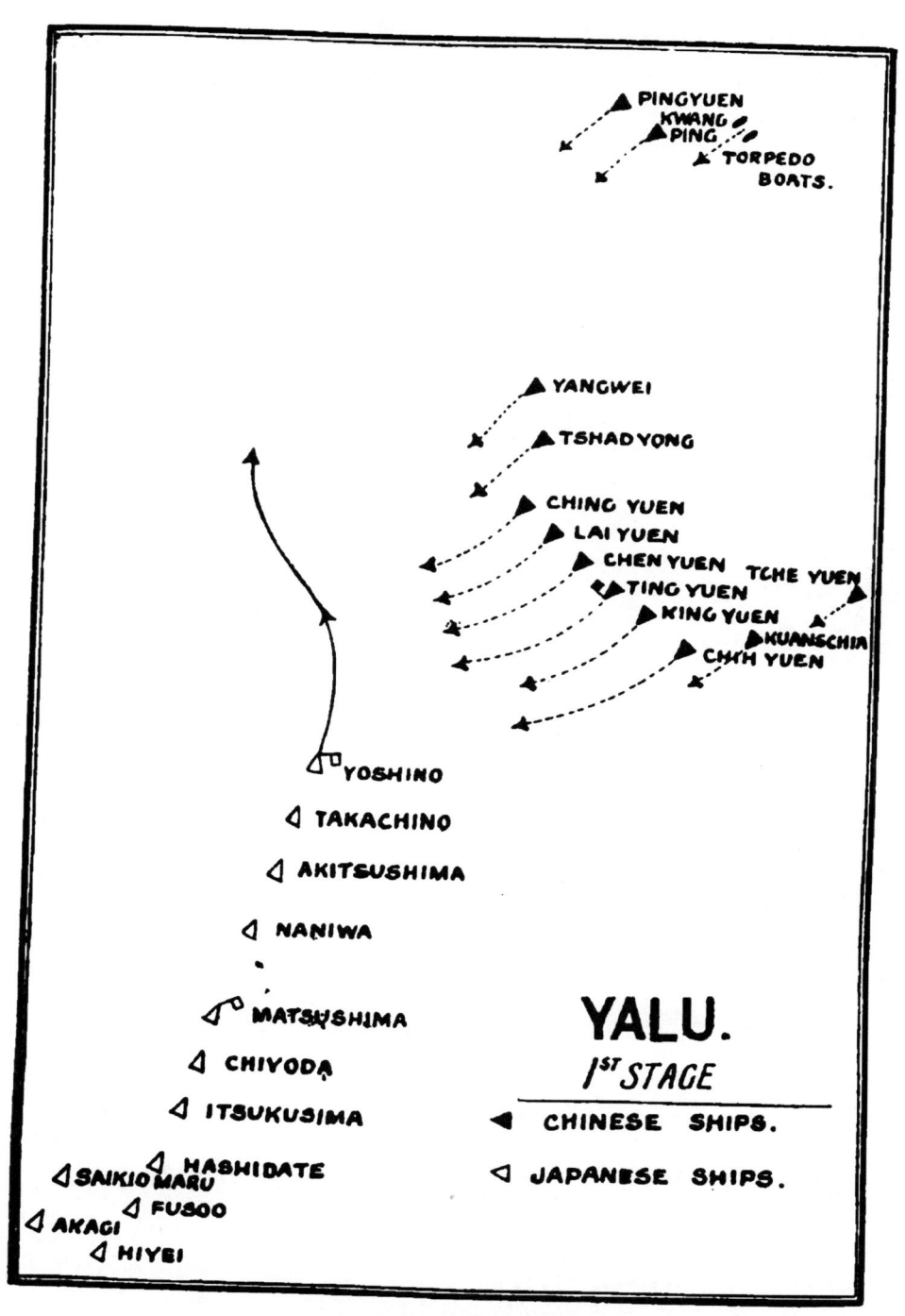

YALU: THE BEGINNING OF THE BATTLE.

of Q.F. guns, in part because the Chinese were very badly supplied with shell. Had they had a good supply of shell, there is little question but that, with their preponderance of large-calibre guns, they would have destroyed the Japanese fleet, especially as Admiral Ito made a considerable error at the outset.

The first shot, which fell short, was fired by the Ting Yuen at 12.30. A moment later the battle was general.

The sea was smooth—almost glassy—the sky dull. There was, however, a growing breeze, and this blew towards the Chinamen, so that the black smoke from the Japanese cruisers acted as a helpful screen.

The Japanese came on, and passed right across the Chinese front, turning in succession eight points to port, when they opened on the Chinese at 3000 yards. This passing across the front was dangerous, and the Chinese nearly succeeded in cutting the Japanese line. They lost station in doing so, masking each other; and to this the Japanese fleet owed much, and only their tail was endangered. The Fuso was badly hit. The Hi Yei, in danger of being rammed, had to alter her course. She passed between the Chinese battle-ships at short range, getting badly hit as she cleared them. The Akagi was badly knocked about; the Saikio alone passed on unhurt.

The Chinese had by now half won the battle, but they were in such a muddle with their ships that the advantage was never followed up. At this time the flying squadron, which had cut off the two old gunboats to starboard of the Chinese line, was masked by the remaining four vessels of the main fleet; and an inspection of the plan of the second stage will show how near victory was for the Chinamen had their fleet only been in hand. Overwhelming heavy gunfire was theirs.

They lost the opportunity, however, and the flying squadron, after a short engagement with the Ping Yuen division, circled and came round on the Chinese front, while the main squadron, also turning, assailed its rear. The Ping Yuen devoted herself to a fruitless attempt at chasing the main Japanese fleet, while the bulk of the Chinese wasted effort in an attempt to complete the destruction of the little Akagi. In doing this they came under fire of the flying squadron, which sank both the King Yuen and Chih Yuen with its 10·2-in. guns.

Attempts by one of the torpedo boats to sink the Saikio-maru failed; she also survived a fire from the Chinese battleships. The Lai Yuen was by now ablaze; the Ching Yuen was no better off. Both battleships were also on fire. The pendulum had swung round, and everything pointed to a complete victory for Japan.

Matters were thus when, at 3.30, the Matsushima was put out of action. The incidents enabled the battleships to recover, and they took, without much serious harm, a hammering from the entire Japanese fleet that remained.

This stage continued till nightfall, when the Chinese

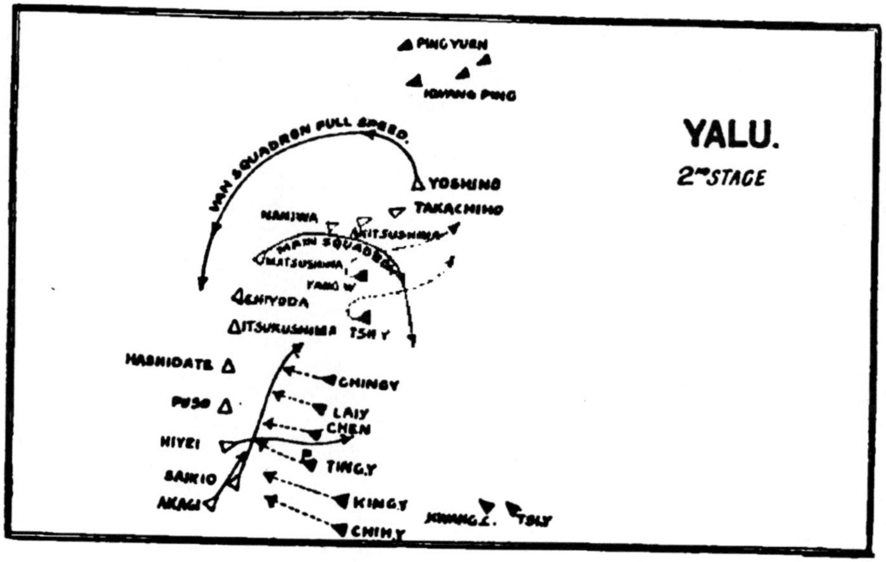

YALU.
2ND STAGE

got into line and steamed away, followed for a short distance only by the Japanese.

Both sides claimed the victory; as a matter of fact, it was a drawn battle. When the length of time the battle took is considered, the damages were relatively small. In detail, they were as follows:—

Japanese Fleet's Damages.

The Japanese flagship, Matsushima, went through the battle without any particular harm for a considerable while, when one of the Chinese ironclads fired a 12-in. common shell at her, which hit her, making a big hole. It went in and wiped out practically the entire battery, disabled two or three guns completely, and exploded some spare ammunition. Altogether 100 men were killed or wounded by that one shell, and she had to be hauled out of action. When that 12-in. shell hit, the majority of the men were in working dresses, in cotton things and so on, and a great many of them were men with beards, and a Japanese officer who was on board the ship at the time tells me that every single one of these men with cotton dresses was set on fire, and all the men with beards and long hair also had their beards and hair set on fire, and were rushing all over the ship, whereas several officers, who happened to be in serge uniform near by, were comparatively little hurt. The ship was set on fire to a certain extent, but a few buckets of water very easily put the fire out.

This ship was also hit by a 10·2-in. shell a little earlier in the action. It hit her torpedo-room, glanced up, and knocked up against the barbette; but as the shell was loaded with cement its burst did not do very much harm.

The second ship in the Japanese line was the Chiyoda. She was also hit by a 12-in. shell, but that was another cement or coal-dust shell, so did not burst. It went through just above the belt. Had it hit the belt it ought to have sunk her; above, it simply made a large hole through and went out again, and the ship was none the worse; there was not a single man killed or wounded.

The Naniwa was hit by an 8·2-in. on the water-line, which went into the coal bunkers, but it did no particular harm there. The shell was afterwards picked up and pieced together, and a photograph taken of such sections as were got. Twenty-seven pieces were recovered, and they say there must have been a great many more. But that 8·2-in. shell practically did no harm whatever to the ship. The coal bunkers acted very efficiently.

In the Itsukushima there were shells in the torpedo-room, but none of the torpedoes exploded—if there were any there with war-heads, which is rather uncertain. There was also a shell in the engine-room, which, curiously enough, did no harm.

The Hashidate had a 6-in. shell burst right up against the barbette of a big gun, which was not hurt at all by it.

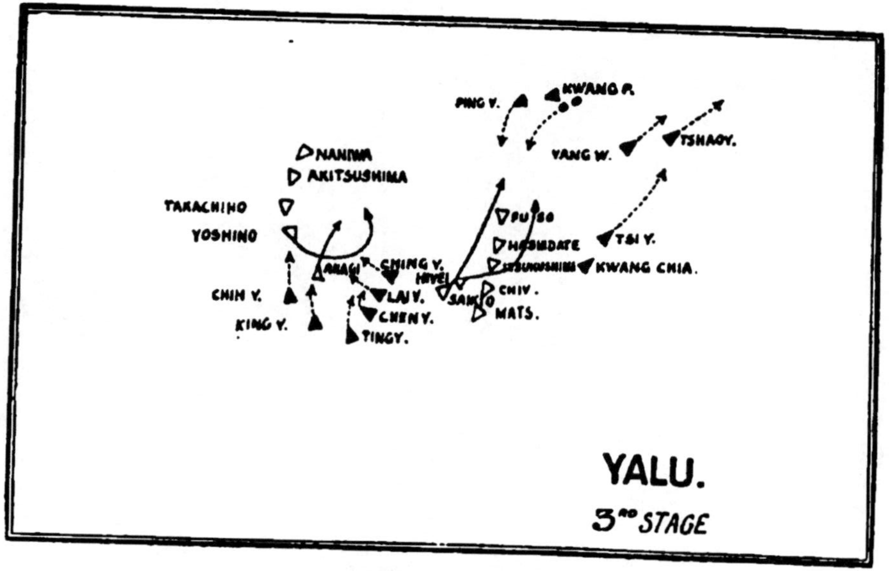

BATTLE OF YALU: THIRD STAGE.

The Hi Yei, an oldish ship, was raked by a 12-in. common shell, and also by some smaller shells, which set her on fire and practically blew the ship to pieces.

The Sakio-maru was quite a small vessel. She was hit first of all by a 12-in. common shell, which, in theory, ought to have blown her to atoms. It disabled her steering-gear and wounded one man. She altogether got eleven hits from pieces of 4·7-in. or over. Of these, four were 12-in. shell, of which two burst inside; and the net result of those eleven hits was to wound eleven men, to kill nobody, but to make the ship leak a bit. The torpedoes fired at her missed, as has already been stated. The reason was that the boat fired as she turned, and the torpedo went under. Two others fired at longer ranges missed badly. The torpedo boat was not hit. The Chinese version of the affair runs to the effect that the Japanese on board the Saikio deserted their guns in panic at the attack. This statement rests, of course, only on the Chinese assertion.

The Akagi was hit by a 12-in. common shell, which struck the mainmast and sent it overboard, and killed the captain. The peculiar thing about it was that all the hits took her about that part; there was not a single hit forward, but the bridge, which stands somewhere aft, was continually swept, and the second in command was wounded almost immediately after he went on the bridge. The third officer, Lieut. Sato, then went up, and was hit by a fragment of shell that scraped the top of his head off, and he went down below. A fourth man went up; he got wounded, and the third man went up again and carried on. She was able to steam and go home quite comfortably after the battle.

A gun shield, about two inches thick, was struck, and the shell that hit it is supposed to have been a 6-in. common. It simply scooped out the shield about an inch or so, and did no harm to the men inside, who were just round the corner, and did no harm whatever to the gun.

One shell burst on the upper deck, wrecked everything, made a tremendous mess, and riddled the deck all over, but the harm was practically *nil*.

The old battleship Fuso was hit more than any other Japanese ship, but every hit upon her has been kept confidential. Still, so far as can be guessed, the Japanese opinion of the result of the fire on this ship was that armour under the peculiar circumstances of the Yalu tended to aggravate hits rather than the reverse, and it is certainly interesting that this ship, with an armoured battery, completely armoured belt, and fairly thick armour which could not be penetrated by any of the Chinese 6-in. shell, should have been one of the most damaged ship of any.

Chinese Fleet's Damages.

The Chinese flagship was an ironclad of 7000 tons displacement, the Ting Yuen. The first thing that

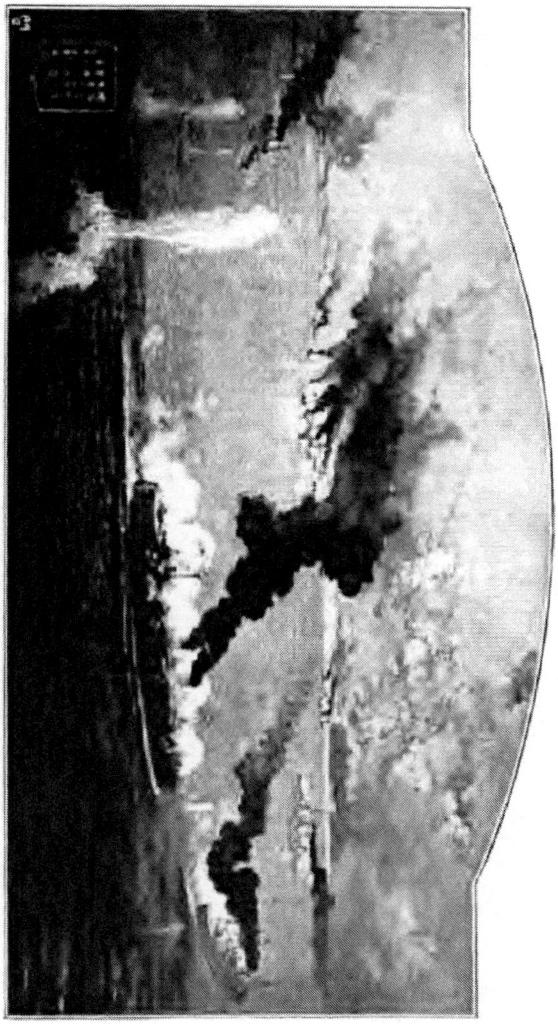

hit her was a big ricochet which flew up and knocked the mast, carried it over the side, and killed all the men in the fighting-top. She was peppered all over by the Japanese, and hit something like 300 times, the result of the 300 hits being 14 men killed and 25 wounded. She was set on fire practically continuously all through the action. As soon as one fire was put out she was set on fire again in another place; but the Chinese managed to get these fires out without any bother, and no harm was done to her that way.

The second principal Chinese ship was the Chen Yuen. She was hit 400 times. The photograph of her in dock is how she appeared shortly after the battle. The funnel was peppered over everywhere. All the men in the fighting-tops were killed. The fore 6-in. turret was hit; it is only about an inch thick, and this shell went through and killed or wounded the gun's crew, but did not hurt the gun. The only gun that was disabled at all in the battle was one of the 12-in., and it appears to have been disabled by something very big—probably one of the Japanese 12·6-in. shell hit the barbette of the ship, and the concussion upset the training gear of the guns in some way. Nothing could be done with them for about ten minutes. After that they were got in working order and fired again. This ship was also set on fire all over the place, but was perfectly able to fight when the battle was over.

The Chen Yuen had on board her the famous

Captain McGiffin, who wrote a great deal about his adventures in the fight. He was an American, who was usually described as commander of the ship and as having fought the battle. He was photographed against the hits in a desperately wounded condition, but afterwards it was surmised that he was not blind to dramatic effect. His narratives can hardly be accepted as historical evidence, save in a general way.

The next ship of interest at the battle of Yalu was the Elswick cruiser, Chih Yuen. She is described in most accounts of the Yalu as having very gallantly charged the entire Japanese fleet, attempting to ram; a tremendous fire was poured into her till she went down, and there was an end of her. According to Japanese officers, what really happened was that at an early stage in the action her steering gear got disabled; she was simply wandering about unable to do anything. She was simply a cloud of white smoke drifting along. The Takachiho, one of the Japanese cruisers, had a 10-in. gun. She waited until the Chih Yuen was within something like 400 yards, when they could not miss, then let drive with this 10-in. They did not attempt to pick out any particular part of the Chih Yuen; they simply fired "into the brown." They hit her somewhere rather high up near the funnel; there was a tremendous cloud of white smoke, which became red, and when that cloud went the ship was gone. There is no idea that any magazine was hit, or that there was any ammunition on deck to account for it, and

SINKING OF THE KING YUEN (p. 131).

[*Sketch by a Japanese Officer.*

the favourite theory of the Japanese officers is that this particular hit upset her stability in some way and did the finishing touch, and thus caused her to capsize.

Opposite is a sketch by a Japanese officer of the sinking of the King Yuen, which was a small Chinese ironclad. There is a great deal of mystery in all the histories as to how that ship really did go down. The Japanese account of it is that "she was on fire, and apparently the fire could not be put out; she began to roll very much indeed—first very heavily over one way and then very heavily over the other way; she continued rolling like that, and one time she rolled and did not come back."

She had a sister ship, the Lai Yuen. This ship was set on fire at an early stage of the action, and the Chinese apparently did not trouble to put the fire out. The consequence was it got a large hold and burnt every scrap of woodwork in the ship. But the extraordinary thing is that her people managed to go on fighting. Of her deck nothing was left but twisted beams. The ship was nearly white-hot, and a number of men got roasted to death in her; but she was still in fighting condition when the battle ended. Probably only Chinamen could have fought in such conditions.

The Ching Yuen was set on fire, but not badly hit in any way.

There were two other Chinese ships lost, the Tchao Yung and the Yang Wei. These were set on fire at a very early stage, and most of the accounts that we hear of the danger of fire in action are based upon these two particular ships. It appears that their captains were economical men, who liked to make a little money; so when the ships were painted they did not scrape off the old paint, and as the ships were about twelve years old the paint got very thick. Moreover, as they found kerosine cheaper than linseed oil, they mixed the paint always with kerosine. The ships, therefore, were of a somewhat inflammable nature. When they got hit, the men trying to put the fire out got hit also, and the ships were then simply left to blaze away. That is the true cause of most of the fire scares that happened just after Yalu.

The Chinese shell were very defective indeed. They had very few shell with any charges; nearly all they had to fire with were solid shot or cement shell, the very worst possible thing for firing at cruisers with; and this fact that they had no good shell must, perhaps, account for the survival of the Japanese fleet. For although just after Yalu the Japanese said that their shooting was 15 per cent. and the Chinese 10 per cent., they have since stated that the Chinese hits were something like 25 per cent. and their own about 12 per cent., and they say that in the early stages of the battle the Chinese never missed a single shot with their big guns—they hit every ship that they fired at; and they describe them as being some of the best gunners in the world—that these No. 1 Chinese gunners were born shots; but gradually, as the battle went on,

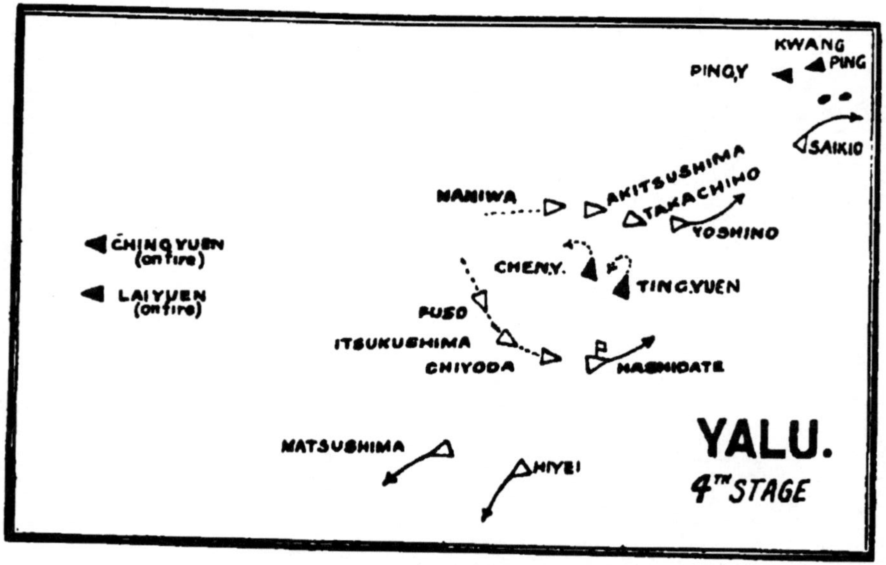

BATTLE OF YALU: FOURTH STAGE.

THE BATTLE OF YALU

the Japanese 3-pounders and machine guns playing on the Chinese ships took off the heads of those men, and they were replaced by other men who were not such good shots, and this went on until, towards the end of the battle, practically no hitting at all was done by the Chinese. But in the early part of the fight their shooting was very good indeed.

The Japanese in their fleet had three enormous guns, each of 66 tons, which would penetrate something like double the thickness of any armour opposed to them. Only one of those guns seems to have been in a condition to fire. In the excitement of the battle the Japanese got something wrong with the gear, and had to manipulate them by hand; and the consequence was that two of those guns fired about once each, and the third once an hour. It is unfortunate that these guns did not secure at least one fair and square hit — the data of it would have been extremely valuable.

After the battle of Yalu the Chinese ships were patched up. The Tche Yuen, which had already taken part in the battle of Asan, took part in Yalu, but was then knocked about and ran away. Although she had been so badly hit in the battle of Asan, when she was doing the strategical movement at the rear, she only took eight days to patch up, and she was then able to go out to sea again. After Yalu she was very quickly got ready once more.

The first conclusion one is forced to is that penetration does not seem to have done anything in this battle. Where a gun was matched against some very inferior armour, it went through and smashed it up, but wherever the armour that it ought to penetrate was anything like equal to the gun, the result was failure.

The second point is the astonishing amount of hitting that all these ships seem to have been able to stand. There are many cases of quite little ships that in theory one single shell would finish, but it has taken five or six shells to disable them at all, and in a week or two they have been fit to go out fighting again. The Saikio-maru, and the way she was hammered and still managed to go on fighting and remain in a fairly good condition, is a particular case in point. Although the upper works may be knocked about and splintered, and so on, it does not seem much good splintering the upper works and making a mess of the ship unless there is a gun near it, and somebody to be disabled. Now, this conclusion is dead against the "moral effect" theory. It is almost a gospel that if the upper works are shelled enough the crew somewhere else will get demoralised. I do not believe it; they will not in a modern war be aware of it. I think this point should be laid to heart and thought over by those who have 6-in. guns to attack ships with. To do harm, they must fire those guns with all the intelligence they can bring to bear.

On the other hand, it is well to remember, as in the case of the King Yuen and Chih Yuen, that hits in the upper works caused the loss of these ships by affecting stability, so far as can be gathered in

145

THE BATTLE OF YALU

the absence of the hulls now at the bottom of the Yellow Sea.

A third point is, that the danger from fire in action is grossly exaggerated. As to the Japanese, they one and all say that they had no trouble with fire at Yalu. They have not entirely done away with woodwork in their ships. Following the fashion set by the Germans, they have done away with a fair amount, but their ships are by no means without wood, like German ships and others which have not been in action—though even Germans are now reverting to a certain amount of wood. The Japanese say that they had buckets of water standing round; the men ran to the buckets of water, and the fire was under. The Chinese had exactly the same system, and they had no trouble till about the end of the action, when they got demoralised, and then the fire began to get headway. Hose pipes seem to have always been untrustworthy, too liable to be holed by splinters. Wet sand proved excellent. It may be noted that hits on the sea near the ships deluged all the exposed parts of ships at Yalu with water.

The loss of life was returned as follows:—

Japanese—90 killed, 204 wounded.

Chinese—36 killed, 88 wounded, 700 drowned (approximate).

Details (official) of the losses are:—

JAPANESE.

	Killed.		Wounded.	
	Officers.	Men.	Officers.	Men.
Matsushima	2	33	5	71
Chiyoda	0	0	0	0
Itsukushima	0	13	1	17
Hashidate	2	1	0	9
Hi-yei	3	16	3	34
Fusoo	0	2	2	10
Yoshino	0	1	2	9
Takachiho	0	1	0	2
Akitsusu	1	4	0	10
Naniwa	0	0	0	1
Akagi	2	9	2	15
Saikio	0	0	1	10
Total	10	80	16	188

Total killed and wounded, 294. Wounded who died subsequently were: Matsushima, 1 officer and 21 men; Itsukushima, 1 man; Hi-yei, 4 men; Fusoo, 1 officer and 2 men; Yoshino, 1 officer; and Saikio, 1 man.

CHINESE.

	Killed.	Wounded.	Drowned.	Total.
Ting Yuen	14	25		39
Lai Yuen	10	20		30
Chen Yuen	7	15		22
Ching Yuen	2	14		16
Tche Yuen	3	0		3
Ping Yuen	0	12		12
Kuang Chi	0	2		2
Chih Yuen	?	?	200	200
King Yuen	?	?	200	200
Tchao Yong	?	?		?
Yang Wei	?	?		?

During the battle both the Tche Yuen and Kuang Chi ran away. The first reached Port Arthur, and her

THE BATTLE OF YALU

captain was beheaded; the other ran ashore at Talienwan, and remained there till she was found on the 23rd by the Naniwa and Akitsushima, which destroyed her. The Yang Wei was finished by a spar torpedo on the 18th.

The remaining Chinese ships reached Port Arthur without adventure, and "victory" was celebrated by the draping of all guns, save those of the Tche Yuen, in red. They refitted very slowly.[1]

The Japanese, on the other hand, kept the sea, repairing ships—except the Matsushima—in secluded bays. The least damaged cruisers watched Port Arthur and Wei-hai-wei.

On October 20th the Chinese were all repaired, and went to Wei-hai-wei, whence Admiral Ting meanwhile cruised aimlessly; but no action took place, and on November 7th he returned to Wei-hai-wei. Here the Chen Yuen ran ashore while entering harbour, and did not get off for three weeks. She was not repaired till the middle of January, a great hole in her bottom having to be mended. This was done with cement.

Meanwhile the Japanese, ignoring Ting, concentrated efforts on Port Arthur, the Lao Tung Peninsula being invaded while the Japanese fleet lay blockading the enemy in Wei-hai-wei. On the 20th he returned to Port Arthur, leaving a few cruisers to watch Ting, and the rest of the fleet took part in the fighting there.

[1] Some of the dead were not removed for a fortnight.

The fleet was in four divisions:—

I.

| Matsushima. | Itsukushima. |
| Hashidate. | Chiyoda. |

II.

| Fuso. | Hi-Yei. |
| Takao. | Yayeyama. |

III.

| Yoshino. | Naniwa. |
| Akitsushima. | Takachiho. |

IV.

Two divisions of 5 torpedo boats each, and some gunboats inshore.

[This fleet moved parallel with the army on shore, and occasionally shelled the Chinese.]

On the 21st the fleet steamed past the harbour entrance, about seven miles out. They then detached the Chiyoda, which went to Pigeon Bay, and shelled Port Arthur at extreme range till 4 p.m.

At that time the Chinese fired at the fleet without result, till a heavy squall came on, in the midst of which the torpedo boats rushed the harbour. Excellently manœuvred, they got in untouched, and shelled the disorganised Chinese in the town. Outside, the Japanese soldiers were carrying fort after fort, the defence being poor, as the Chinese grew panic-stricken.

"THE MASSACRE AT PORT ARTHUR."

Then followed the Port Arthur massacre, horrible stories of which flooded the world for the next few days. It has been strenuously denied that any massacre took place, but this is not correct. Few, if any, civilians were killed; there were next to none in the place, the supposed dead civilians being Chinese soldiers, who had discarded the overcoats, which were the only uniform they had, in order to continue the fight on guerilla lines. But very little quarter was given.

A Japanese disavowal and explanation will be found below:—

To the Editor of the *Japan Mail*.

SIR,—In September last, for the purpose of studying the practical application of International Law, I joined the fleet, and embarked in a man-of-war of the Imperial Japanese Navy. I am now staying in Port Arthur, after witnessing several battles. Being a subscriber to your paper, I saw in the issue of the 21st January some singular statements by Mr. Creelman, to which you refer. It being impossible for an eye-witness like me to pass over such a matter in silence, I enclose an explanation of this affair, in the hope that you will kindly have it translated at your office, and published through the columns of your valuable paper. What I write is an accurate and faithful description of the things that actually happened, and I vouch for their truth in the sight of Heaven. Convinced that the contents of my letter are of value to the public at large, I venture to trouble you, especially since my facts may furnish material to strengthen the position you take in the matter. Harassed by official business of various kinds,

I cannot find leisure to write at greater length, and must crave your kind indulgence.

I am, sir, your obedient servant,

TAKAHASHI SAKUYE,

Hogakushi,

Professor at the Naval University, and Ex-legal Adviser to the Commander-in-Chief of the Regular Imperial Fleet.

ENCLOSURE.

On the occasion of the battle of Port Arthur I was on board the Itsukushima, and accurately observed the fight as carried on both on shore and at sea. I saw how the Imperial troops fought, and how the squadron co-operated with the army off the coast of Port Arthur, and I watched the movements of the enemy with the utmost vigilance. Similarly, I carefully looked out for any incident that might furnish material for the study of my special subject, and I do not therefore hesitate to say that I am among those best informed as to what actually took place on that occasion. Equally, I do not hesitate to declare that I saw nothing blameworthy about the assault on Port Arthur.

I have seen to-day in a copy of the *Japan Mail* that reached me, that Mr. Creelman, the war correspondent of the *New York World*, wrote to that paper to the following effect: "Torpedo boats were going through the waves, sinking junks loaded with men, women, and children endeavouring to escape. Ten junks, laden with terror-stricken people, were thus sunk, and the water was filled with drowning inhabitants." While regretting, for the sake of Mr. Creelman, whose honour as a gentleman may be impaired by such absurd fabrications, I fear that the public might be led astray by what he has written, and therefore I feel constrained to refute the false statements made by him.

In the first place, the assertions of Mr. Creelman are entirely imaginary; for his allegation that he saw from the shore, on the day of the assault upon Port Arthur, that is, on November 21, 1894, Japanese men-of-war and torpedo boats in motion, cannot be founded on actual fact. It is true that on the 21st men-of-war and torpedo boats were off the coast of Port Arthur, but for two days, from the evening of the 21st, they were away from the coast, owing to stress of weather. Now, Port Arthur was not entirely taken on the 21st. Severe struggles were still in progress on that day. Hence it was practically impossible at such a juncture to see the warships and torpedo boats in motion off the coast of Port Arthur, and the fictitiousness of any statement to the contrary will be admitted by any one actually at the scene of the battle. On that same day certain staff officers of the Army, desiring to communicate some intelligence to the fleet, could only effect their object by braving extraordinary dangers and hardships, and by passing through the lines of the enemy. How, then, could Mr. Creelman have seen the movements of the fleet and the torpedo flotilla except in pure imagination!

Secondly, while the fleet and flotilla were lying off the coast of Port Arthur and in the vicinity, from 5 a.m. to 6 p.m. on the 21st, not a single Chinese junk was captured. Only two junks escaped that day, at a little past 5 p.m. But the commander of the fleet had specially ordered that any small vessel of the kind should be let alone, attention being paid to the larger only. No other junk escaped. It is true that there were five or six junks on the shore, close by the foot of Lao-Tie-Shan, but they were all beached. Thus the statement that junks, loaded with men, women, and children, were sunk is not only absolutely groundless, but the very allegation that such a number of junks attempted to escape is a fabrication.

Thirdly, it is a fact that at a little past 4 p.m. two steamers emerged from Port Arthur. It was subsequently known by the confession of Chinese prisoners that a number of Chinese officers were on these vessels. It is also a fact that torpedo boats pursued these steamers. It would have been a neglect of duty on the part of the fleet to disregard the escape of such vessels. When the torpedo boats gave chase to the steamers, they signalled, "Heave to, or take the consequence." The steamers not obeying, two blank cartridges were fired after them, but they still kept on their course. Moreover, they returned the fire of their pursuers, and the latter therefore began to chase them with more vigour. Thereat one of the steamers turned back into the harbour, and the other changing its course, ran ashore, and all the persons on board fled. Was not this procedure on the part of the Japanese officers perfectly proper, and in strict accordance with the canons of western nations?

The foregoing explanations are sufficient to prove the falsehood of Mr. Creelman's statements. I regret that he should be so lost to the sense of honour as to fabricate such injurious stories. In order that the public may not be deceived, I beg you to give publicity to these facts.

Your obedient servant,
TAKAHASHI SAKUYE,
Hogakushi.

Port Arthur,
February 11, 1895.

This disposes of the most gruesome fictions about the massacre, but it does not deal with what took place on shore.

The true story, as I had it from a Japanese army officer who was there, is as follows:—

The battle was over, and the Japanese were marching into the town, a few Chinese retreating before them. Isolated fighting continued; but the place was, to all intents and purposes, captured.

As the victorious Japanese pressed forward, a young officer suddenly came across the remains of his brother, who had been captured, wounded, a day or two before. The body showed that death had been inflicted with atrocious Chinese tortures.

Maddened at this dreadful sight, the young officer

practically ran amok. Crying "No quarter," he began to kill. His men, understanding the cause, started on the same career of vengeance; and it spread like wildfire through the army, that the town was full of the corpses of tortured Japanese prisoners, and two or three regiments got out of hand. For some time "Vengeance" was the battle-cry, and terrible things happened that night.

Before we blame the Japanese, we should remember that our own hands are not quite clean in this matter; human nature has its limitations, and there are many men still living who can recall what they did when, in the Indian Mutiny, they found rebels red-handed among the tortured and outraged bodies of British ladies and children. Armchair ethics may condemn; but the armchair critics sit at home doing the condemnation. It is less easy to be philosophical in the hour of battle. The philosopher must have been through it, and abstained from slaughter, for his strictures to be worth anything. Personally, I think few things come more under the head of "excusable" than the Port Arthur massacre, so long as human nature remains human.

Port Arthur was converted into a Japanese base, and for a few weeks events languished, while preparations were made for the attack on Wei-hai-wei.

VII

WEI-HAI-WEI

ON January 18, 1895, the Japanese fleet bombarded Teng-chow-foo, facing Port Arthur on the Chinese mainland. It is about eight miles west of Wei-hai-wei.

On the 19th the bombardment was continued; on the 20th the army was landed to the east of Wei-hai-wei.

Wei-hai-wei was moderately fortified, chiefly with 8-in. Krupp guns. There were a few larger ones, and a sprinkling of modern pieces. Mostly, however, the guns were old. On Leu-Kun tau[1] were some more forts, a gunnery school, and a coaling station. The Chinese fleet lay behind this island, the Japanese watching both entrances, which were protected by booms.

On the 30th the Japanese fleet and army opened fire on the defences. In this affair the Chao-pei-tsui defences were silenced by the Naniwa, Akitsushima, and Katsuragi, the division being under command of Captain (now Admiral) Togo. The magazine was exploded, and the forts taken possession of by the Japanese soldiers.

[1] *Tau* means island.

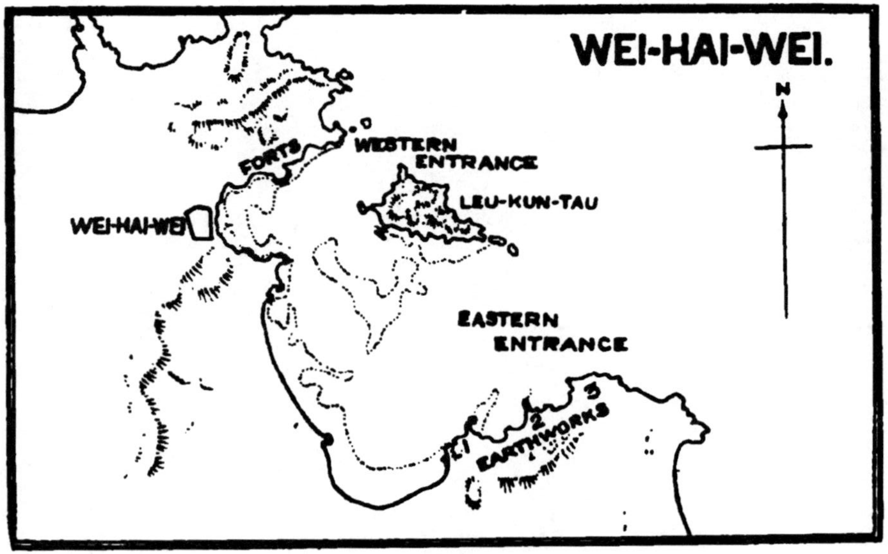

MAP OF WEI-HAI-WEI.

Before retreating, however, the Chinese destroyed all save a few old guns.

The rest of the fleet bombarded Leu-Kun tau without much result on either side. The Chinese warships took part in the defence. A photograph of this battle, taken from a captured fort, is given.

The net result, however, of the operations of the 30th to 31st was that the Japanese took practically everything except the island. On the night of the 31st, Admiral Ito decided on a torpedo-boat attack. Both entrances had some boom defence, with gaps here and there. The Japanese attempted to attack by the east with sixteen boats.

    Division I. . . six boats.
      ,, II. . . six ,,
      ,, III. . . four ,,

The Japanese soldiers in the forts took them for Chinese, so they retired.

A heavy gale came on next day, and the whole Japanese fleet ran to shelter at Teng-chow, returning on February 2nd, when another ineffectual bombardment at 2500 metres took place. An equally ineffective torpedo attack was tried in the night. It failed, as the Chinese sighted the boats, and they wisely did not try to force their way in.

Next day, and the next again, the bombardment was violently renewed, but on both sides it led to nothing save expenditure of ammunition. Landings on Leu-Kun tau led to nothing, and the only incident of real moment was the rushing out of twelve Chinese torpedo boats on the 4th.

Several were sunk as they came out; the rest ran ashore, and were captured or destroyed. So far as can be gathered, Ting had found his boats a nuisance, and was in terror of the Japanese boats being allowed in in mistake for Chinese ones. He also appears to have imagined that a daylight attack might produce something in his favour; but the balance of evidence seems to point to the fact that the boats were a nuisance to him.

Whatever was intended, the Chinese boats made no attack on the Japanese cruisers; escape was their only objective. Only two succeeded in getting away.

On the night of the 4th the third torpedo attack was made. The boats went in in three divisions of four each, though only the second and third divisions went in—the first being employed to create a diversion at the western entrance.

The eastern boats crept in slowly, in a cold so intense that an officer and two men were frozen to death. Two boats (8 and 21), their steersmen frost-bitten, grounded as they tried to enter.

By four o'clock a boat had got quite near the Chinese, and fired two torpedoes without result; a second boat was no luckier with three. Not till then did the Chinese open fire, and this boat ran ashore immediately afterwards.

Two more boats collided in the confusion, another had her boilers burst, yet another was badly hit. Only

CELEBRATING SURRENDER OF THE CHINESE FLEET, AT THE NAVAL CLUB, TOKIO.

one boat came out unscathed. As mentioned further on in " Personal Characteristics," the real truth of the attack has never been known, and never will be, save vaguely.[1]

Its result, however, is well known, the battleship Ting Yuen was hit in the stern and sank in the mud, where she lay with her upper works above water and guns still firing.

Throughout the 5th the bombardment continued unabated, and though no harm was done, the ceaseless worry told heavily on the Chinese.

On the night of the 5th a fourth attack was made by the first division. It met with little resistance, torpedoed the Lai Yuen and a despatch vessel, the Wei Yuen, and also hit the Ching Yuen in the bow without sinking her. The boats met with no defence worth mentioning; the Chinese look-outs, worn out with the ceaseless bombardments, were mostly asleep.

On the 6th a landing was effected on Leu-Kun tau, and on the 7th the usual bombardment continued. The Matsushima, Naniwa, and Yoshino were hit, but the Chinese lost a magazine, blown up.

On the 9th the Ching Yuen sank, her end being accelerated by a water-line hit from a shore gun. The Itsukushima was hit on the water-line this day by a shell from the 12-in. guns of the Chen Yuen, but the shell failed to burst. On the 10th and 11th the bombardment still continued. Only one fort now remained to the Chinese, but their ships still afloat

[1] See this chapter for the reason why.

were comparatively little hurt. The moral effect of the continuous firing finally broke them down, and on the 12th, in the midst of the firing, a gunboat flying a white flag came out.

The Japanese ceased fire, and the gunboat came to the Matsushima. Two officers from the Chinese fleet came on board, and delivered a letter from Admiral Ting to Admiral Ito, suggesting terms of surrender. It is worthy of note that, so one of the Matsushima's officers told me, these two Chinamen, on being taken to the wardroom to await Admiral Ito's reply, promptly and instantly fell asleep, and were only awakened later with the greatest difficulty. They were absolutely worn out. It is stated, also, that the whole of the beleaguered crews did the same thing directly firing ceased; want of sleep was, indeed, the immediate cause of Admiral Ting's surrender, though, of course, his position was absolutely hopeless.

Ting surrendered on condition that the lives of his men were spared, but he and his principal officers committed suicide. The whole of the defenders were executed by the Chinese at the first available opportunity.

Japanese naval losses during this affair were officially given as :—

    2 officers and 27 men killed.
    4   ,,   ,, 32 ,, wounded.

On shore the army lost much more heavily, as during the fighting the entire force occupying one captured fort were destroyed by the Chen Yuen, which steamed up close to them and opened fire.

JAPANESE FLEET BOMBARDING WEI-HAI-WEI DURING THE WAR.

[*Official photo.*

Chinese losses were never stated, but they are believed to have been much less than was expected. The entire crews of the Lai Yuen and Wei Yuen were lost, and most of those in the Ching Yuen.

Wei-hai-wei was won chiefly through sheer human inability to stand the strain of the everlasting bombardment and torpedo menace. Guns accomplished practically nothing directly towards it, and even the torpedo *per se* was not decisive. The principal factor was Admiral Ito's persistent and unremitting attack.

With Wei-hai-wei the war was practically over. The only remaining incident of note was an attack on Formosa, in which, if all accounts are true, the Japanese did not shine very greatly, or else there are problems in war which in peace cannot be conceived. It is stated that the Japanese began to bombard at 8 a.m. The Chinese had loaded all guns; they left a few men to fire them, and then retired. Reply ceased about 8.30, but the Japanese did not, it is said, discover it till about 2 p.m. An explanation, of course, is that they did not trust the silence of the forts—which is reasonable enough. That they did not notice it is the accusation of their critics.

VIII

AFTER THE WAR WITH CHINA

SAVE for a few torpedo boats lost, the war left the Japanese fleet unimpaired; the ships damaged at Yalu were in trim again when peace was declared. On the other hand, beyond the Chin Yen, Japan gained little in the ships she took. The Tche Yuen is of very small fighting value, the Ping Yuen of none, and none of the gunboats are of any utility. Of the captured torpedo boats, one was superior to any Japanese boat; the rest, from long neglect, were in a bad way.

Towards the end of the war the Esmeralda (now Idzumi), already described, passed from the Chilian to the Japanese Navy, and at its close the Tatsuta, detained *en route*, proceeded on her way.

Just before war broke out—in May, 1894—the Akaski, a sister to the Suma, had been laid down at Yokosuka; the two battleships Fuji and Yashima, of an improved Royal Sovereign type, were progressing in England, the former at the Thames Ironworks, the latter at Elswick.

The Suma was launched at Yokosuka on March 9, 1895. Unlike the Akitsushima and other ships which

SUMA.

AFTER THE WAR WITH CHINA

had preceded her, she is of entirely Japanese design and workmanship, and nothing more Western than an odd "stand-by man" or two assisted in her construction. Practically, she is the first Japanese-built ship. Particulars of her are:—

Displacement	2700 tons.
Material of hull	Steel.
Length	305 ft.
Beam	41 ft.
Draught	16¼ ft.
Armament	Two 6-in. Q.F. 45 cals.
	Six 4·7-in. Q.F. 45 cals.
	Twelve 3-pdr. Q.F.
	Four Nordenfelts.
	Two torpedo tubes.
Horse-power (forced)	8500.
Boilers	Cylindrical.
Number of boilers	Eight.
Screws	Two.
Type of engines	Vertical triple expansion.
Where made	Yokosuka.
Trial speed (forced draught)	20 knots.
Coal (normal)	200 tons.
„ (maximum capacity)	600 tons.
Nominal radius at that	11,000 miles.

Protection is afforded by a steel deck 2 ins. on the slopes and 1 in. on the flat.

The Akashi, launched two years later, is a sister, without fighting-tops and more built-up amidships.

The Yashima was launched at Elswick on February 28, 1896; the Fuji at the Thames Ironworks on March 31st in the same year. Mr. G. C. Mackrow, of the Thames Ironworks, was the designer.

The following are particulars:—

Displacement	12450 tons.
Material	Steel.
Length between perpendiculars	374 ft.
,, over all	400 ft.
Beam	73½ ft.
Draught	30 ft.
Armament	Four 12-in. 40 cals.
	Ten 6-in. Q.F. 40 cals.
	Twenty 3-pdr. Q.F.
	Four 2½-pdr. Q.F.
	One torpedo tube in bow.
	Four broadside tubes (submerged).
Horse-power (natural draught) on trials (10,000)	Fuji, 10200.
	Yashima, 9750.
Speed (natural draught)	Fuji, 16·8 knots.
	Yashima, 17·7 knots.
Horse-power (forced draught) (14,000)	Fuji, 14,100.
	Yashima, 14,075.
Speed (forced draught) (contract 18 knots)	Fuji, 18·5 knots.
	Yashima, 19·2 knots.
Boilers	Cylindrical (with Humphrys' ferrules).
Engines (by Humphrys and Tennant)	Triple expansion.
Screws	Two.
Weight of armour	3000 tons.
Material of armour	Harvey steel.
Normal coal	700 tons.
Bunker capacity	1100 tons.
Complement	600.

These ships are, as has been before noted, improved Royal Sovereigns. As designed, they would have differed from these ships only in that, being some 1500

PLAN OF FUJI AND YASHIMA.

178

tons smaller, they are able to carry less weight in the way of coal, etc. Their big guns, 12 in. against 13·5 in., are lighter, but against this must be put the fact that they carry heavy shields to them. Further, the introduction of Harvey steel in the place of compound armour greatly increased the value of their armour without adding to its weight. Regarded in the light of present-day developments, they are defective in protection to the secondary armament nearly as much as the Royal Sovereigns were before reconstruction. A comparison of the two ships, Fuji and Royal Sovereign, is of interest.

	Fuji.	Royal Sovereign.
Guns	4 A (12-in.).	4 A (13·5-in.).
	10 D (6-in. Q.F.).	10 D (6-in. Q.F.).
Steel armour deck on slopes	2½ ins.	3 ins.
Belt (water-line)	18–16 ins.	18–8 ins.
Length of belt	226 ft.	250 ft.
Lower deck	4 ins.	4 ins.
Barbettes	14 ins.	17 ins.
Barbette guns	Inclined thick shields.	No protection.
Bulkheads	14 ins.	16 ins.
Casemates (main deck), thickness in front	6 ins.	6 ins.
Casemate backs	2 ins.	2 ins.
Coal carried normally	700.	900.
Capacity	1100.	1450.

The difference in armour value, caused by the introduction of Harvey process in time to allow of its adoption on the Fuji, is very marked. Since then, of course, Harvey has given place to Harvey nickel, and this in its turn to Krupp process armour, of which 9 ins. would

FUJI.

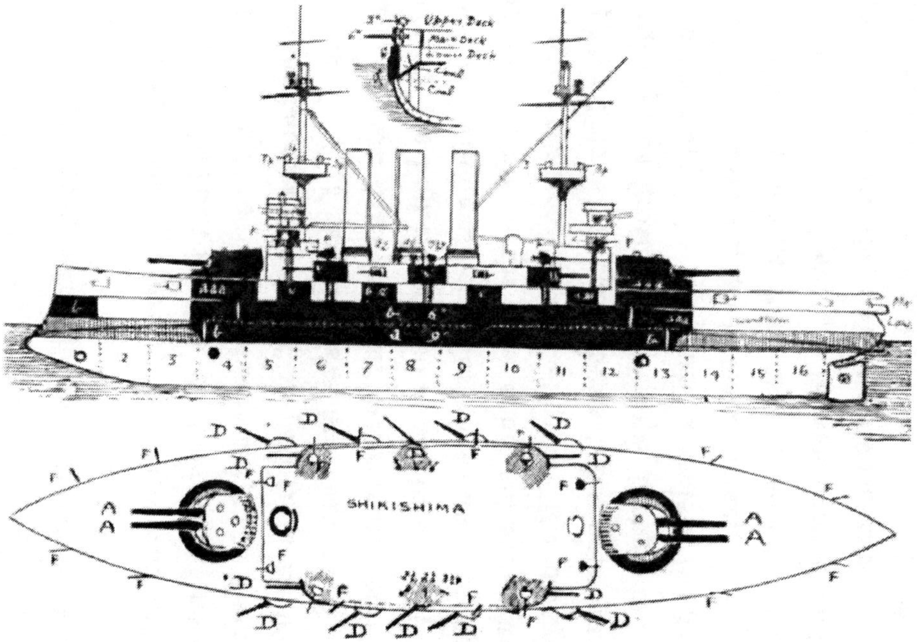

PLAN OF SHIKISHIMA.

nearly equal 17 ins. of Royal Sovereign armour. But their fine 12-in. guns, as powerful still as any afloat, keep the Fuji class still in the ranks of good fighting ships.

In appearance the two ships are almost identical, the only difference being in the arrangement of the ventilators.

Between them, however, an important difference exists; the Yashima has her dead wood cut away aft, while the Fugi has not. Consequently, the Yashima is much the handier vessel, but, in part from the fact that she was the first ship to have the dead wood aft cut away, in part from inherent weaknesses thereby engendered, the Fuji is regarded as the better ship of the two. The Yashima, being docked without proper precautions suitable to the case, exhibited some dropping aft, in consequence of the effect of the unsupported weight. This led to such sterns being countermanded for subsequent Japanese battleships, though in cruisers it is always applied. The turning circle of the Yoshima, it may be mentioned, is extremely small.

Finally, it may be noted that these two ships were the first to be fitted with the Elswick submerged torpedo tube. They have the earliest pattern, and it will not deliver torpedoes very successfully when the ship is at high speed.

The "After-the-War Programme."

After the war Japan decided to have a really first-class modern fleet of four battleships, six cruisers, and a proportionate number of smaller craft.

HATSUSE.

[*Photo, Symonds.*

The four big battleships are practically sisters, though differing in appearance and detail. The main differences are as follows :—

FUNNELS.

Shikishima	3
Hatsuse	3
Asahi	2
Mikasa	2

Little differences in rig have been purposely introduced; thus the Hatsuse is shorter-masted than the Shikishima, and the Asahi and Mikasa have their funnels differently placed, those of the latter being more amidships.

Also, instead of casemates, the Mikasa has her 6-in. battery protected by a continuous armoured wall. Essentially, however, the ships are sisters.

They were produced as follows :—

Shikishima, by Thames Ironworks, launched 1898.
Asahi, „ Clydebank, „ 1899.
Hatsuse, „ Elswick, „ 1899.
Mikasa, „ Vickers-Maxim, „ 1900.

Although she differs considerably from the Shikishima in appearance, the Asahi is practically a sister ship, the sole points of difference being (1) funnels; (2) distribution of the 2½-pounders; (3) absence of a bow torpedo boat; and (4) mounting of the big guns. There are, of course, certain minor structural differences —such, for instance, as the fact that the Asahi has a slightly larger wardroom, and that this wardroom is a trifle further aft — but, generally speaking, for fighting purposes they are identical, save for the points of difference noted above. There are unseen differences of detail also, such as the thickness of the armour deck, but none of these affect the fighting value. There is a difference, too, in the coal carried, but coal capacity does not show to the eye.

The details of the Asahi, with those of the Shikishima and the British Formidable, are as follows:—

	Asahi.	Shikishima.	Formidable.
Displacement	15,200	14,850	15,000
Material of hull	steel	steel	steel
Length	400 ft.	400 ft.	400 ft.
Beam	75¼ ft.	75¼ ft.	75 ft.
Draught	27½ ft.	27¼ ft.	26¾ ft.
Guns—12-in.	Four 12-in. Mark IX. for all		
6-in.	14	14	12
3-in.	20	20	16
Smaller	Six 3-pdrs. Six 2½-pdrs. Eight Maxims	Six 3-pdrs. Six 2½-pdrs. Eight Maxims	Twelve 3-pdrs. Eight Maxims
Torpedo tubes, submerged	4	4	4
" above water	0	1	0
Armour belt	9 ins.	9 ins.	9 ins.
" at ends	4½ ins.	4½ ins.	3 ins.
" deck	4 ins.	5 ins.	3 ins.
Lower deck	6 ins.	6 ins.	9 ins.
Casemates	6 ins.	6 ins.	6 ins.
Barbettes	14 ins.	14 ins.	12 ins.
Bulkheads	14 ins.	14 ins.	12 ins.
Armour material	Harvey nickel, all three		
I.H.P., forced	15,000	14,500	15,000
Boilers	Belleville, all three		
Speed (contract)	18	18·5	18
Coal (normal)	(?) 1,400	700	900
Screws	Two in all three		

There is some doubt about the Asahi's coal, 1400 tons may be the maximum and 700 the normal. Japanese ships do not need to carry much coal, being designed to operate in waters where friendly coal stations are numerous. True, ships thus kept short

PLAN OF MIKASA.

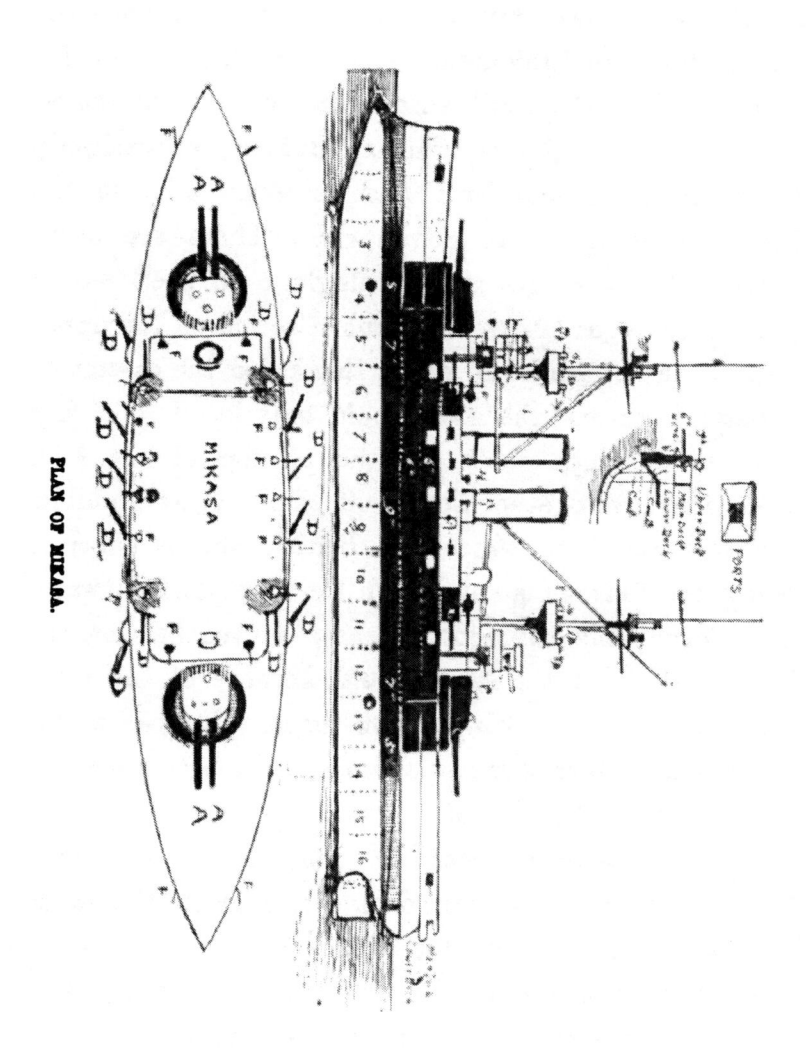

are likely to be out of action because they are coaling, about once a week; but, on the other hand, as they get two extra 6-in. quickfirers and four 12-pounders for this sacrifice, they are rather envied by our naval officers. After all, the primary duty of a battleship is to hit the enemy hard, and an extra 6-in. in the broadside is no mean advantage. There are other incidental advantages too—a single 6-in. shell would put all the eight 12-pounders out of action on the upper deck of the Formidable, while, thanks to the casemates acting as screens, the Asahi could only lose four of her 3-in. by a single shell. In the placing of her 3-in. guns she is altogether better off than the Formidable, the sole point in which the British ship is superior being the four guns carried on the main deck forward. The Formidable can fight all these on the broadsides; it is doubtful if the Asahi could, because of the blast from the big guns firing above them. But *per contra* she has her other 3-in. quickfirers much better placed; they are more distributed.

The positions of these are: four on the main deck forward; four on the main deck aft; four on the upper deck amidships; two on top of the forward upper deck casemates; two beside the fore conning-tower; and four beside the after conning-tower—a total of twenty. Those of the Shikishima are placed in exactly the same fashion. Those of the Formidable are: four on main deck forward (extreme bow); four on main deck aft; and eight on upper deck amidships; a total of sixteen. Three units instead of six; or, to put it another way, work for only three shells instead of six shells.

The Asahi is an improvement on the Shikishima in the matter of the 2½-pounders—a very small detail. In the Shikishima these are grouped on top of the amidship upper-deck casemates; in the Asahi only two are over these casemates, the other four being distributed, a couple on each bridge. Two theories are at work here, and it will need a war to say which is the better. In the Shikishima it is easy to concentrate three 2½-pounders on a single torpedo boat or portion of a big enemy, while, as a price for this, they are at the mercy of a single shell. Those of the Asahi are not thus at the mercy of one shell, but it will be far less easy to concentrate them.

The next point of difference between the Shikishima and the Asahi is that the former carries a bow above-water torpedo tube, with 6-in. Harvey nickel protection to it. This tube, similarly protected, is in the Fuji, Yashima, Asama, Tokiwa, and Yakumo. After some experiments and practice the Japanese authorities decided that this tube was of no use practically, and decreed its abolition. That of the Shikishima had, however, already been built in, so this ship has it. In the Asahi the design was modified, and the bow tube dropped out. It is absent also in the Hatsuse, a sister, and in the Iwate and Idzumo.

Under certain circumstances such a tube might be of great use in action—for instance, approaching an enemy who presented his broadside while the ship possessing the tube wished to make a feint to close. But to use it it would be necessary to slow down or reverse engines—both things that might be awkward to do in an action. Still, the real objection does not lie there, so much as in the trouble with sea that a bow tube causes. Bow guns, even high up, are always liable to get "washed out," a bow torpedo tube is still more likely to be so. In addition to this, it raises an unnecessary large bow wave.

In comparison with the Formidable, the Asahi and Shikishima have—beside the 6-in. and 3-in. guns— other points of distinct difference. They have (1) complete instead of partial belts; (2) 6-in. instead of 9-in. armour protecting the lower deck; (3) much higher barbettes; and (4) quite differently shaped hoods to the big guns.

Of these differences the armour one is of no immediate moment at present. The Asahi, in the matter of armour, is practically a Majestic with 3-in. stripped off the lower deck amidships and disposed on the ends plus some extra armour paid for in the weight of coal carried. Now, the 6-in. lower deck armour of the Asahi is proof against any 6-in. projectile at any range, and though a steel-pointed 9·2-in. common shell has been through 6-in. Harvey nickel at Whale Island, this is probably an isolated proving-ground case, and nothing but an armour-piercing shell of large calibre is ever likely to get through such armour in actual warfare. Also it is at least doubtful whether such a shell would do more harm than a solid shot, and against a 12-in.

MIKASA.

[*Photo, West.*

AFTER THE WAR WITH CHINA

solid shot 9-in. armour is no more protection than 6-in. In either case the shot will go through and dance about inside, and it is this "dancing about" that makes shot dangerous, and all armour save the very best a snare and a delusion so far as solid projectiles are concerned. However, medium armour is imperatively needed to keep off shells, for it is good-bye to any ship inside of which a big common shell is comfortably planted. The Admiral class, for instance, would do no more fighting once a big common shell got them amidships.

As for the complete belt, the Formidable, of course, has something on the bow, and this may be considered proof against 6-in. shell in action, save at short range. It is, at any rate, proof against the deadly little shell from 12-pounders and the like. As for any 6-in. shot —well, very few 6-in. shot are carried in any ship, and holes made by them are easily plugged.

The real gain of the Asahi is the extra gun-power, but since it is held essential that British ships shall have a large coal supply, it is useless to decry the Formidable over the two missing 6-in. guns. The defect of the Formidable, and one that might have been remedied, is the position of the 12-pounders. These could and should have been either more distributed, or else placed right up above everything and clear of everything, much as the French place their 4-in. quickfirers. Such a gun is extremely unlikely to be actually hit, whereas if it is crowded about with bulwarks, boats, and so on, a shell coming anywhere near is bound to burst with devastating effect.

In appearance it is difficult to tell the Asahi from our Canopus class, save for colour. A critical eye could detect the much higher barbettes of the Japanese vessel and their different shape, but that is about all, for the extra casemate would hardly be visible at any appreciable distance. Like the Canopus class, the Asahi has the huge after funnel, and the resemblance is increased by the tautness of her masts. The sign manual of a British man-of-war is the rake forward of the top masts, in the smartest Channel Fleet ships this is most noticeable; but the Asahi also is taut.

The Asahi has a slight sheer forward, like all our new ships, in consequence of which, though both pairs of guns are at the same height above the water, the after barbette looks a good deal higher than the fore one. The shields are peculiar. The plan gives a general idea of their appearance—sloping fronts but straight sides. The British pattern slopes all round, and is generally more squat—and of the two is more favourably regarded afloat. If by any off chance a big shot hit the side of the Asahi shield it would get through, from the inclined sides of the British pattern it would rebound at any range. However, a shot is very unlikely to hit the sides of the shield, and probably the mere shock of a big projectile would effectually displace everything and put the turret out of action. Wherever a big projectile hits it must do some harm, whether it gets through or not, and the old American idea of battering in preference to penetration is not so unsound as many folk are now disposed to regard it. Especially must this be so with certain foreign-built ships; the least little thing wrong and the colossal blow will find it out.

The guns and mountings of the Asahi are from Elswick. They embody some slight improvements upon those of the Shikishima, but are on exactly the same general principle. The 12-in. can easily do a round a minute, and should be able to do a round every two minutes in action. The rate of the 12·5-in. Canet gun at Yalu was one round per sixty minutes, but there were special circumstances involved. Still, there is no doubt that big guns have made enormous strides towards quick-fire in the last year or two, and two of the Asahi or Formidable 12-in. are equal to three of those in the Majestic probably.

The Asahi is fitted with the Barr and Stroud transmitters, each casemate having an indicator—in English and Japanese—to give the range automatically from the conning-tower. The official British view is against these transmitters, on the grounds that action will derange them; but there is no getting away from the fact that, even so, till deranged they will be exceedingly useful. Our methods of passing the range are cumbersome, and, in addition, by the time it is passed it has probably altered. Moreover, gunnery is not so much a matter of good shooting as knowing the range; the wrong range given accounts for most misses—at any rate, in the British Navy.

All the hoists in the Asahi are electrical, with auxiliary hand-power in case of need.

All the ships have twenty-five Belleville boilers each, fitted with economisers.

Full-speed trial results were:—

Shikishima . 6 hours . 16,370 = 18·78 knots.
Asahi . . 6 ,, . 16,360 = 18·3 ,,
Hatsuse . 6 ,, . 16,117 = 19·11 ,, (maximum).
Mikasa . . 6 ,, . 16,400 = 18·6 ,,

IZUMO.

[*Photo, Elswick.*

ARMOURED CRUISERS

THE armoured cruisers are of two classes. The first comprises the British (Elswick) built Asama, Tokiwa, Idzumo, Iwate; the second the Stettin-built Yakumo, and the St. Nazaire-built Azuma.

These last were the original Japanese design; Elswick put the extra guns at its own discretion, and rearranged the positions as the plans indicate.

Particulars are :—

	ASAMA TYPE.	AZUMA TYPE.
Displacement	9750.	9436.
Length	408 ft.	446 ft.
Beam	67 ft.	59 ft.
Draught (mean)	24¼ ft.	24¼ ft.
Guns	Four 8-in.	Four 8-in.
	Fourteen 6-in.	Twelve 6-in.
	Twelve 3-in.	Twelve 3-in.
	Seven 2½-pdrs.	Twelve 1-pdrs., etc.
Torpedo tubes (submerged)	Four.	Four.
,, ,, (above water)	One.[1]	One.

All six have four of the 6-in. guns unprotected, the other 6-in. and the 8-in. guns are in casemates and turrets (for the 8-in.).

All have 7-in. belts reduced to 3½ ins. forward, with 5-in. armour on the lower deck side. Their decks reinforce the belts.

The Iwate, Idzumo, Azuma, and Yakumo have Belleville boilers, the other two cylindrical. The

[1] Not in Iwate and Idzumo.

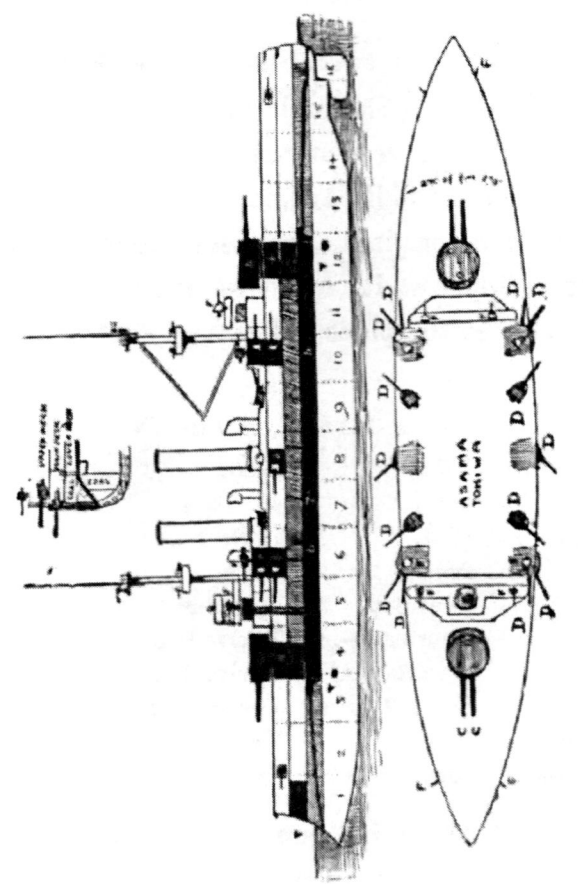

PLAN OF THE ASAMA.

YAKUMO.

[*Photo, Steinitz.*

type ship had very high horse-power; in the later vessels this was reduced, and the saving effected spent in substituting Krupp process armour for Harvey nickel on the sides.

Trial (full-speed) results were:—

	Designed speed.	Indicated horse-power.	Trial result.
Asama	22 knots	19,000 =	22 knots.
Tokiwa	"	(?) =	22·7 "
Idzumo	20·75 knots	15,739 =	22·04 "
Iwate	"	(?) =	21·8 "
Yakumo	20 knots	15,500 =	20·7 "
Azuma	21 knots	18,000 =	21 "

The first two have a pair of funnels only.

The ships are very good ones, equal in many ways to second-class battleships, but not calculated to stand battleship fire, I fancy.

The Kasuga and Nisshin were launched for Argentina in 1902 and 1903 respectively, by Messrs. Ansalds, of Genoa, Italy. They were purchased by Japan immediately before the war with Russia.

Details are—

Displacement	7700 tons.
Length	357 ft.
Beam	61½ ft.
Draught (mean)	23 ft.
Guns (in Kasuga)	One 10-in. 45 cals.
	Two 8-in. 45 cals.
" (in Nisshin)	Four 8-in. 45 cals.
The secondary armament is in both	Fourteen 6-in. 45 cals.
	Ten 12-pdrs.
	2 Maxims.
	Two field-guns.

あづま

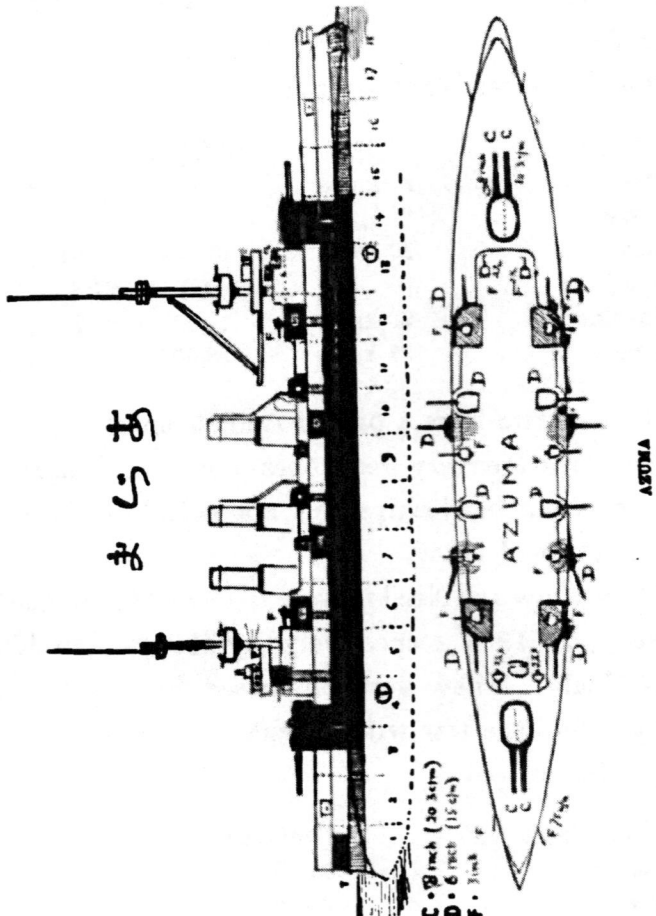

C = 8 inch (20 3cm)
D = 6 inch (15 cm)
F = 3 inch

AZUMA

NISSHIN.

[*Photo by favour of C. de Grave Sells, Esq.*

AFTER THE WAR WITH CHINA

Torpedo tubes	Four (above water).
Designed horse-power	13,500.
Speed	20 knots.
Coal (normal)	650 tons.
„ (maximum)	1100 tons.
Boilers	Cylindrical.

These ships belong to the well-known Garibaldi class. The belt is 6-in. Terni armour reduced to $4\frac{1}{2}$ ins. at the ends, and reinforced by a deck $1\frac{1}{2}$ in. on the slopes.

Above the main belt is a 6-in. redoubt, with $4\frac{3}{4}$ in. ends, above again a 6-in. battery containing ten 6-in. guns.

The primary guns are protected by $5\frac{1}{2}$-in. armour.

The remaining 6-in. guns are carried without protection on the upper deck. Six 12-pounders are carried between them, the remainder under the poop and forecastle.

The torpedo tubes are in special casements.

The ships originally had a single military mast, but just before completion the fighting-tops were removed.

They are the heaviest-armed armoured cruisers of their size in the world. Compared to the Russian Bayan, of about the same displacement, this superiority is manifest.

NISSHIN.	KASUGA.	BAYAN.
Four 8-in.	One 10-in.	Two 8-in.
Fourteen 6-in.	Two 8-in.	Eight 6-in.
Ten 12-pdrs.	Fourteen 6-in.	Twenty 12-pdrs.
	Ten 12-pdrs.	

The Bayan is the product of La Seyne. She

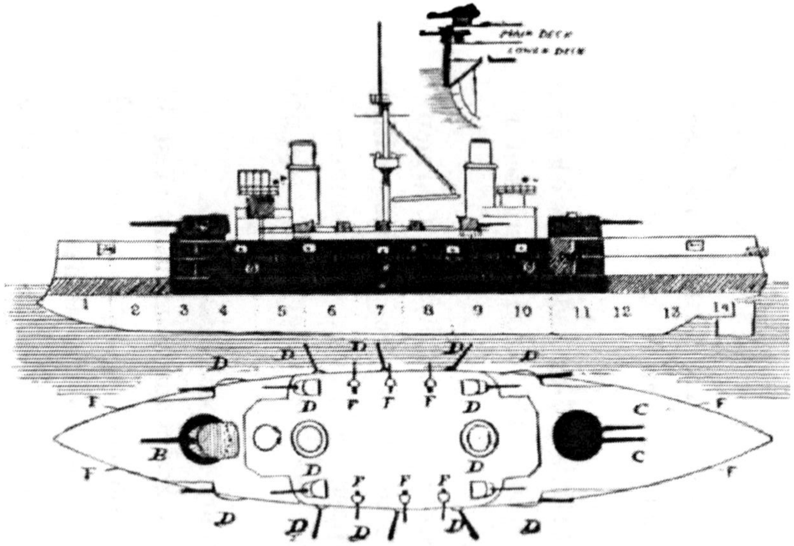

NISSHIN AND KASUGA.

(Nisshin has two 8-in. in forward turret where Kasuga has a single 10-in. The fighting-tops were removed on completion.)

KASUGA.

[Photo by favour of C. de Grave Sells, Esq.

is somewhat faster, better protected by 2 ins. on the water-line, but less protected on the guns, and with only half as many. She would take more punishment than the Nisshin and Kasuga; but, given equal crews and tactics, the heavy fire of the Nisshin type would seem to convey an immense advantage.

PROTECTED CRUISERS

THE three ships Takasago, Kasagi, and Chitose, are slightly improved editions of the Yoshino already described. The first was built at Elswick, the other two in America.

There are slight differences in dimensions, otherwise the description of the Yoshino stands for them. The armament is not quite the same as in the Yoshino, as these three later vessels carry two 8-in. guns in heavy turrets, ten 4·7's on the broadsides, and 12-pounders instead of 6-pounders.

They are very fast, but the heavy gun turret forward does not improve their behaviour at sea. *Per contra*, the 8-in. guns give them the power to deal a knock-out blow to other cruisers of their size; so their value depends on whether scouting or fighting is the more important *métier* for a second-class cruiser. The Yoshino type is intended to be both, and the Yoshino herself in a great measure is; the others are too heavily armed to be ideal scouts.

The Niitaka and Tsushima were launched in 1902. A sister, the Otawa, was laid down in 1903. They are improved Sumas, and entirely of Japanese design and construction.

Particulars are:—

Displacement . . . 3420 tons.
Length . . . . $334\frac{1}{2}$ ft.

KASAGI.

TAKASAGO.

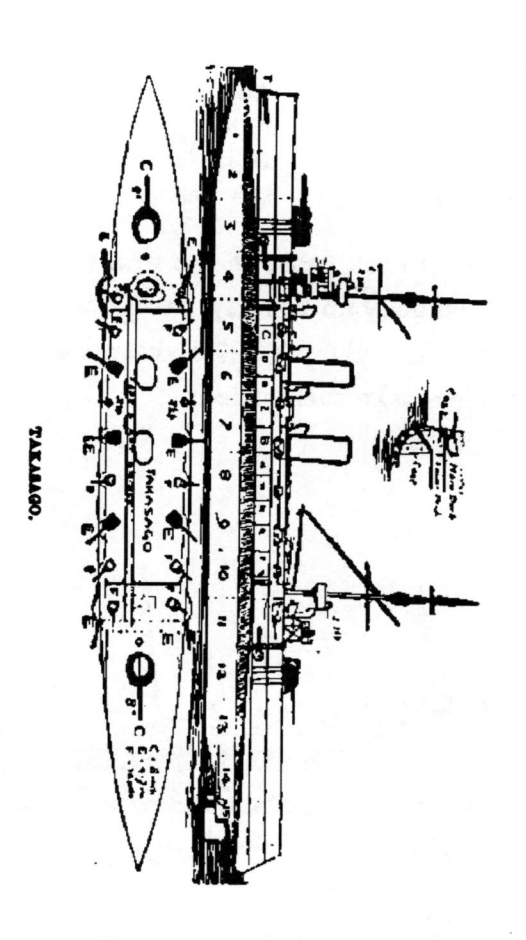

Beam	44 ft.
Draught	16½ ft.
Guns	Six 6-in.
	Ten 12-pdrs.
	Four 2½-pdrs.
Machinery	Two sets triple expansion.
Screws	Two.
Designed I.H.P.	9500.
Speed	20 knots.
Coal (maximum capacity)	600 tons.

A 2½-in. steel deck protects the vitals.

The ships embody no novelty, except in the selection of armament. The Suma's 4.7's disappear, and 6-in. and 12-pounders take their place.

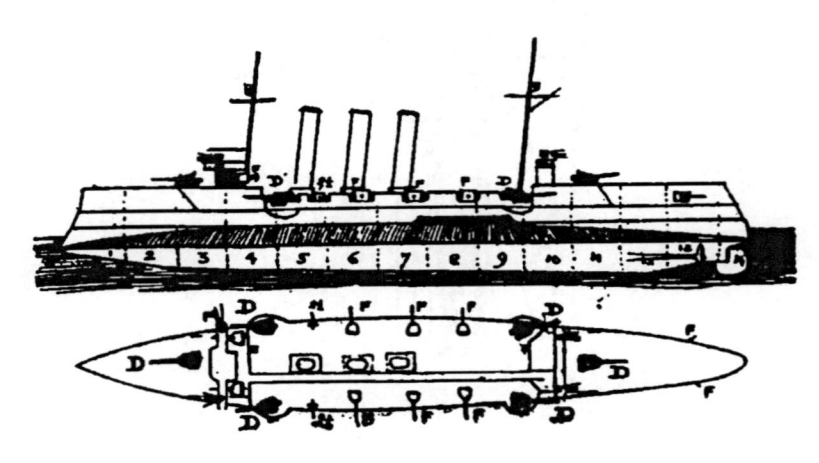

PLAN OF NIITAKA.

TORPEDO GUNBOATS

THE Miyako was launched in 1897. Details are:—

Displacement	1800 tons.
Length	304 ft.
Beam	35 ft.
Draught (mean)	13 ft.
Armament	Two 4·7-in.
	Eight 3-pdrs.
Indicated horse-power	6130.
Speed	20 knots.
Coal	400 tons.
Boilers	Cylindrical.
Complement	220.

The Chihaya was launched in 1901. Details are:—

Displacement	850 tons.
Length	314¾ ft.
Beam	36 ft.
Draught	13 ft.
Armament	Two 4·7-in.
	Four 12-pdrs.
	Three torpedo tubes.
Indicated horse-power	6000.
Speed	21 knots.
Coal	250 tons.
Boilers	Cylindrical.

There is no armour protection.

MIYAKO.

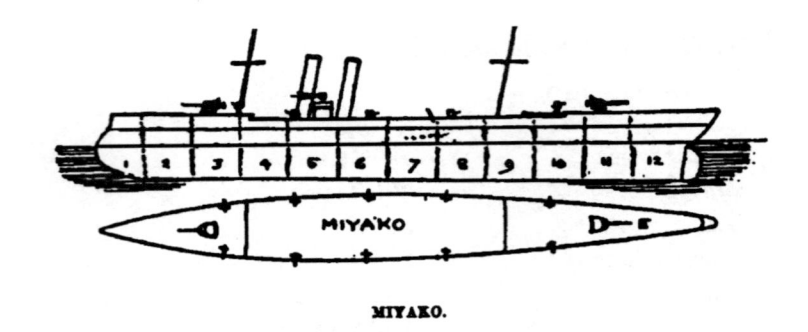

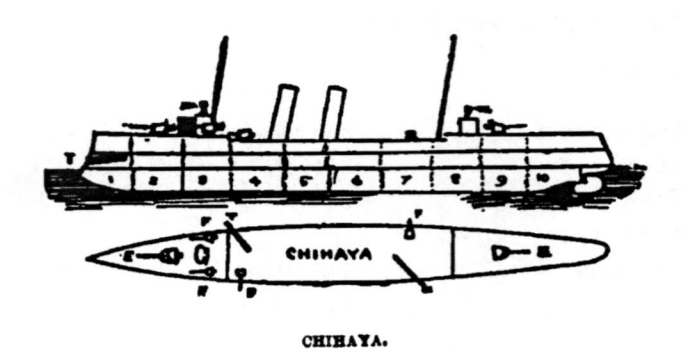

CHIHAYA.

DESTROYERS

JAPAN has selected two types of destroyers, the Yarrow and the Thornycroft. The Thornycroft boats are practically replicas of similar boats in the British Navy, and the Yarrow boats do not greatly differ, except that they have the usual Yarrow stern.

Details will be found in the Appendix.

The feature of most interest concerns the disposition of the guns—the 12-pounder being carried aft instead of forward. This is a preferable system to the usual one of the 12-pounder forward, as the bow is thus less weighted down.

Mention may also be made of the fact that a railway is fitted on deck for the conveyance of torpedoes. This is convenient, but the raised rails are apt to get in the way of the crew a good deal.

In the war with Russia the Japanese destroyers appear to have stood the strains to which they have been subjected remarkably well, and no cases of "broken backs" and similar catastrophies which had been foretold seem to have occurred.

TORPEDO BOATS

TILL recently, the fastest Japanese torpedo boat was one captured from the Chinese at Wei-hai-wei. Some very fast boats were built in the period 1898–1901, the types being Normand and Yarrow (Viper type), mostly the former. Details will be found in the Appendix. Some recent boats reached 29 knots on trial, and they are practically small destroyers.

The early Japanese torpedo boats were of the "second class" variety, usually of the Normand or some similar French type, and the boats which sealed the fate of the Chinese Fleet at Wei-hai-wei were mostly of this pattern.

THE FIRST TORPEDO BOAT BUILT IN JAPAN.
(Nos. 5–19 are of this type.)

SUBMARINES

JAPAN had no submarines when the war with Russia broke out, but orders for an experimental Holland type boat are said to have been placed.

IX

THE NEW PROGRAMME

THE new programme began, in 1904, with the ordering of two 16,400-ton battleships at Elswick and Barrow respectively. They have been named Kashima and Katori.

The following description of the Elswick battleship appeared in the *Engineer*:—

Her length on the water-line is 455 ft.; her breadth, 78 ft. 2 ins.; her draught, 26 ft. $7\frac{1}{2}$ ins.; and her displacement, in tons, 16,400; and she will carry for her armament four 12-in. guns, twin mounted in barbettes; four 10-in. guns, mounted singly in barbettes; twelve 6-in. guns in the citadel; twelve 12-pounder guns; six Maxim guns; three 3-pounder guns; and five torpedo tubes. The plan shows the disposition of the above-named armament, the arrangement of which has been most carefully considered, so that there is no interference with one another in the firing of the different guns, which, however, are all capable of being trained through large arcs. The 12-in. guns are 26 ft., and the 10-in. 22 ft., above the water-line. The 6-in. guns in the battery are from 13 ft. to 14 ft. above the water-line.

The general disposition of the armour protection is that adopted in the latest and most powerful battleships, the armour amidships being carried from below the water-line right up to the upper deck. Above the level of the upper deck additional protection has been adopted, a 4-in. screen being worked to a height of 7 ft. 6 ins. above the upper deck, and extending between the 10-in. gun positions. The main armour belt, which extends the whole length of the vessel, has a thickness of 9 ins. for more than half its length, tapering to rather less at the extremities. The depth of this belt is from 5 ft. below water to 2 ft. 6 ins. above water. Immediately above this is a belt of 6-in. armour, extending in length from the after 12-in. barbette right forward to the stem. Above this again is the 6-in. citadel armour carried to the height of the upper deck, and enclosing the two 12-in. barbettes. In this citadel are placed ten of the 6-in. guns, divided from one another by screens of 80-lb. armour plating, and firing through ports similar to those adopted in casemates. This citadel arrangement, which is one of the most important features of this and other recent battleships, is really a revival or development of the old box battery arrangement adopted in some of our battleships built in the seventies, such as the Shannon and Alexandra. This arrangement fell into disuse when the great improvement made in ordnance—which for a time kept so far ahead of the improvements in armour—made it necessary to increase the thickness of the armour to make it efficient, and therefore it was only possible to cover a comparatively small area of the vessel's side. However, the recent improvements in armour have been such that again comparatively thin armour is efficient in keeping out projectiles, which has once more made it possible to protect a greater area of side. In more recent years the same system with protective divisions between the guns in the battery was adopted in the Nile and Trafalgar, but as the 4-in. armour protecting the battery of each of these vessels was not of a quality to keep out even the smaller armour-piercing shell, the system was not repeated until the latest and most improved armour was adopted in such vessels as our King Edward VII. class, and in the much-talked-of Swiftsure and Triumph. The remaining two 6-in. guns fire through similar ports in the 4-in. screen armour on the upper deck amidships. The barbette armour of the 12-in. guns is 9 ins. thick on the upper portions where exposed, and 5 ins. thick where protection is afforded by the citadel armour. The barbette armour of the 10-in. guns has a thickness of 6 ins., the conning-tower armour is 9 ins. thick, and the observer tower 5 ins. thick. In addition to these two armoured positions for commanding officers, three officers' shelters are to be built of 3-in. armour, one above the conning-tower and one on each side. Besides the armour described above, a steel protective deck runs throughout the entire length of the vessel, the whole of the machinery, magazines, etc., being kept below. This protective deck has a thickness of 2 ins. on the flat portions amidships, and 3 ins. on the sloping sides, which are carried

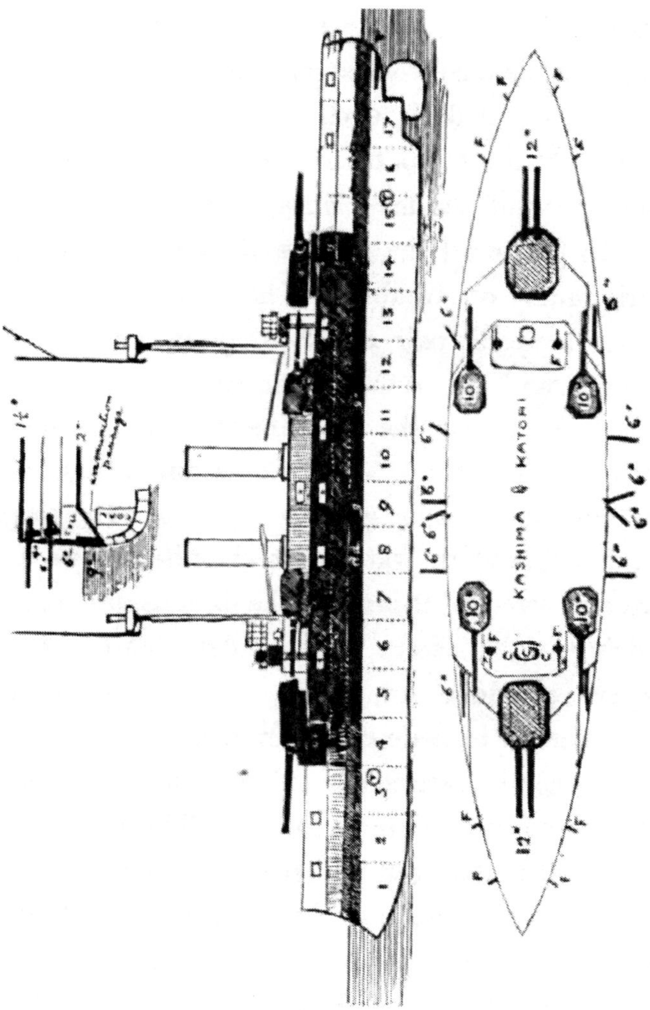
KASHIMA & KATORI

down to meet the bottom of the main armour belt. At the ends where the armour protection is reduced, this deck has a thickness of 2½ ins. all over. Thick protective plating is also worked on the top of the screen armour at the boat deck level.

Special attention has been paid to the arrangement and disposition of the magazines, so that the ammunition can be got to all the guns with the greatest speed and minimum of trouble. There are independent magazines for each pair of 12-in. guns, and for each 10-in. gun, and an ammunition passage is provided running right round the machinery spaces below the protective deck for the supply of ammunition to the various 6-in. and smaller quickfiring guns. The torpedo tubes are situated in watertight chambers—two tubes forward and two aft firing on the broadsides, and one tube firing right astern, also under water. Special means are provided for rapidly clearing water from these submerged torpedo-rooms in case of emergency.

The general particulars of the main propelling machinery and boilers are as follows: There are twenty Niclausse boilers disposed in three separate boiler-rooms. These boilers will have a working pressure of 230 lbs., and a grate surface of 1300 sq. ft., and a heating surface of 43,000 sq. ft. The twin engines will have four cylinders each, of 36 ins., 56 ins., 63 ins., and 63 ins., with a stroke of 48 ins., and the horse-power will be sufficient to give a speed of at least 18½ knots. The coal bunkers are so arranged as to reinforce the protection given by the armour and protective deck to the engines and boilers, whilst their disposition is such as to require very little trimming to get the coal to the furnaces. The bulk of the coal can also be got to the stokeholds without opening any of the doors in the main watertight bulkheads—a point of very great importance when the vessel is in action. In addition to the coal-bunkers below the protective deck, reserve bunkers are arranged on the slopes of the protective deck up to the height of the main deck over the length of the machinery spaces amidships, the total capacity being approximately 2000 tons, which is sufficient to give the vessel a very large radius of action.

A very complete outfit is being provided for the vessel, including the following boats: Two 56-ft. vedette torpedo boats of high speed, one 36-ft. steam pinnace, one 40-ft. launch, one 32-ft. pinnace, three 30-ft. cutters, two 30-ft. gigs. For lifting these boats two powerful electrically worked derricks are provided—one on each side of the vessel.

There is also a powerful electrical equipment, both for providing energy for the numerous machines on board, and also for lighting. The latter will include provision for six searchlights and some 1250 incandescent lamps.

The equipment of anchors and cables includes three stockless bower anchors of 120 cwt. each, and other smaller anchors. There are also three main cables of 150 fathoms each of 2⅝ ins. stud chain.

The vessel being of such an immense weight—over 17,000 tons with her full equipment of coal, stores, etc

—special arrangements have been provided for docking her with safety, and, in addition to shoring ribbands for giving special support to the armour in dock, two docking keels are provided on the flat portions of the bottom under the bilges amidships. These keels will rest on separate lines of blocks in the dock, as well as the usual blocks along the middle line of the vessel. Bilge keels are also provided to reduce rolling in a seaway.

The watertight subdivision of the vessel is of a most thorough description; the inner bottom extends over the whole length of the vessel, and is minutely subdivided, and above this the number of transverse and longitudinal watertight bulkheads is too numerous to mention.

An elaborate system of pumping and draining has been worked out, and in addition to the main pumps in the engine-rooms, which can be used in case of emergency for dealing with a large inrush of water, are two 9-in. pumps, two $5\frac{1}{2}$-in., and one $4\frac{1}{2}$-in., besides pumps for fresh and salt water services.

In a vessel of this description the ventilation arrangements are not the least important of the many items which have to be thought out, and every precaution has been taken for efficiently ventilating spaces both above and below the protective deck. In addition to the natural ventilation, artificial means have to be largely adopted, even in the upper portions of the vessel where she is entirely enclosed in with armour and protective plating, and here, as well as below the

THE NEW PROGRAMME

protective deck, numerous electrical fans, with air trunks, branches, pipes, etc., are being provided for.

Two complete sets of steering engines, independent of one another and in separate watertight compartments, are fitted, with steering positions both forward and aft. Hand gear is also provided, and appliances for changing as quickly as possible from hand to steam gear, and *vice versâ*. Tiller indicators are fitted in all the steering and conning-tower positions. Helm signals are provided for the purpose of communicating the position of the helm to other vessels in the neighbourhood. Voice-pipes, telegraphs, and telephones are fitted throughout the vessel to communicate between all the important positions. The vessel is also to be supplied with a wireless telegraphy installation. Torpedo net defence is to be fitted around the greater part of the vessel, which, in view of recent experience, appears to be not an unnecessary precaution.

With the exception of the main propelling machinery and boilers, which are being supplied by Messrs. Humphrys, Tennant and Co., the whole of the ship, with armour, armament, fittings, etc., will be supplied by Sir W. G. Armstrong, Whitworth and Co., Limited.

The 12-in. guns will weigh approximately 59 tons each. The length is 46 ft. $9\frac{1}{2}$ ins. (46·7 calibres). The weight of the projectile is 850 lbs. The charge will be cordite, probably of the modified type. The exact weight of the charge is not yet fixed, and neither can the velocity be given, but these guns will be the most powerful 12-in. guns which have yet been constructed.

No armour which any ship can carry can hope to cope with their penetrating powers at 3000 yards. The breech-screw is arranged for a parallel motion, which obviates the necessity of having a steep cone at the seating of the obturating pad. It is yet early to speak of the rapidity of fire to be obtained with these guns, but it is anticipated that, in conjunction with the mounting described, the hitherto obtained rate of approximately two rounds per minute from each gun will be exceeded.

The 10-in. guns will weigh approximately 34 tons each. The length is 39ft. (46·76 calibres). The weight of the projectile is 500 lbs. The charge will be cordite, probably of the modified type. As in the 12-in. guns, the exact weight of the charge has yet to be fixed, but here again this will be the most powerful gun of its calibre in existence. As a gauge of the power of these guns, it may be noticed that their penetrating power is equal to the penetrating power at 3000 yards of any of the 12-in. guns at present afloat in any navy. The breech mechanism will be somewhat similar in design to that of the 12-in., and will embody all the essential advantages of that design. The rapidity of fire of these guns on the Elswick mounting it is anticipated will at least be at the rate of three rounds per minute with a well-drilled gun's crew.

The 6-in. guns will weigh approximately $8\frac{1}{2}$ tons. The length is 23 ft. 6 ins. approximately (47 calibres). The weight of the projectile is 100 lbs. The charge will be probably M.D. cordite; but here again this is not definitely fixed, but these guns will be the most powerful guns of their description made, having a penetrating power at 3000 yards equal to, if not exceeding, any 6-in. guns hitherto built. The breech mechanism will be of the Elswick modified coned type, actuated by the single motion of the lever, and, as in the other gun, the necessity for the steep-coned obturator is obviated. The exact type of the smaller guns is not yet settled, but they will also follow the general advances in power and efficiency noted in the case of the heavier armaments.

12-IN. GUN MOUNTINGS.

The 12-in. guns are mounted forward and aft on the midship line, as shown in the sketch on the ship. Owing to the powerful nature of the guns, these mountings are necessarily stronger than any hitherto manufactured in this or any other country. The design is arranged with a view to occupying the least possible space in the ship, and, at the same time, to give ample room for working the machinery. The general features of the design are the turn-table proper containing the mountings for the gun, the working chamber underneath into which the ammunition is received from the magazine and shell-rooms in preparation for sending up into the secondary or loading hoist, the trunk connecting the working chamber with the magazines and shell-rooms, and the hoist connecting the working chamber and the gun. This latter hoist is so arranged that a gun can be loaded at any angle of elevation or training. The charge for each gun, consisting of the projectile and the cordite charge, the latter in two halves, is brought up at one time in a loading cage, which is automatically stopped in its proper position in line with the breech opening of the gun. It is then rammed home by means of a chain rammer actuated by a hydraulic motor. The breech block of the gun is opened or closed by a hydraulic motor, thus enabling this operation to be performed with great rapidity. In the working chamber, by an ingenious arrangement, the projectile and the two halves of the cordite charge are simultaneously transferred from the cage which works in the trunk connecting the shell-rooms and magazines with the working chamber, to the cage working in the hoist connecting the working chamber with the gun position. The ammunition trunk is of a new design, which enables the ammunition cage always to come to the same position in the magazines and shell-rooms; but when it is brought up to the top of the trunk the cage is in its proper position with respect to the ammunition loading hoist, although the turret may be revolving at a quick rate; or, in other words, the ammunition trunk does not revolve at the bottom, but revolves with the turn-table at the top. The guns are protected by 10-in. hard armour in the front, and 8-in. at the sides and back. The feature of the turret is that it is quite balanced, thus enabling it to be readily trained by hand, although the ship may have a heel at the time.

THE NEW PROGRAMME

There are three systems for performing the operation of training, primarily by hydraulic power, and should this fail through any of the piping being shot away, electric training gear can be quickly put into operation; and finally, should this be disabled, the turret can be trained by hand. Similarly the operation of elevating and depressing the gun can be performed by working primarily by hydraulic power, and then either by electric or hand. The operations of loading can also be performed by hand should the hydraulic system be disabled. To safeguard against accident by freezing in the intense cold which is found in the China seas during the winter months, heating apparatus is fitted throughout the turret installation. The gun mountings are so arranged as to give the gun 18 deg. elevation and 3 deg. depression, a greater range of elevation than has hitherto been provided for mountings of this description. The training angle is arranged for 270 deg., that is to say, from right ahead or right astern to 45 deg. before or abaft the beam. The turret can be trained at the rate of one complete revolution (viz. 360 deg.) per minute. In the shell-room, suitable overhead hydraulic lifting and traversing arrangements are made for lifting the shell out of the bays and placing them in the cage, but this operation can also be done by hand should necessity require it.

The sighting of the guns is provided for by a central sighting station and two side sighting stations, one on the left and the other on the right. By an ingenious arrangement the captain of the turret is enabled by working one lever to train or elevate the gun or to perform both these motions at the same time. Voice-pipes and other apparatus are fitted to enable the officer in charge of the turret to communicate his orders to the magazines and shell-rooms. A complete system of electric circuits enables the guns to be fired from any one of the eight positions either simultaneously or independently. Percussion firing arrangements are also provided.

10-in. Gun Mountings.

Each 10-in. gun is placed in an armoured revolving gun-house, or turret. The ammunition is sent up in a lifting cage from the magazine and shell-room direct to the gun platform, each cage containing a projectile and cordite charge in two parts. On reaching the gun platform the projectile is quickly transferred to a hinged loading tray fixed on the gun-cradle by means of an intermediate resting tray, the cordite being transferred by hand to the loading tray. By this arrangement three projectiles are always in waiting for loading, ensuring rapidity of fire. The projectile and charges can then be rammed into the gun by a telescopic hydraulic rammer. This rammer is arranged to follow the gun in elevation or depression, so that it always remains in line with the gun axis, enabling the operation of loading to take place at any angle within the usual fighting limits. The training of the gun-house is performed as in the case of the 12-in., primarily by hydraulic power; then by electric, and finally, if necessity occasions it, by hand, and, like the larger mounting, it is balanced so that the operation of training by hand can be readily performed although the ship may have a heel. The breech-block of the gun is arranged to be operated either by hydraulic power or by hand. The gun can be elevated by hydraulic power as in the 12-in. The operations of training and elevating are performed by the single motion of a lever. These guns also have the large range in elevation of 18 deg., with 3 deg. depression. The sighting of the gun is provided for by two positions, placed on the right and the left of the gun respectively. A complete set of electric firing circuits is fitted to enable the gun to be fired from either of these positions. Percussion firing gear is also provided. The guns are protected in front by 9 ins. of hard armour, and on the sides and back 6 ins. The training angle is from right ahead to 30 deg. before or abaft the beam, or a total angle of 120 deg.

6-IN. GUN MOUNTINGS.

The 6-in. guns are mounted on the well-known central pivot principle. This principle was first introduced by Sir W. G. Armstrong, Whitworth and Co., and has since been adopted for mounting guns of medium calibre by all the Governments and armament constructors in the world. Briefly, to describe this system, it may be said that the gun is mounted in a cradle in which it recoils, the recoil being absorbed by an oil buffer attached to it forming a part of the cradle, the piston of which is attached to the gun. The cradle is mounted by means of trunnions on a Y piece, which revolves on hard steel balls placed on a fixed pedestal. This pedestal is bolted to the ship's structure, the elevating arrangements are attached to the cradle, thus enabling the elevating gun number to work the gear even during the firing of the gun without injury to himself. Telescopic sights are fitted in a convenient position. Electric circuits are fitted to enable the guns to be fired by the simple operation of pressing the trigger of a pistol. Arrangements for percussion firing are also provided. A circular shield is attached to the revolving Y piece, so as to keep the port opening in the ship's side blocked up at any angle of training. This port opening allows for the guns to be trained through a range of 120 deg., viz. 60 deg. before the beam and 60 deg. abaft.

12-POUNDER GUN MOUNTINGS.

The 12-pounder mountings are similar in principle to the 6-in. above described, but, of course, arranged to suit the smaller size of the gun. They are protected by revolving shields attached to the Y pieces by elastic stays.

TORPEDO TUBES.

The vessel carries four 18-in. torpedo tubes on the Armstrong-Whitworth principle, which has been fitted to all the Japanese warships built either in this country or abroad since the date of the Fuji and the Yashima, which were the two first ships to have this apparatus. The vessel will also be fitted with a torpedo tube for firing 18-in. torpedoes in the line of keel astern. This also will be a special design by the builders.

The ammunition supply to the 12-in. and 10-in. guns has been described under the heading of mountings for these guns. The ammunition supply for the 6-in. and 12-pounder guns is arranged for by supplying to each 6-in. gun an electrically driven ammunition hoist of the improved Elswick design. These hoists will bring up the projectile and the cordite charge, and maintain a continuous supply. The operation of the hoist is extremely simple, and necessitates the minimum personal attendance. The seaman working the hoist has only to start it in motion and then keep it supplied with the necessary ammunition, which is automatically discharged in a position best situated for the working of the gun. The hoists for supplying the 12-pounder guns are of similar design; eight of them will be placed in suitable positions for supplying the 12-pounder guns.

X

THE JAPANESE DOCKYARDS

YOKOSUKA.

YOKOSUKA is the oldest Imperial dockyard in Japan, and was a going concern in the sixties. It is at present expanding considerably as a building yard. There are large engine shops for machinery construction. There are three dry docks opening into the outer basin, their dimensions being—

No. 1 (stone).

	Feet.
Length	392
Width	82
Depth	$22\frac{1}{2}$

No. 2 (stone).

Length	$502\frac{1}{3}$
Width	$94\frac{1}{4}$
Depth	$28\frac{1}{3}$

No. 3 (stone).

Length	308
Width	$45\frac{1}{4}$
Depth	$17\frac{1}{4}$

No. 2 is able to take any ship in the Japanese Navy; but the others are not available for any of the large battleships or armoured cruisers.

THE JAPANESE DOCKYARDS 235

There are two slips. On these, amongst others, the following ships have been built: Hashidate, Akitsushima, Suma, Akashi, Takao, and Yaeyama.

The dockyard lies at the foot of a picturesquely wooded hill, in the Bay of Tokio, and is well defended by sea forts. To the landward the defence is, however, poor, and Yokosuka could be taken by an army that could secure a foothold on the southern coast, supposing it able to defeat the defenders.

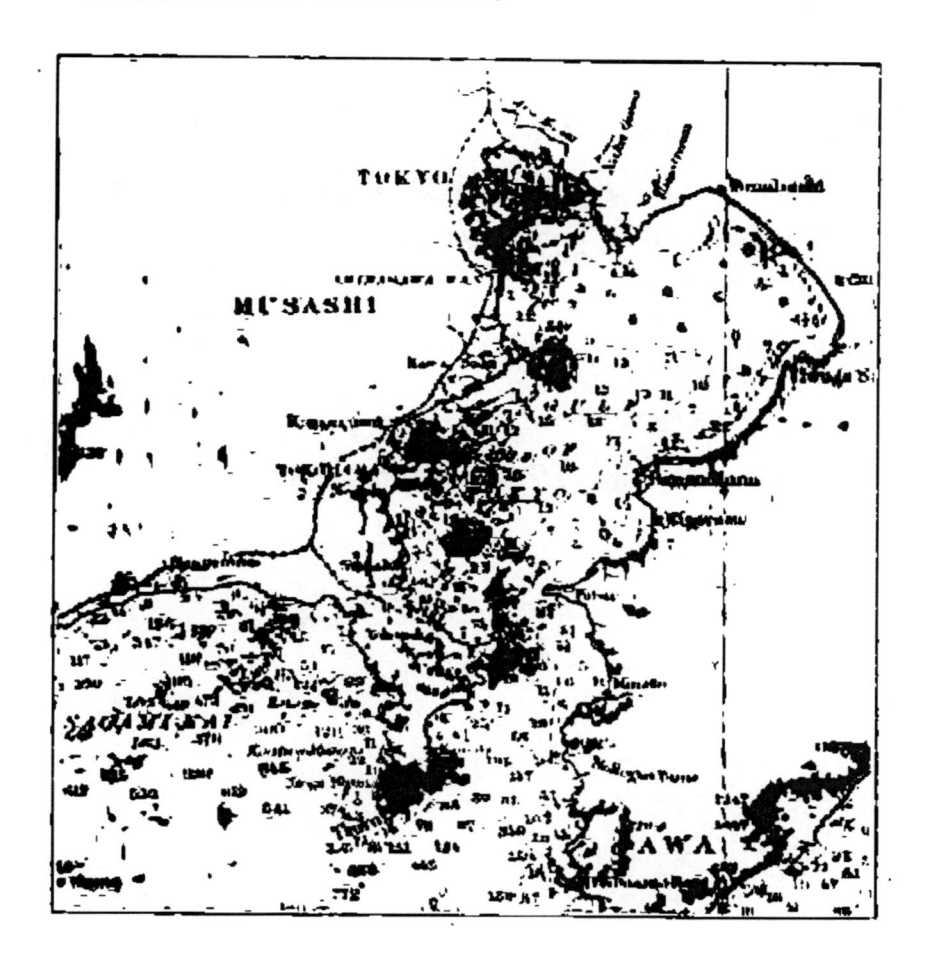

Tokio.

AT Tokio, roughly twenty-five miles from Yokosuka, there is a small dry dock belonging to the Japanese Government. It is, however, only suitable for gunboats and destroyers.

Dimensions—

	Feet.
Length	300
Width	52
High-water depth at springs	$14\frac{2}{3}$

There is also a private dock here, belonging to the Tokio Shipbuilding Company.

Dimensions—

	Feet.
Length	220
Width	42
High-water depth	14

The water front of Tokio is very shallow.

Kuré.

KURÉ, in the province of Aki, is the coming dockyard of Japan. Situated on the Inland Sea, it is almost impossible of access by an enemy, while it is far nearer any possible base of operations than Yokosuka. Two large dry docks have been built here, but the larger is not yet complete.

Dimensions—

No. 1.

	Feet.
Length	464
Width	69
High-water depth	29

This dock is able to take the Asama class, but not the battleships.

No. 2 (building).

	Feet.
Length	525
Width	125
High-water depth on sill	$33\frac{1}{2}$

This dock is building for the new 16,400-ton battleships, and its dimensions indicate that still larger vessels are expected in the future. It will be the largest dry dock in the world.

Sassebo.

SASSEBO, in Hizen, near Nagasaki, is not of much account as a dockyard. It has neither dry docks nor slips, and is essentially a place for minor repairs. For these it is very fully equipped.

It was found most useful in the Chino-Japanese War, and its utility continued in the war with Russia.

The dockyard lies well inside a deep, sheltered bay. The navigation around it would be very difficult to a hostile fleet, as many shoals exist.

NAVAL CLUB, SASEBO.

THE JAPANESE DOCKYARDS

MAITZURU.

MAITZURU, in the province of Tango, lies at the end of an inlet which has a uniform depth of seven fathoms at low water. The position is not very unlike that of Kiel, in Germany.

A dockyard is building here, but its resources are *nil* as yet.

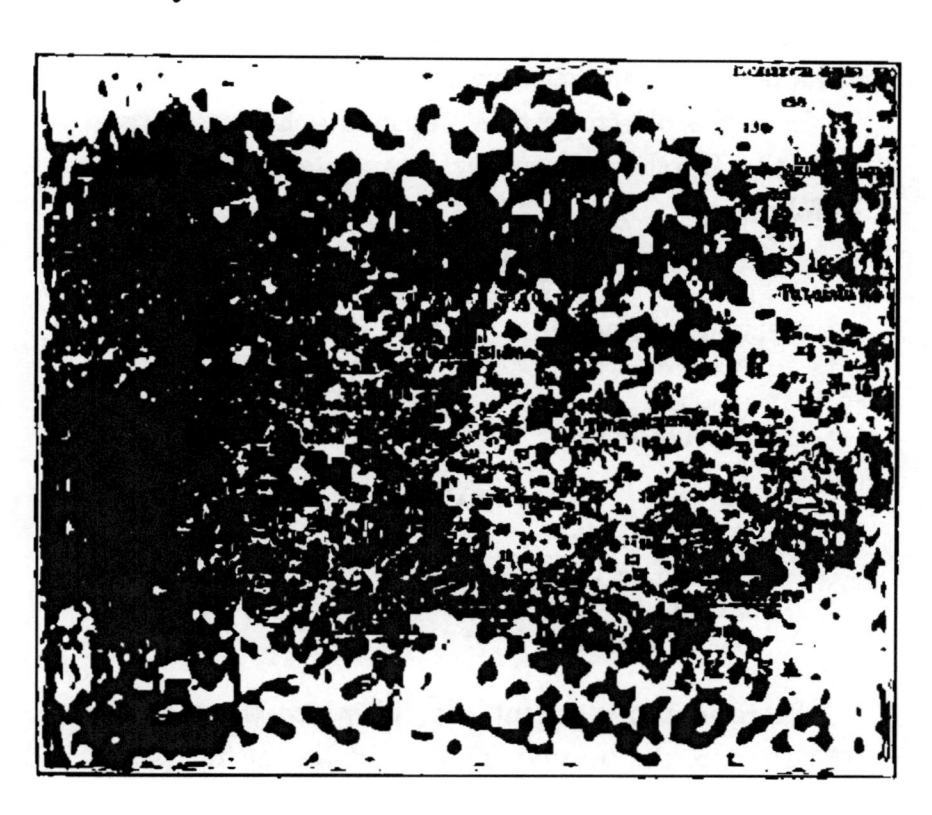

XI

NAVAL HARBOURS

NAGASAKI

NAGASAKI is not a dockyard town, though it is generally supposed to be outside Japan, on account of its being a naval harbour.

It is the oldest port in Japan, its history dating from the Dutch trading days. It contains two docks, as follows:—

1. TATEGAMI.

	Feet.
Length on blocks	510
Extreme length	530
Breadth	99
Depth (maximum)	$27\frac{1}{2}$

2. MUKAIJIMA.

Length on blocks	360
Extreme length	371
Breadth	53
Depth (maximum)	$24\frac{1}{3}$

There is also a patent slip, of which the rails are 750 ft. long, the breadth 30 ft., and the lifting power in tons 1200.

It has already been mentioned that Nagasaki was

an old Dutch station; but the present Tategami yard was established about the time of the Crimean War, by the Tokugawa Government, with the assistance of Dutch engineers. After the civil war it was taken over by the Imperial Government, who in 1884 sold it to the Mitsu Bishi Company, to which it now belongs.

This company built the present granite dry docks. In 1889 they had begun to build ships—a tug of 206 tons gross being their first effort. Since then quite large vessels have been constructed, not always with success; but, as an invariable rule, the failures on one have led to successes on another, and the yard is now a very going concern, employing about 4000 men.

The harbour and docks are extensively used by men-of-war.

As yet, judged by European standards, no really excellent work has been turned out at Nagasaki. The main trouble has been with riveting; but this is being steadily overcome, and it is purely a question of time before ocean greyhounds will be turned out at this yard.

The work is not entirely Japanese; "stand-by" Westerners still exist. These are kept in the background, in case their services are needed. So far as I can gather, they are not requisitioned unless a difficulty occurs, which is another way of saying that they are less and less in demand. The majority of these stand-by men have Japanese wives, and have adopted Japan as their country; as often as not they are naturalised Japanese subjects.

TAKESHIKI.

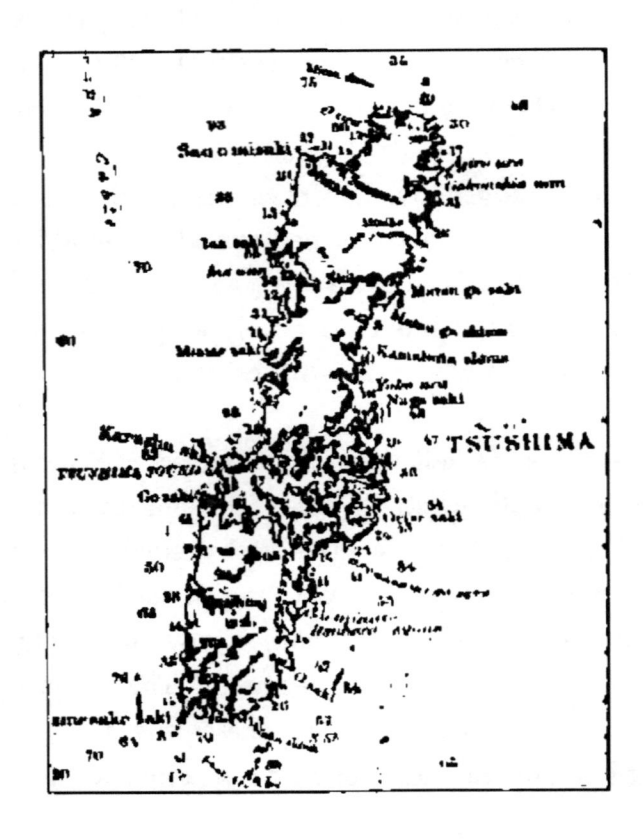

TAKESHIKI, on the island of Tsushima, is the advanced coaling station of Japan. There are two approaches, on the west and on the south-east, but only the first is possible to big ships. In the centre of the western entrance is a large shoal, three and a half fathoms below low-water mark, leaving very deep channels close inshore on either side. As the whole entrance is only some two thousand yards wide, flanked by high hills, it will be seen that it is impregnable. Inside is a large and very deep harbour, where the whole Japanese Fleet could lie.

The coaling station of Takeshiki lies six miles from the entrance by water, and five as the crow flies. It is, however, only some three thousand five hundred yards from a fourteen-fathom bay on the south-east, and so susceptible to a long-range bombardment from this quarter. It is to be bombarded also from several other east-coast inlets.

The port is very strongly fortified with Canet 9·4's on disappearing mountings.

OMINATO.

OMINATO, on the north coast of the principal island, is a torpedo-boat base. The town lies in a huge bay (Rikuoko Bay) that runs out of the Tsuguru Straits, on the opposite shores of which Hakodate stands.

The country is very mountainous, the highest peak being 3264 feet high, and the lower ones seldom less than a thousand feet.

In the war the Russians once passed through the Tsuguru Straits, but it was a risky proceeding.

KOBÉ.

KOBÉ, on the Gulf of Osaka, on the Inland Sea, is a fine roadstead, with western and southern entrances twenty miles apart, the island between them being nearly two thousand feet high in places.

There is a yard here, where all the Japanese-built torpedo craft are constructed.

KURÉ.

AT Kuré, no great distance away, the Japanese armour-plate plant is being laid down; but at the time of writing things are still in an elementary stage, and it will be some years yet before Japan is able to armour plate her own battleships. Probably, as Russia did, Japan will begin by building her own battleships and importing the armour plates.

KOBÉ HARBOUR.

XII

THE MERCANTILE MARINE

THE Japanese mercantile marine is of a steadily increasing character. Quite a few years ago it had no existence, and though in past centuries Japan had a very considerable merchant fleet, few people are aware of it, and fewer still realise that the present fleet of merchant ships, instead of being a wonderful new development, is merely a return to what previously existed. In this matter Japan is rather reasserting herself than striking out a new line.

The principal trade ports are—

Yokohama.	Nagasaki.
Kobé.	Hakodate.
Osaka.	Niigata.

There are twenty other ports which have some export trade.

The principal imports are: cotton and seed, sugar, rice, wines, food, etc., wool, manufactured cotton, drugs, dyes and paints, petroleum, manure, iron and steel manufactures, arms and machinery.

The principal exports are: manufactured silk,

copper, food, rice, drugs, and colours, matches, mats for floors, coal.

The principal import trade is from: Great Britain, the United States, British India, Hong Kong, Korea, China, Germany, Russian Asia, France, and Belgium.

The principal export trade is with: United States (72,000,000 yen), China and Hong Kong (about 40,000,000 yen each), France (about 27,000,000 yen), Korea (11,000,000 yen odd), Great Britain (11,000,000 yen), and British India (9,000,000 yen).

The following (from the *Statesman's Year Book*) are the shipping statistics of the Japanese ports (without Formosa), exclusive of coasting trade, each vessel being counted at every Japanese port it entered:—

	Entered.		Cleared.	
	No.	Tonnage.	No.	Tonnage.
Japanese steamships	3,042	3,861,659	3,064	3,883,782
„ sailing ships and junks	1,344	67,139	1,408	68,902
Foreign steamships	2,998	7,018,077	2,990	7,016,357
„ sailing ships	105	104,505	102	95,910
Total	7,489	11,051,380	7,564	11,064,951

Of the total foreign ships entered, 1644 of 4,080,583 tons were British; 385 of 1,192,153 tons German; 284 of 455,243 tons Russian; 188 of 240,906 tons Norwegian; 175 of 404,724 tons American; 154 of 303,690 tons French. Of the total shipping in 1901, 1094 vessels of 2,050,201 tons entered Nagasaki; 770 of 2,001,233 tons Yokohama; 1446 of 2,998,955 tons

THE MERCANTILE MARINE

Kobé; 207 of 85,952 tons Shimonoseki; 1683 of 2,870,640 tons Moji.

In 1901 the merchant navy of Japan (without Formosa) consisted of 1321 steamers of European type, of 543,258 tons; 3850 sailing vessels of European type, of 320,572 tons; and 911 native craft above 200 "koku," of 415,260 "koku."

In 1901 the total ships for foreign trade entered to the ports of Formosa were 2017 of 184,192 tons, of which 140 of 125,222 tons were steamers, 1877 of 58,970 tons were sailing vessels.

The total ships cleared the ports of Formosa were 1946 of 174,814 tons, of which 139 of 118,912 tons were steamers, 1807 of 55,902 were sailing vessels.

The principal steamship line is the Nippon Yusen Kaisha, the ships of which are usually white with black funnels, and a white house-flag carrying two red horizontal lines in the centre. It has a dozen good steamers and many smaller ones. None are very swift, and so there are none of any account as "armed liners," supposing such craft even to be of value. On the other hand, all are very useful as transports. Both in the Chino-Japanese war and in the war with Russia they proved very valuable.

XIII

THE JAPANESE ADMIRALTY

THE Japanese Admiralty is modelled closely on the British one.

The supreme command is vested in the Emperor.

The Minister of Marine—the present holder of this office (1904) is Admiral Yamamoto Gombey—is a member of the Cabinet, and superintends administration. He is selected from the admirals on the active list, and responsible under the Emperor for everything.

The coast is divided into four naval districts:—

Yokosuka.   Sassebo.
Kuré.   Maitzuru.

A fifth district, that of Muroran, is in process of formation.

Each district has its headquarters at the arsenal from which it takes its name, and barracks, etc., are at each of these places.

The men belonging to any district wear the name of that on their cap ribbons, not the name of the ship in which they serve.

ADMIRAL GOMBEY.

FINANCE

THE expenditure upon the Japanese Navy for the years preceding the war with Russia was—

	Yen.
1900–1	17,518,354
1901–2	20,161,010
1902–3	28,425,630

In 1903 the new programme was authorised, to spread over a series of years.

The Chinese war indemnity paid for most of the ships of the after-the-war programme. The war with China cost £3,595,400 for the Navy, while the Army part totalled to £16,455,200.

Japan is not a wealthy country, and, but for the probability of war with Russia, it is quite possible that the new naval programme would never have been authorised — at any rate, on so extended a scale as now.

XIV

ENTRY AND TRAINING OF OFFICERS

EXECUTIVE.

THEORETICALLY, the Imperial Japanese Navy is a democratic institution; actually, it is no more so than the British Army. All classes are eligible for commissions, but, owing to the low rate of pay, only those with some private means care much to become officers. Eighty-five per cent. or so belong to the old fighting class, the Samaurai.

The regulations as to the entry of cadets are as follows :—

They must be between the ages of 16 and 19. On the day appointed they must present themselves for a physical examination, and about 33 per cent. fail to satisfy the medical board in this respect. The remainder are then entered for a competitive examination in the following subjects :—

    Japanese literature.
    Chinese literature.
    English grammar.
      ,,   dictation.

English conversation.
    ,,   translation (English to Japanese and Japanese to English).
Arithmetic.
Algebra.
Plain trigonometry.
Elementary geometry.
History (of the world).
Geography.
Elementary physics.
Very elementary chemistry.
Freehand drawing.

Competition is severe; for each vacancy there are about five competitors; consequently, of those that originally enter only about 15 per cent. become *ko-hoshi* (naval cadets).

The successful competitors are sent to the Naval College at Yetajima, near Kuré (pronounced Kōūrā), where they remain three years, at the entire expense of the Government nominally, but generally costing something to their relatives.

Here they go through a very extensive course, which, in addition to a number of subjects not specified here, includes :—

    Seamanship,
    Gunnery,
    Torpedo,
    Navigation,
    Field drill,
    Physics,
    Chemistry,
    Mechanical engineering (elementary),
    English,

and all the other subjects of the original competitive examination in advanced stages.

There is a feeling in Japan that this curriculum is rather too liberal for the time allowed.

Some gunboats are attached to the college, and in these classes of the cadets go out for a day or two's practical instruction now and again; speaking generally, however, the three years are shore-service.

After the three years at college a cadet becomes a *sho-i ko-hoshé* (midshipman), and is sent to sea for one year in a training ship (masted), drawing a trifling pay.

At the expiration of this period, when between the ages of twenty to twenty-three, the midshipmen enter for a technical pass-examination for *sho-i* (second-class sub-lieutenant). If he fails (as a proportion do) he is put back six months. He then has a second try. If he fails in this attempt his services are dispensed with for good and all.

Passed midshipmen become sub-lieutenants, not by virtue of the examination only, but in order of seniority obtained in the examination, and as vacancies occur.

As sub-lieutenants they leave examinations behind them, but they have to write essays on naval subjects. According to how the *sho-i* does in these, he passes up through into the higher class of sub-lieutenants. The best take about one year to become a *tchu-i* (first-class sub-lieutenant), the worst take much longer.

After two years' service as first-class sub-lieutenant a *tchu-i* is eligible for promotion to *taï-i* (lieutenant).

Promotion is entirely by selection in this and all

senior ranks. The very youngest age at which an officer can become a *taï-i* is twenty-three. Twenty-four to twenty-five is nearer the average. A non-promoted *tchu-i* is compulsorily retired at the age of forty-two; but there are none so old as that.

After eight years' service a *taï-i* is eligible for promotion (by selection entirely) to lieutenant-commander. Thirty-one is the youngest age for this. Lieutenant-commander is a distinct rank, intermediate between lieutenant and commander. Its holder is entitled to the courtesy rank of "captain," and officially so addressed. In command of a small ship he is a *scho-sa*; serving in a big ship he is a *hojutsho* (gunnery lieutenant), *suirisho* (torpedo lieutenant) or a *kokisho* (navigator).

A lieutenant-commander is selected for *tchu-sa* (commander) without any definite service time.

Thence, still entirely by selection he can pass on upwards through the usual higher grades of captain, rear-admiral, and vice-admiral (*kancho*, *scho-sho*, and *tucho*). The average age at which an officer becomes a *scho-cho* (rear-admiral) is forty-five. The retiring age is sixty-five, but comparatively few live so long.

To be selected for *taï-sho* (admiral), a *tucho* must have been in command of a fleet two years, and, further, have been so in actual war.

A higher nominal rank still exists of admiral of the fleet—destined for a full admiral who has had meritorious war service in that rank; but there are none at present.

ENTRY AND TRAINING OF OFFICERS

ENGINEERS.

An officer enters for a *kika-no* (engineer) by competitive examination identical with that for those of military rank already described.

Those who pass are sent to Yokosuka, where they spend four years training in the technique of their profession. After that they join ships, having equivalent rank with, but after, the military branch, according to the table on a later page.

Engineers in the Japanese Navy have power to punish their own men, being executive in their own department. They are not, however, granted military titles.

DOCTORS.

A doctor (*quini*) is now a civilian who has a fancy for the sea-service. Like engineers, doctors have equivalent rank with, but after, the corresponding military branch, and are eligible for pensions after twenty years' service.

PAYMASTERS.

A paymaster (*shukei*) is also a civilian, entered as doctors are, and serving under the same conditions.

CONSTRUCTORS.

The constructor (*losin-sokun*) enters by competitive examination much as executive and engineers do.

After passing he is attached to a dockyard, and then sent abroad, usually to England, to learn more than he can acquire in Japanese dockyards, where only small ships are built as yet. A constructor has equivalent rank with the executive, just like the other non-military branches. All these branches at times use for themselves a military title; thus, *taï-i-kikano* (lieutenant-engineer) or *taï-i-losin-sokun* (lieutenant-constructor); but the military branch being, naturally enough, jealous of their titles, the prefix is non-official, and never applied to civil branches by the executive. Of the civil branches, constructors most often get the military title, and in the dockyards are always addressed by the employés as *taï-i, houk-cho,* or *kan-cho,* without the word constructor at all. In the British Navy, of course, constructors are almost as entirely civil a profession as Admiralty clerks, and are absolutely unknown to naval officers afloat; but in the Japanese Navy the tie is closer, and every officer knows them.

ENTRY AND TRAINING OF OFFICERS

JAPANESE NAVAL TITLES WITH ENGLISH EQUIVALENTS

NOTE.—
    a is pronounced as *a* in f*a*ther.
    ai ,, ,, *i* in *i*dle.
    i ,, ,, *e* in f*e*et.
    u ,, ,, *ou*, or as *ue* in cl*ue*.
    ei or *e* ,, ,, *a* in f*a*te.
    Example: *taï-i* is pronounced "ti-ss."
To follow French pronunciation is a tolerably safe guide.

THE system under which the Japanese name their deck officers is extremely simple. They are divided into three groups—big, medium, and little. For each of the three grades in these groups there are three similar prefixes—*taï-*, *tchū-*,[1] and *shŏ-*. The affix is the same for all grades in each group, *-shō* for the big, *-sá* for the medium, and *-i* for the lowest.

Thus they get:—

Prefix.		Affix.	
	Big.	Medium.	Little.
1. *taï-*			
2. *tchū-*	*-shŏ*	*-sá*	*-i*
3. *shŏ-*			

The various ranks, with the corresponding English equivalents, are as follows, working upwards:—

    Sho-i (Ko-hoshei) = midshipman.
    Sho-i = 2nd class sub-lieutenant.
    Tchu-i = 1st class sub-lieutenant.

---

[1] Might also be transliterated "su," "s" having the pronunciation of "tch" here.

Taī-i = lieutenant.
Sho-sá = lieutenant-commander.
Tchu-sá = commander.
Taī-sá = captain.
Sho-sho = rear-admiral.
Tchu-sho = vice-admiral.
Taī-sho = admiral.

In addition, there are the following branches of lieutenant-commanders :—

Ho-jūt-sho = gunnery lieutenant,
Sui-ri-sho = torpedo lieutenant,
Ko-ki-sho = navigating lieutenant,

which means principal officer connected with guns, torpedo, or navigation, as the case may be.

As for the other branches :—

Kika-no = engineer.
Gui-ni = doctor.
Shukei = paymaster.
Zosin = constructor.

The affix *kwan* (pronounced "kuàrn") denotes junior rank, and is equivalent to our "assistant." *Tdi-kikansh* is also "assistant-engineer," while the chief of any ship is *kikan-sho*.

The ordinary warrant officer is known as a *juin'shi-kwan* ("jivēntsh kuàrn").

XV

ENTRY OF MEN

Bluejackets

BY the law of Japan, every male of the age of twenty has to draw lots for the conscription, unless he is already serving. As a matter of fact, however, there are comparatively few conscript sailors in the Imperial Navy, as young Japanese volunteer for service in large numbers.

All candidates undergo a physical examination; and also a literary examination in elementary writing, reading, and arithmetic.

Volunteers are accepted between the ages of seventeen and twenty-one years, and sign on for six years' service.

Conscripts are compelled to serve four years.

Both classes may volunteer to continue serving up to the following ages, when they are pensioned off:—

Seamen	40 years.
Petty officers	45 ,,
Warrant officers	50 ,,
Chief warrant officers	55 ,,

Warrant and chief warrant officers in the Japanese Navy never undertake watch-keeping as in the British Navy. In no cases do they mess with the commissioned officers, as in our destroyers, torpedo boats, and torpedo gunboats, but, even in destroyers, have always their own mess.

They are not eligible for promotion to commissioned rank.

XVI

PAY

PAY in the Japanese Navy is, save in one important particular (mess allowance), very much on all-fours as to system with pay in the Russian Navy. There is, in all ranks, the same distinction between shore pay and sea pay, only, unlike the Russian, the Jap is not confined inside his harbours by Nature for two-thirds of the year.

Like Russian pay, too, it varies according to the station and varying living expenses. The distinctly Japanese element—and a very democratic one to boot—is that mess allowance is the same for all ranks: an ordinary seaman, a lieutenant, and a vice-admiral all draw exactly the same sum for messing, and that the modest one of 4s. 7d. and a fraction per week—a pound a month. The idea of the Japanese Government appears to be admirable enough in theory; it has certainly the merit of simplicity.

It must be borne in mind that the cost of living in Japan is about one-third the cost of living in the same style in England, about half the cost of living in Russia, and one-fifth the cost in the United States.

Details of pay for the various ranks are as follows :—

OFFICERS.

Naval cadets and engineer students, while at college, are allowed £5 (50 yen) a month to cover all expenses.

Midshipmen, during their year at sea, receive £3 a month.

Sub-lieutenants get from £3 5s. to £4 a month, plus a sea allowance of £1 a month and the £1 mess allowance. Altogether they draw about £70 a year, the equivalent of £200 a year in England; while, if serving abroad, their sea allowance is nearly trebled. It is said to be practically impossible for sub-lieutenants to live on their pay. A first-class sub-lieutenant draws £5 a month as ordinary pay.

Lieutenants and Equivalent Ranks.

Lieutenants draw £8 a month, plus a sea allowance of from £1 to £8 per month, according to the station. Exclusive of mess allowance, a Japanese lieutenant in England gets a little under £200 a year—more or less the same as a British naval lieutenant.

Flag, gunnery, and torpedo lieutenants draw some additional pay for these duties. Unlike British specialists, all specialist lieutenants are watch-keepers in the Japanese service.

Lieutenant-Commanders.

A lieutenant-commander is paid £10 a month, while his sea allowance varies from £2 to £12, according to the service on which he is engaged. Destroyers are lieutenant-commanders commands, and those who are captains of destroyers draw more accordingly than those serving in big ships as senior lieutenants.

Commanders.

Commanders are paid £15 a month. Sea pay ranges from £2 10s. to £10—the maximum in a big ship; but if captain of a gunboat, a commander's sea pay may rise to £15.

Captains.

The pay of a captain is £22 a month. Sea pay runs from £3 to £16. He may also draw additions for entertaining expenses.

Rear-Admirals.

Rear-admirals draw £29 a month, and the extra sea pay may run to £23, plus entertaining allowances.

Vice-Admirals.

Vice-admirals draw £35 per month ordinary and £30 extra sea pay. In Japan this is equivalent to over £2000 a year in comparison with life on the English scale.

Admirals.

The pay of admirals is fixed at £52 per month and £30 sea allowance.

In addition to these sources of pay, all officers on the active list in the senior ranks are eligible for extra pay—a species of good-service pensions. Meritorious conduct and medals are qualifications.

Engineers, doctors, and paymasters draw identical pay with the corresponding naval ranks, and extra pay for special duties.

Constructors are on the same footing.

The equivalents in the different branches are:—

Military.	Engineer.	Doctor.	Paymaster.	Constructor.
Cadet	Cadet		Clerk	
Midshipman	Assist.-Engineer (junior)	Assist.-Surgeon (junior)	Assist.-Paymaster (junior)	
Sub-lieutenant	Assist.-Engineer (senior)	Assist.-Surgeon (senior)	Assist.-Paymaster (senior)	Assist.-Constructor
Lieutenant	Engineer	Surgeon	Paymaster	Constructor
Lieut.-Commander				
Commander	Staff-Engineer	Staff-Surgeon	Staff-Paymaster	
Captain	Fleet-Engineer	Fleet-Surgeon	Fleet-Paymaster	Chief Constructor Inspector
	Inspector of Machinery	Deputy Inspector of Hospitals and Fleets	Paymaster-in-Chief	
Rear-Admiral	Chief Inspector of Machinery	Inspector of Hospitals and Fleets	Paymaster-General	
Vice-Admiral				
	Inspector of Machinery General	Inspector-General		
Admiral				

Men.

Ordinary seamen get 7*s*. a month. In addition, they have a varying sea allowance. The pay of seamen ranges up to 30*s*. a month, plus sea allowance. Altogether the average Japanese sailor, while in England, gets about 3*s*. a day.

Petty Officers.

The normal pay of petty officers, according to class and length of service, runs from 17*s*. to £2 a month, with allowances extra.

Warrant Officers.

Warrant officers draw from £3 to £5 a month, with numerous allowances.

Allowances to the men include clothing, or money for clothing, etc.

Altogether the Japanese sailor is very well paid. In our naval ports he is looked on as something of a Crœsus. He spends his money freely, as all sailors do, and his purchases run to practically everything, from top-hats to trinkets, and heavy technical books to musical instruments. Many of them talk English, and still more are able to read it, and these are prone to buy books. It is quite a common thing for them to tender five-pound notes in payment; but further particulars of this sort will be found under the head of Personal Characteristics.

RETIREMENTS, PENSIONS, ETC.

AS already stated, the retiring age (nominally) of a sub-lieutenant is 42. Other officers are retired *pro rata* up to 65 years of age for vice-admirals.

Officers of good conduct are promoted on retirement as a rule. Pensions vary from a minimum of £20 to £76 per annum upward in each case. In the admirals' ranks, the minimum ranges from £105 to £150 per annum. There is no exact maximum.

Intentionally or otherwise, there is one excellent thing that obtains in the Japanese Navy. By the system of selection of captains to be admirals the "duffer officer" has little chance of blocking the way of better men. He, however, as a rule is ready to recognise his own shortcomings, and it is not at all uncommon for such officers to exhibit their patriotism by retiring to make room for those who are likely to do better than they. It is only in the Japanese Navy that this happens: and it is in very marked contrast to certain other navies.

JAPANESE FLAGS.

XVII

FLAGS

TILL comparatively quite recent times the Japanese naval ensign was the same as the present jack and mercantile flag. The first battleships flew this white flag with the red ball, and the now well-known Japanese naval ensign only dates from the Itsukushima. It is very rarely correctly represented. The accompanying illustration shows it as it actually is; usually the sun is put in the centre instead of in its proper place.

Admirals' flags are remarkable in that they follow the Russian system of marking by bands at the edges, instead of the almost universal balls or stars which other nations employ.

The other flags illustrated do not call for comment to any extent, as they follow existing custom in all navies.

The device on the Imperial Standard is the national chrysanthemum. It is the personal flag of the Emperor. This badge, by the way, is found upon the device on the caps of all officers.

XVIII

UNIFORMS, ETC.

(1) Officers

JAPANESE officers' full-dress uniform is very like full-dress English. The difference lies in the sword, which is a dirk, and the cap, which is rather Russian in shape, and has a gold band round it.

The reefer jacket does not exist. In place of it they wear a dark blue military undress tunic, buttoning at the neck with stand-up collar, and black braid down the front. There are no gold insignia of rank; these are of black braid, with a loop for the military branch, just like the gold ones. Engineers, paymasters, and doctors have their stripes in black; but, being without the mauve, white, or red distinguishing badge between the stripes with their undress, it is impossible to distinguish. Cocked hats and frockcoats are identical with ours. Owing to the extra number of ranks, the stripes vary slightly from ours. They are:—

Sub-lieutenant or equivalent . . .	1
1st class sub-lieutenant or equivalent .	$1\frac{1}{2}$
Lieutenant	2
Senior lieutenant	$2\frac{1}{2}$

Lieutenant commander	3
Commander	3½
Captain	4

These are the usual gold stripes.

Admirals have stripes just like ours. No special illustrations of these various stripes are given, as the photographs of officers of different ranks throughout the book show them clearly.

There is no dress uniform in the Japanese Navy, but the national kimino is often worn at dinner.

Constructors wear a uniform identical with that of paymasters in undress.

Warrant officers wear a uniform closely akin to that of commissioned officers. Ordinary warrant officers have no stripes. Chief warrant officers wear a half stripe.

(2) Men.

The uniform of Japanese seamen is identical with that of British seamen, save that the cap is a little flatter and nearer the French shape. The cap ribbon is just like ours—the name of the depôt instead of ship is on it in Chinese characters.

XIX

PERSONAL CHARACTERISTICS

Officers.

JAPANESE naval officers, like as they are to European ones in many characteristics, are yet of a more distinct class by themselves than any other body of men in the world. The likeness to European officers is superficial, a first impression; the real Japanese officer is not to be known or understood at a casual glance; he needs knowing.

Whether the Western brain can ever get to truly comprehend the Oriental is a favourite question, usually answered in the negative. But, true as the negative may be in a general way, it is only true to that extent. Sea service marks all its votaries as a class apart; and additionally apart as the Japanese may be by race, they are not more so than Russians or Frenchmen. It is just as easy or just as impossible to "bottom" a Japanese as a Russian. Still, Japanese officers as a class are, as before stated, a unique class.

Their primary and principal characteristic is that they are utterly different to the Japanese that we read about in books. Art books tell us of Japanese art instinct, of their feeling for decorative art, and so forth. Japanese artists may possess, or have possessed, this feeling, but it is conspicuous for its absence in Japanese naval officers, who are as "Philistine" as British officers —if possible, more so. The decorative art that their nation is supposed to live for they cordially despise. I have never heard one admire a picture for its colour, but light and shade (that decorative art knows not) appeals to many. Effects, action, motion, sentiment they will understand, but abstract art, never. They are truly and healthily "Philistines."

So much for art, which I have touched on because it is said to be, over here, the keynote of Japanese character. Illustrated as a good deal of this work is with Japanese drawings and photographs, selected for the book by Japanese officers, this matter deserves mention apart from the question of artistic influence on national life. We may note, therefore, that "art-instinct" was the first thing flung behind him by the Japanese when he "advanced." If the so-called taking to civilisation of the Japanese means anything, it means having abandoned art for something more utilitarian and more forceful.

Some slight recapitulation is now necessary. When Japan, as the saying goes, "adopted Western civilisation," she did little but adopt Western methods of war and business, and, in the strictly ethical sense, discarded a good deal of civilisation rather than adopted it; she abandoned all those forms of civilisation that have a decadent tendency. Her advance was not the birth of a new empire with a new civilisation, but the awakening of an old nation that for centuries had been sleeping, steeped in ultra-civilisation. In this fact lies her strength and her weakness.

A forgotten history was studied, and with that study slumbering ambitions were revived. The man of action, relegated to the background by ultra-civilisations,[1] again began to loom upon the stage. Disputes with foreigners called him on to it; Japan awoke determined to be again a nation. "Let us have intercourse with foreigners, learn their drill and tactics, and ... we shall be able to go abroad and give lands in foreign countries to those who have distinguished themselves in battle,"—this sentiment every Japanese officer has imbibed with his mother's milk. The introduction of Western social institutions, such as newspapers, railways, telegraphs, the new criminal code, the abolition of torture as a punishment, all these things are side issues. They have contributed to build commercial Japan; but they have had small part in making her Navy; the Navy, indeed, would perhaps have been stronger without them. The mechanical arts and *the food*[2] of the West, not its social institutions, have made the new Japan an empire.

Now, having decided to adopt Western methods, the Japanese sought Western instructors. The British

---

[1] The drift of ultra-civilisation is towards peace and the arts. The man of action must embody something of the savage, and the seeker after universal peace draws his chief recruits from the ranks of those who supply those luxuries of life that civilisation makes into necessaries.

[2] See p. 310, where the food question is fully gone into.

being the premier navy, they sought naval instruction from us, and were chiefly supplied with officers of what even then was the "old school." In one of Major Drury's books of naval stories [1] there is a British admiral who always read his Bible in his shirt-sleeves, because the sight of his uniform made it difficult for him to realise the existence of a Higher Power! Absurd, no doubt; but this seemingly far-fetched yarn exactly represents the "old-school" sentiment, and the sentiment upon which every Japanese officer has been dry-nursed. Even to-day a British admiral is encircled with a halo of pomp, formula, and etiquette equal to that of any Court; in the old days the reverence was greater still. The young Japanese officers' first lessons in "sea-power" were in reverence to its chief practitioners. With their reverential loyalty to their Emperor, they proved apt pupils. As the seat of power the quarter-deck is revered in the British service; lesson number two taught this to the Japanese, and included the bridge and a few other places. Practical work they were taught on our model; the theoretical they more or less taught themselves. Japanese naval strategy and tactics are much less the result of European tuition than we suppose. What they learnt from the West was after the Nelson model...

To understand a Japanese naval officer at all, we must fully realise that he has been brought up with the things mentioned above as his religion—indeed,

[1] "The Tadpole of an Archangel," by Major Drury, R.M.L.I.

it is the only religion he knows. Whether a professed atheist, or a Christian, or a Buddhist, the only semblance of reality in his creed is this religion of "Sea Power," and the worship of its visible embodiment. Such god as he has is the navy to which he belongs.

We are more or less given to understand nowadays that Japan has adopted Christianity. A Japanese told me that, to a certain extent, they have. "Render unto Cæsar the things that are Cæsar's," struck him as an excellent text for the common people—Cæsar being translated Emperor of Japan. He preferred Christianity too, he said, "because it was more modern and general." Had the leading Powers been Mahomedan, I have no doubt that official Japan would revere Mecca. It was, I think, this same officer who told me that some friends of his who had become Christians were anxious that he should do the same. He agreed, therefore, to go and be baptised on a certain date *if it were fine*. The day was wet, so he did not go. Some other friends were anxious that he should embrace Buddhism. "As their temple was much nearer, I went there," he said; "so I am a Buddhist. But, of course, I do not believe in any religion really."

A Christian Jap, on the other hand, once asked me whether Santa Klaus was one of our gods—the combination of monotheism and pantheism of the Doctrine of the Trinity being altogether outside their philosophy.

Actually the Japanese are members of that "Agnostic Creed" which some of our greater materialists have preached, plagiarising both Christianity and Buddhism. "Do unto others as you would that they should do unto you." And in a great measure they live up to it. Where they seem not to, the difference between ideals of the Orient and the West explains the omission. Our particular type of hypocrite is not known in Japan. But, as I have said before, the only "Power" that they recognise and worship is their fleet. To grasp the true inwardness of this is not over and above easy to our mental processes, but it is the keynote.

One might imagine that a far-seeing administrative brain had evolved this most utilitarian religion, but I have never detected evidences of purpose. The seed was planted by our "old-school" naval officers; it fell on fruitful soil, and grew of its own accord into a weapon of almost indescribable potency. It is not on the lines of fanaticism exactly—the case of the Mahomedan is not altogether analogous. Rather, it is on all fours with Calvinism.

"If people don't like being killed, why do they fight?" a Japanese officer remarked when discussing war. Individually and physically, a Japanese officer is not at all brave, if we define "bravery" in our sense of the word, but he will fight harder and die harder than any Westerner. To him a wound taken in action is on a par with a toothache or more serious ailment in ordinary everyday life; death in battle he views as we view ordinary death in our beds. The risk of death in action is an idea that moves him about as much as an actuary's table affects us. Unlike the Mahomedan warrior, death in battle entails no Paradise with beautiful Houris as a reward; nor does *dulce et decorum est pro patria mori* seem to weigh much. Death is an incident, nothing more. "If people do not like being killed, why do they fight?" is the beginning and end of their ideas on the subject.

In every navy there are men who work at their profession and men who do not. The Japanese Navy is no exception to the rule, but the proportion of those who are casual is very small.

"Working at their profession" has, however, a very liberal meaning in the Japanese Navy. It means the absolute ignoring of everything else. I once inquired of a Japanese naval officer over here what the Japanese military attaché was called. "I cannot tell you," was the answer, "*because I work at my profession.*"

And, judging by his expression, my friend was proud of this little bit of evidence that he wasted no time on extraneous matters. This, too, was in England. His ship was then in an elementary stage at Elswick; he was at Portsmouth on leave.

The "working at his profession" in this particular case, of an officer with his ship a mere skeleton on the building slip, consisted in spending the day poring over naval books. I generally found him deep in Mahan, with halma-pieces on sheets of paper to work out the tactics.

Speaking generally, a Japanese naval officer's (in

England) idea of a holiday appears to be to come to Portsmouth, spend the day going over the dockyard, with a visit to my house to play naval war-game into the small hours as a kind of subsequent dissipation and relaxation! Whatever naval Kriegspiel may or may not be, it takes a Japanese to regard it as a dissipation.

In person, Japanese officers are very short, but the generality of them are far more "physically fit" than popular opinion imagines. The narrow-chested, sloping-shoulder variety is the exception, not the rule. Many are very well proportioned indeed. Height averages about five feet, or an inch or two over. In type of feature there is an immense variety; though black hair, high cheek-bones, and narrow eyes are common to all, general resemblance ends there. Colour varies much. Some have the same pale, yellow complexion that one often meets with in Russians; others have the more olive Italian tint. The former type have the *nez retroussé*, usually small; the latter have a more or less hooked nose. Features vary much according to the province or island from which the owner hails.[1] Occasionally one encounters a swarthy officer, hailing from the Northern islands, while here and there one meets a face almost typically European.

In character they are all more or less after one model. Taking them in the lump, they are the merriest lot I ever came across. No one enjoys the "At Homes" which Japanese officers invariably give before

[1] Those who come from the South are usually nicknamed "Russians."

their ships leave England more than the givers of them; they make the best of hosts for that reason. These "At Homes" are a distinctive Japanese feature; no other foreign visitors in our harbours ever give them. The usual foreigner arrives, official calls are made, one or two of us may perhaps be entertained on board, and there the matter ends. With a Japanese ship, on the other hand, that is about where it begins. As an old waterman on Portsmouth Hard observed, "One Japanee is worth a dozen bloomin' Rooshians and Eyetalians. Give me a Japper here once a month and I'll make my bloomin' fortune," the fact being that the civil population, who never dare venture near a Russian, crowd on board a Japanese ship in season and out, sure that, even if they are not wanted, their invasion will be forgiven. I suppose the Japanese derive some pleasure from watching the enjoyment of these self-invited guests, though their good nature must be a trifle strained at times.

When the Shikishima was docked at Portsmouth, I happened to call, with an officer of ours in uniform. In company with several of the Shikishima's officers, we were doing the round of the upper deck, when a tripper of the regulation type suddenly confronted us, and addressed my companion.

"One moment, sir!" he cried. "I want to see over the ship."

My companion indicated the Japanese officers, telling the man to apply to them.

"Bother the foreigners!" returned the man. "I

THE SHIKISHIMA ENTERING PORTSMOUTH DOCKYARD.

was told that if I went on board the officials would show me round. Can't you send one of 'em? You can tell 'em I ain't a spy. I don't mind showing 'em my card—at least, no; I find I haven't any about me. But here's my return ticket from London; they can see that if they want to. I assure you I'm not a spy, or connected with the Press in any way."

As all the Japanese understood and spoke English perfectly, this was not the happiest of introductions. However, one of them volunteered to show the tripper round, for which the tripper tendered thanks to *our* officer. He then called out to a party of his friends on the jetty that he had "managed to make one of the silly foreigners understand," after which he devoted himself to patronising his guide. He meant no harm, doubtless, but it was a good deal of a tax on Japanese politeness, and had he been kicked off the ship he would have only had himself to thank for it. There are, unhappily, a good many of these tripper-folk who, given an inch in the way of being allowed on board at all, grab a good many ells in the way of taking advantage of it. Nor is it only the tripper-folk who take undue advantage of Japanese hospitality. At the "At Homes" I have seen women, who certainly ought to know better, armed with scissors, with which they cut down any decoration that takes their fancy. The sight of the decorations does not make the Tenth Commandment easy to observe. At the close of the "At Home," the paper flowers are always all given away to the guests. But this sort of thing would

P

never happen on board an English ship in a Japanese harbour.

For an "At Home" the Japanese officers put all the men to work making paper flowers. Chrysanthemums and cherry blossoms are the favourites, but convolvuli and iris are also made, as well as a few others. All are singularly beautiful and realistic reproductions— very different things to the ordinary artificial flower of commerce. With these flowers the greater part of the ship is profusely decorated, numbers of lanterns are hung about, and here and there a "Welcome" is stuck up. In addition, each ship hits on some device of its own; thus the Kasagi went in for a host of Japanese and British naval ensigns, while the Shikishima turned diving-dresses into decorative uses. Generally, as in the illustration of the Kasagi's "At Home," some sports make a programme, fencing, single stick, conjuring tricks, and so on, with some Japanese songs in between the turns. The Shikishima, however, before she left England, capped all these things by rigging up a stage, scenery, platform, and all, upon the quarter deck, and here old Japanese plays, with the proper costumes and everything, were performed, while the entire upper deck was transformed into a paper flower-garden. I have attempted in the illustration to give some idea of the fairyland thus created, but it needs colour to give anything like the real effect.

I have dwelt thus upon Japanese "At Homes," because the way in which the officers put themselves out to enjoy these, and make their guests do the same,

"AT HOME" ON BOARD THE KASAGI.

is an index to one of their leading characteristics. It is a curious thing that no descriptions or illustrations of these gala days of the Japanese war-god ever find their way into print. The whole thing is essentially Japanese, and shows that Western drill and weapons have not killed Oriental charm.

Beyond relegating art to its proper and inferior position, I do not think that Western influence has altered Japanese character to any great extent. A Japanese naval officer of some note, in relating to me his experiences during the war against China, referred to a combined naval and military operation in which he was engaged. Cholera killed them off like rats. "It was one of the funniest sights I have ever seen," he said, "to see the soldiers all doubled up and rolling about by the side of the road as we marched." This frame of mind is distinctly Oriental; it is also distinctly useful for a fighting-man. A British bluejacket might have contrived to see the humour of the situation also,[1] but no other Westerner is so blest—for it is a case of blest; the toughest warrior is the one that wins. Japan is not going to collapse in a war while this sort of sentiment can obtain. Modern warfare is becoming more and more a matter of acting on the *morale* of the

---

[1] The following I can vouch for, as I heard it myself:—A certain warrant man in one of our destroyers came off leave one morning a little late, and thus explained himself to his skipper: "I was waiting for the train all right, sir, when some silly fool walking across the line got run over by a train coming the other way. It took both his legs off, and there was he and the legs lying on the line. *I stood there laughing so that I clean forgot my train.*" This is not exactly typical, but we have a good many such Mark Tapleys in the R.N.

personnel; it is on nerves rather than on bodies that shell-fire is intended to have its most powerful effect, and it will take a good deal of it, and a very deadly deal, to affect those who can see the humorous side of what is primarily a very terrible thing. Probably the root of the " war-instinct " lies somewhere hereabouts, and we should think many times ere we endeavour to " humanise " such ideas out of our own Mark Tapleys.

The Japanese also retains his old native dignity; European uniform has not abated one jot of that dignity which we have all read about as having been beneath the Kimino. Mostly, though not invariably, they are the descendants of the old fighting-men, the Samaurai.[1] In the midst of the new order all the best of the old traditions live, just as, in a few cases in our new social order, pauper members of old families scorn the wealthy mushroom aristocracy around them. Whatever he may do, in whatever position he may be placed, the Japanese officer never forgets his dignity, and, further, is always a *gentleman*. I believe this is the first impression that he creates; it is also the last.

On the whole, though their politeness generally hides it completely, the Japanese are a very " touchy " and sensitive people. Quite unwittingly one is apt to

---

[1] These Samaurai, or officer class—there were three classes in Japan: (1) the nobles, descendants of rulers of provinces; (2) the officer class; (3) the common people—for generation after generation lived very uncertain lives; they were liable to be killed at any moment once they left their homes. In addition, they were used to killing, having the right to do so at pleasure. If they unsheathed their swords, they could not replace them until they had killed some one. Possessing this power, it is little wonder that a strong sense of dignity was acquired with it.

tread on tender corns, without in the least realising it, until one gets to know them a good deal more than casually. They are sensitive about any infraction of the extended laws of etiquette, which they themselves observe most punctilliously. There are numbers of little things to be learnt and observed by one who would come to be on friendly terms with them, and I doubt if any Westerner can acquire all. Still, if he offends through ignorance he will never learn his fault from his hosts.

They carry this sensitiveness a considerable distance, and into a variety of things. For instance, to see themselves represented in print in broken English and queer pronunciation annoys them intensely. An Englishman, seeing his rendering of a foreign language guyed, would laugh at it; but not so the Japanese. I remember well the indignation of a Japanese at reading in a Portsmouth local paper that his countrymen had talked about their vessel as a fine "*sipp.*" He did not like it at all. Incidentally, I may mention that "sipp" was phonetically inaccurate; the majority say the word "ship" just as we do, while the rest would merely give the "i" the same phonetic value that it has in French, Italian, or Russian. On their part, I have known Japanese deliberately pronounce many of their own ship-names wrongly, so as not to offend English ears by emphasising an English error.

It is a legend in our navy that the first English word learnt by a Japanese is always *Damn!* but I have only once heard a Japanese use it. His own language is singularly defective in swear words. Japanese learn English very rapidly, and soon grow to speak it remarkably well. After a year, or less, in England they acquire not merely a mastery of the English, but also—a far more difficult thing for a foreigner—a mastery of our *slang*. Ability to pick this up argues a singularly quick brain, as dictionaries are of no avail here. It is characteristic of them, too, to set about it with a serious thoroughness, essentially Japanese. Recently a sub-lieutenant, not long from the Far East, who had learnt school English out there, took to studying a novel of mine, "The Port Guard Ship," a book that deals solely with social naval life, and so is loaded to the muzzle with current naval slang and phraseology. Every time I met this sub. he used to haul a notebook from his pocket, and reel off a list of slang and, possibly, now and again, profanities culled from its pages, the exact import of each of which I had to explain! In consequence that sub. is now able to join in any conversation without difficulty, or without the talk having to be suited for him. The Frenchman's dilemmas over such expressions as " Look out ! " do not bother him at all. In fine, he knows " English as she is spoke," by virtue of adopting a method.

Curiously enough, Japanese never learn to write English so well as they speak it—thus reversing the condition of all other foreigners. Their caligraphy is fine and bold always, but the phraseology as invariably formal. Possibly it is due to the etiquette of letter-writing in their own country that their letters here almost always begin with a "Thank you for your kind letter," and continue formal all through.

Mentally, the Japanese is adaptive, not originative. If one is explaining anything to a Japanese, he will have seized on the idea and absorbed it while a European is still struggling with the externals of it. Japanese invention has extended to a small quickfirer and a water-tube boiler, but in both cases the invention is merely a change of some existing mechanism. Even so, neither is of great moment; their abilities do not lie in that direction at all. If an entirely new system of naval tactics is ever evolved, it will not be by a Japanese; like their British *confrères*, they shine better at practical work than in the regions of theory.

They are not, however, devoid of views. Every Japanese gives time to thinking of the future, and were any lieutenant suddenly made into an admiral, I fancy that he would acquit himself quite as well as if he had reached his rank by orthodox gradations. He is apt to fail now and again at his present task from this trait, which is in many ways his chief defect, and one that may lead to trouble in war. It is sometimes dangerous to reason before proceeding to obey. A Japanese tends to do this. It is details that they think about. For instance, I once got a Japanese officer to give me his views on the conduct of a naval war. They are worth quoting *in extenso*, because naval opinions invariably run more or less in grooves.

His primary detail was strategical, and referred to the Press. "I shall have no correspondents with my fleet when I am an admiral in war," said he. "If they insist on coming, directly we get out to sea I shall set them all adrift in a boat. If they do their duty to their papers they are a hindrance to me; if they do not they are no good at all."

Detail number two referred to his fleet. "I shall hoist the signal, 'No ship is to surrender; if beaten, it must sink.' If any ship hoists the white flag, the rest of my ships will open fire on it till it sinks."

I shall watch this officer's career with interest if ever he commands a war fleet in the future, for he will go far; every detail was similarly thought out. I fancy every Japanese who stands any prospect of being an admiral in the future does the same, though the matter is not one upon which they talk at all readily to a stranger.

It is also, however, their weakest point, this fondness for thinking of the future. Too often they think of it unduly, and to the detriment of the present. Not invariably, of course, still there is, I fancy, a fair sprinkling of lieutenants who devote as much or more thought to an admiral's duty twenty years hence than to lieutenant work of to-day. It is not, primarily, a bad thing so much as a good thing overdone; but that is a Japanese naval characteristic all through. They are always in more danger of overdoing a good thing than anything else. Curiously enough, this tendency to think for the admiral does not lead to any great evil in the way of an undue corresponding tendency to be critical.

On the other hand, a Japanese naval officer never underrates his own abilities. Every junior officer feels in his inmost soul that he is fully as capable and as fully able to do anything as his senior. None of them suffer from false modesty. On the whole, this, within due bounds, is by no means a defect; self-confidence is a fine thing for begetting ability; but, as before stated, they are prone to overdo many good things. Some of them, doubtless, overdo the confidence in their own abilities.

They are, in a way, a discontented lot of men as a whole, despite all their fatalism, their enthusiasm, and their joviality. Every civilian officer fumes over to himself that he is not an executive; every lieutenant curses the time that must pass before he is a lieutenant-commander, and so on all through. Wherever they are in the professions, they want to be better and higher. Sometimes this is a defect, sometimes not. When it is a defect, it is again a case of the good thing overdone.

With all this, however, they are not ambitious in the exact way that we define the word. A friend of mine was appointed skipper of a destroyer, to take her out to Japan. He had worried everything and everybody for the post. Now, he could have gone back to Japan as a passenger in a steamer, drawing more pay, and without the risks and heavy responsibilities of being a destroyer captain; but, having got his wished-for ship, there the matter ended. There was no "another rung in the ladder" about it; it was simply "a good opportunity to get experience."

He got it. He left the Thames in a blizzard. Down Channel he had a gale, a head sea, and a thermometer well below freezing-point. Not having been to sea for some time, he was seasick continually, and the weather gave him neuralgia and bronchitis in addition. Having a crew new to the ship, he had to spend nearly the whole trip from the Thames to Portsmouth on deck, and when he snatched a brief watch below a defective cowl gave him shower-baths in his bunk. Yet, when he put into Portsmouth Harbour to coal, I found him sitting in the wardroom, expatiating to his officers on his good luck in having thus early been favoured with some bad weather experience.

"Duty," in the sense in which one finds it in the British or Russian navies, is not much of a motive-power to Japanese officers. The religion of war, the interest of their profession, the longing to put theories to a fuller practical test—here lie the springs of their motive-power. To quote one of them, they "like being killed." I believe they do.

Personal glory is, again, discouraged rather than otherwise; a solidarity of glory is rather aimed at. In the torpedo attacks at Wei-hai-wei some boats "got in," some failed. No Japanese officer who participated will tell you his share. I once asked one of these, whom I met, about the famous action. "Oh yes," said he, "I was there. It was a very cold night."

Subsequently I learnt from another officer that this particular one had commanded the boat that sank the Ting Yuen. "But," added my informant, "he would not tell you, and you should not ask. All did well; some were lucky, some not; since all did well, they agreed not to speak of it after and say who did this or did that, *for all were equally worthy of praise.*"

Ethically our socialists theorise on this sort of thing, but only the Japanese have actually practised it. Such are Japanese naval officers. To sum up, they have little ambition, little thirst for personal glory, but a good deal of thirst for the thunder of battle. The only religion that they wot of is the worship of their fleet; their only heaven, that fleet in action. They cannot originate, but they are peerless at practising the things that they have learnt. And there is only one possible way of beating a Japanese fleet—by sinking it.

In many of these things the trail of Samaurai may be visible. The Samaurai were trained to kill and to be killed; it was the thing they lived for. Take the case of the old Japanese duelling laws, which ceased to exist quite recently comparatively. No French *affaire* about these duels. To a Japanese serious European duels are as comic as French duels are to us. With the Japs the vanquished had to die, only death or a mortal wound stopped the duel, and the victor had then to commit suicide.

Hari-kari, though now illegal, is not yet entirely dead. It is not very many years ago that a Japanese sub-lieutenant disembowelled himself because of the disgrace of some affront that he felt had been put on him; in the war with China there were one or two cases. *Hari-kari* is not a nice thing to describe, and has been described in detail often enough before to-day. It has altered somewhat from the orthodox manner. The torpedo-gunner who, after his frozen-in torpedo failed to leave the tube at Wei-hai-wei, committed *hari-kari*, slit his stomach across with a knife, and then fired a pistol at his throat—according to the captain of his boat, who told me about it. This was not quite after the orthodox manner, but it was a singular painful means of death for a man to choose of his own accord. The ancestors of Japanese officers, near and remote, lived for centuries under the *hari-kari régime*. In other ways human life was cheap, and torture was common. Their descendants reap the results in an age when war has become so much a matter of "moral effect." And this is one great reason why a Japanese fleet will have to be sunk *en masse* for it to be defeated.

I will close this chapter with one anecdote, a trifle shocking to our convictions possibly, but so eminently characteristic that I must give it. One Japanese I know was studying naval history, noting the most effective dying words of great commanders (the distant future in his mind's eye very probably). "They are pretty, some of them," he said, "but I do not think them very useful. Now, if I get killed, I think I shall say, 'I die a good Christian, and shall soon be an angel with very pretty wings.'"

I can quite imagine him saying it, and his comrades finding the jest useful.

XX

PERSONAL CHARACTERISTICS

MEN.

I SOMETIMES wonder who it was first coined that well-known phrase, "little Japanese sailors." As phrases go it is very "catchy," but in the matter of accuracy it is very general only. Save for Russians and Italians, some of the biggest sailors going are Japanese. Beside their own officers they look giants, while actually they average nearly an inch higher than British bluejackets, and in breadth fully equal them. One and all, they are fine men physically, able to hold their own in size with almost any other nation's bluejackets, except Russians and Italians. They are almost invariably stout and well set up, and they are always smiling; they take to their profession much as their officers do.

As previously stated, they are recruited chiefly from the northern islands, and chiefly from the lowest classes. These make the bravest sailors, and they have been educated from early youth upward into a disregard for death. Till quite recently, most Japanese villages had feuds with neighbouring hamlets, and these resulted in a good many broken heads and a fair amount of blood-letting, all of which the Government, if it did not actually encourage, at least viewed with a very lenient eye on account of its practical utility in rearing fighters.

Japanese officers have, on the whole, a preference for sailors of little education. Their view is that such are less hampered by appreciating danger. Apparently some of the better class sailors—artificers and others drawn from a rather better class socially, acquire with their education an inconvenient ability to realise some of the frightful dangers of modern naval warfare. Either from experience or instinct, these more educated men are not looked on with favour. "The less a man knows the better sailor he will make," is the saying.

A rabid anti-Japanese of my acquaintance, who has spent his life in the Far East, allows the Japanese only one virtue—general and complete bravery. "No Japanese," said he, "is ever afraid." It is not easy to reconcile this statement with the Japanese estimate of educated sailors given above; but I am not in a position to deliver a verdict of any value on the question. The officers' contempt of danger, alluded to some pages back, has little bearing on the point. The fact that "cowardice" exists as an offence in the Japanese naval code of punishments may, perhaps, throw a little light upon the matter; but, even so, we need an exact definition of what the word "cowardice" means to a Japanese. It does not mean cowardice as we should understand it. I incline to fancy that it means the absence of an utter disregard for life; and that what the Japanese call a coward we describe as a waverer—which is by no means the same thing. It is not impossible that their more liberal definition of cowardice would include a man who got unduly excited in action. After Yalu, several men were punished for that.

The general intelligence of Japanese bluejackets is high, they have the national aptitude for "picking things up" with marvellous rapidity—wherein they form a marked contrast to the Russian sailors, who learn very slowly. They—some of them—also forget rapidly; a national defect in Japan.

In many ways they are replicas of their officers. Like their officers, their ideas of dissipation centre round learning something. Parties of fifty or so "do" London and our chief industrial centres when they are in England. On these occasions, and, indeed, always in foreign ports, their behaviour leaves nothing to be desired. At Portsmouth, where public houses are thick as can be, and where leave is given very freely, a hundred or so will roam the town all day in groups, fraternising and being made much of by the populace, but any disorder or trouble with the police in consequence is almost unknown.

On ship-board drinking is said to be on the increase; but it is rarely a cause of trouble, though a drunken Japanese is a nasty customer. Most are temperate.

Stealing is practically unknown. Natural causes

operate here. If by any chance a Japanese sailor steals, he is a marked man. His shipmates refuse to have any dealings with him whatever, he is an absolute outcast; and his crime is passed on against him by his comrades should he be sent to another ship. This perpetual ostracism is a most effectual safeguard.

Till recently Japanese sailors were not over and above obedient. A marked change has since sprung up, and they are now, as a rule, very amenable and willing, as well as able. They still, however, need some tact in management; and attempts to knife officers are not unknown.

Cleanliness is a national characteristic. Japanese sailors, like all of the lower class in Japan, bathe more frequently even than the upper classes—twice each day every Japanese sailor has a bath. If from war, or any other cause, they are prevented from bathing for a couple of weeks or so, the lower class Japanese suffer a great deal from skin diseases. Hence they are ill-adapted for lengthy torpedo boat service.

In general neatness their average is high; on whatever work they are engaged—except, of course, coaling ship—they are usually spick and span.

Despite his good qualities, however, the average Japanese bluejacket is not on a par with his officers in value. He lacks stolidity; and, take him all and all, he is inferior to a Chinese sailor. The Chinaman is braver, or, rather, what the Japanese call braver. According to the Japanese, Ah Sin is the finest material for blue-jackets in the world, and they are not alone in this opinion.

To return to the Japanese bluejacket. Like his officers, he has little, if any, religion—though, nominally, a certain proportion may be Buddhists or Shinto. They have, however, a species of semi-religious code over some minor matters—for instance, no Japanese sailor will accept a tip for small services, such as showing visitors round a ship, or because he is coxswain of a boat in which you have taken passage. According to their ethics, it is a *crime* to accept special payment for anything done in the way of duty, and if a man by any chance did accept anything, his shipmates would render his life unbearable by their contemptuous ridicule of him. So, though they will as readily and gladly take any amount of trouble for a stranger, to try and give them a tip annoys them. I once kept a Japanese boat's crew, which had been sent for me, waiting a long time, on a bitterly cold day, through some misunderstanding as to time. It was a long row to the ship, against a strong tide, in which they were soon wet through. Arrived at the ship, my first attempt to tip the coxswain was greeted by a shake of the head. Thinking he had misunderstood my intention, I repeated the attempt. He at once called out, "No. Go away!" in a most indignant tone, and his whole expression was that of a man on whom I had put a deadly insult.

Japanese sailors are very quick in everything. In the Far East brawls between them and Russian sailors, before the war, were very frequent, and though the Russians are physically much the superior, yet, from their quickness, the Japanese were more frequently the victors.

When Japanese sailors are in England, some of our missionary societies keep an eye on them—taking them about, and generally trying to help them. One old lady is particularly kindly remembered by the crews of those destroyers that fitted out at the West India Docks. She gave the crew of one of them a good many texts of the usual ornamental sort when they left. They hung all these up, giving the post of honour to one that said, "The wicked shall be destroyed." They regarded this as a very kindly compliment and good wish to their destroyer! I do not think that the texts stand any chance of fulfilling a missionary *rôle*—however, there they hung, in the fo'k's'le, and over the officers' bunks in the ward-room also, in the hopes that "the old lady, who had been so good to the men," would derive some *quid pro quo* in the way of satisfaction at the sight.

XXI

MESSING

IN the Japanese Navy, as in ours, there are many messes—admirals being by themselves, captains by themselves, and below them the ward-room, gun-room, warrant officers, and petty officers' messes.

The officers have three meals a day—

> Breakfast at 7.0 to 7.30 a.m.
> Lunch at 12 noon.
> Dinner at 7.0 p.m.

The food is alternately English and Japanese—thus, one day there are two meals European and one Japanese; the day following two Japanese and one European. Preference is probably towards our food, but sentiment retains the national diet. At the Japanese meals chopsticks are used. The staple of these meals is rice.

In the way of liquids, our whisky-and-soda has now as great a vogue as anything; but in all ships the national *saki* still abounds. This is a light wine made from rice—a sort of cross between hock and thin cider—disagreeable at first to most European palates, but for which one soon cultivates a liking. It is apt to play unexpected tricks on the stranger who imbibes it too freely. In the winter time *saki* is drunk warm.

Japanese tea is always "on tap." It bears no resemblance to tea as we know it, being a strong green tea made with water just off the boil. Neither milk nor sugar is taken with it—sweets are, however, eaten beforehand.

So far from these national drinks being in abeyance, if a visitor in a Japanese warship elects to take one or the other in place of whisky or champagne, it is taken as a compliment by his hosts.

Japanese sailors are fed entirely, or nearly so, on European food. It was found that they could not work so well on Japanese diet, and they prefer European. They cook it, however, in more or less Japanese fashion, and always eat it with chopsticks.

24-CM. (9·4-IN.) 36-CALIBRE SCHNEIDER-CANET ON DISAPPEARING MOUNTING FOR THE JAPANESE COAST SERVICE. FIRING POSITION.

XXII

ARMAMENT AND EQUIPMENT

1. Guns.

THE early Japanese warships were equipped with Krupp guns, the Naniwa and Takachiho being so fitted. At a later date Canet guns were introduced, but only for the heavy pieces, and the Matsushima class carried a big 12·6 Canet and Elswick guns for the smaller pieces. Subsequently, with the Fuji and Yashima, Elswick guns alone were employed, and a factory for the construction of guns on the Elswick model was established in Japan. The pieces selected were the 12-in. 40-calibre, the 8-in. 40-calibre, the 40-calibre 6-in., and the 45-calibre 4·7-in. Up to and including the Mikasa, all ships were mounted with these guns.

In 1902-3 the Vickers 50-calibre 6-in. was experimented with and adopted.

The guns at present mounted in the Japanese fleet, excluding a few old pieces about to be replaced or already removed, are as follows:—

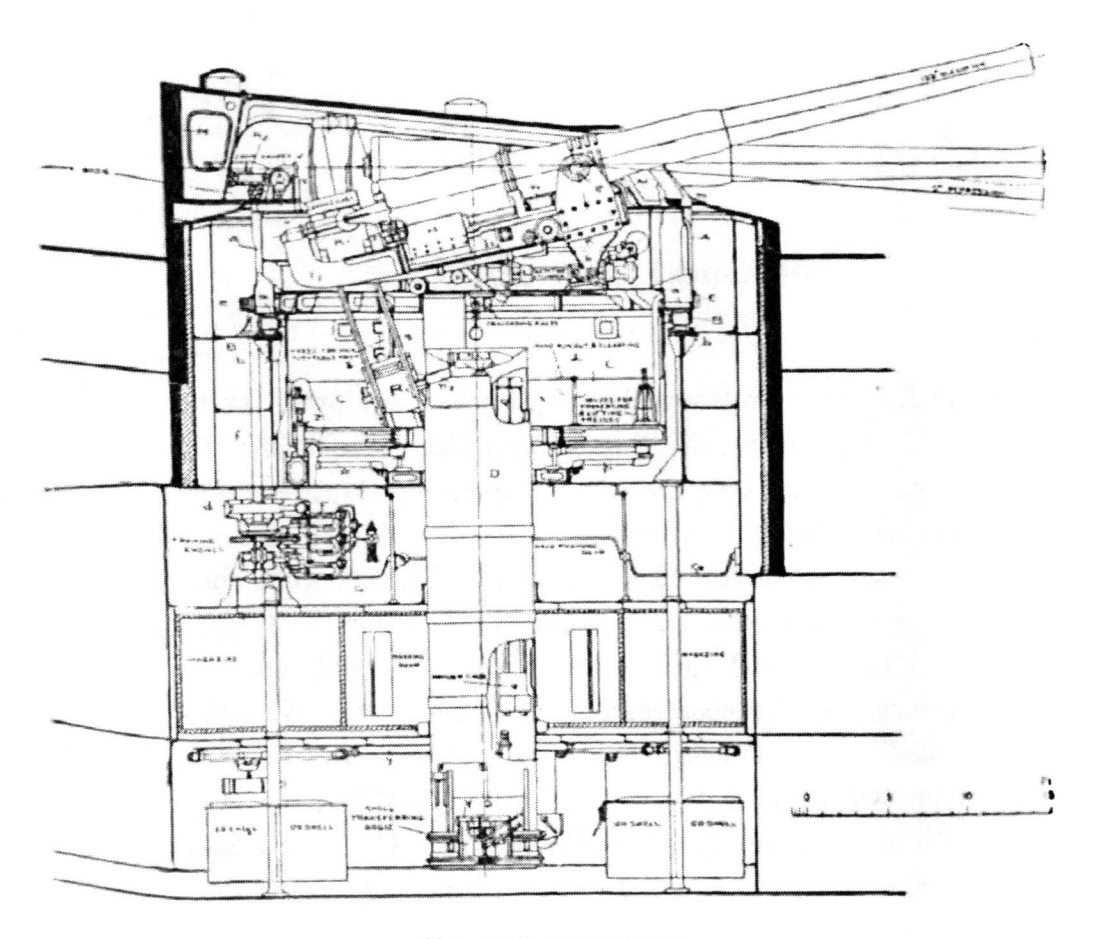

12-IN. GUNS OF THE MIKASA.

24-CM. (9·4-IN.) CANET GUN OF 36 CALIBRES ON DISAPPEARING MOUNTING, AS SUPPLIED FOR JAPANESE COAST FORTS. LOADING AND TRAINING POSITION.

ARMAMENT AND EQUIPMENT

Nominal calibre.		—	Long.	Initial velocity.	Initial energy.	Shell.	Weight of gun.
in.	cm.		cals.	foot secs.	foot tons.	lbs.	tons.
12·6	32	Canet [1] . . .	40	2306	35220	990	66
12	30·5	Elswick [2] . . .	40	2423	34600	850	49
12	30·5	Krupp [3] . . .	20	1755	14750	725	35·4
10·2	26	Krupp [4] . . .	25	1640	8400	450	..
8·2	21	Krupp . . .	30	1935	6167	..	13
8	20·3	Elswick . .	40 {	2242 / 2068	7319 / 7413	210 / 250	} 15½
6	15	Vickers . . .	50	3000	6240	100	8
6	15	Elswick . . .	40	2500	4334	100	6¼
6	15	Elswick . . .	40	2220	3417	100	6
6	15	..	35	1958	2554	100	5
4·7	12	Elswick . .	40	2150	1442	45	2
4·7	12	Elswick [1] . .	32	1938	900	36	1¾
3	7·5	Elswick . . .	40	2200	420	12	2

All guns of 40-calibres and over—that is to say, all the modern pieces—fire a smokeless nitro-cellulose powder of Japanese invention, and the maximum service velocities of all, save the 50-calibre Vickers, are now up to the nominal initial velocity.

A.P. shot, A.P. shell, and common shell are fired by all guns, and, in addition, those of 8 ins. or less calibre fire a special Japanese high explosive of the lyddite type.

In smaller pieces, a 2½-pounder exists, which is to a certain extent a Japanese invention; but it differs from models existing elsewhere only in a few minor

[1] Matsushima class.   [2] In Fuji to Mikasa.   [3] Chin Yen.   [4] Hei Yen Naniwa, Takachiho.

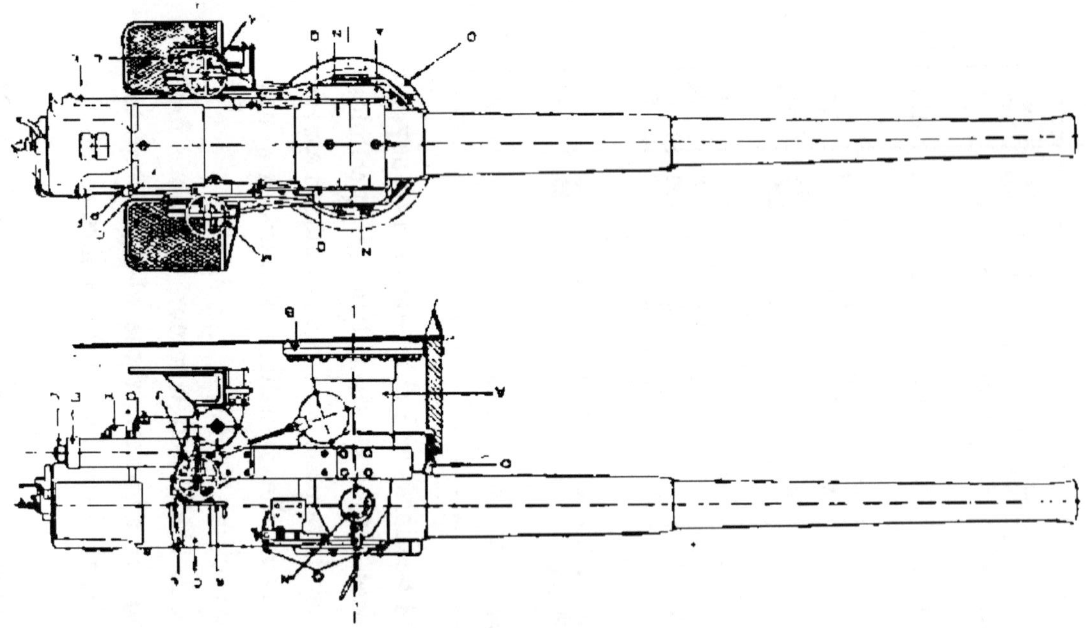

VICKERS 50-CALIBRE 6-IN. JAPANESE GUN.

6-in.

7·5-in.

THE VICKERS 6-IN. AND 7·5-IN. OF 50 CALIBRES.
(*The former is adopted, the latter under consideration.*)

ARMAMENT AND EQUIPMENT

details of a semi-automatic nature. From what I have seen of it, the piece would be better without these innovations.

The maximum penetrations of the larger pieces through Krupp cemented armour at 3000 yards are as follows:—

	Capped.	Uncapped.
Schneider-Canet 12·6-in.	16	13
Elswick 12-in.	15½	12½
Elswick 8-in.	7½	6
Vickers 6-in.	6½	5
Elswick 6-in.	4	4

For coast defence, Schneider-Canet guns are mostly employed, many 9·4's on disappearing mounting having been supplied for forts.

2. Gunnery Accessories.

THE Barr and Stroud range-finder is used in all Japanese ships, and acted excellently at the bombardments of Port Arthur in February, 1904.

The Barr and Stroud transmitters are also fitted to all first-class warships. By means of these the range, projectile, and so forth is telegraphed from the conning-tower to a dial in each turret and casement. Without some such device a range-finder is of no particular service, as by the time the range is passed down it will have altered.

The Grenfell system of transmission is also understood to be under experiment. This differs in details from the Barr and Stroud, but in general principle is much the same thing.

The theoretical objection to the Barr and Stroud is that the electric leads may be cut by a hostile shot. They might be, but as the wires are carried in duplicate under the armour deck the chances of failure are about one in a million! Throughout the war with Russia all these instruments have worked perfectly, and proved particularly serviceable in the bombardments of Port Arthur.

CANET 27-CM. (10.6-IN.) JAPANESE COAST GUN OF 36 CALIBRES.

3. TORPEDOES.

THE Japanese service has three torpedoes:—

    14-in. Whitehead, for torpedo boats and small cruisers.
    18-in.   „   for destroyers and large ships.
    24-in.   „   for defence of channels.

This last torpedo has an effective range of over 3000 yards. It is not, however, carried on shipboard.

The Whiteheads are identical with those in the British service. So, too, are the above-water tubes. The submerged ones are of Elswick pattern—Mark I., which was not satisfactory at high speeds in the Fuji, Yashima, and Shikishima; Mark II., which delivers fairly well at all speeds in the later ships. All ships that carry submerged tubes—that is, all first-class battleships or cruisers—have four fitted: two forward on the broadside and two bearing 45° abaft the beam, just abaft the after barbette.

Above-water tubes are condemned, and several of those in existence were under orders of removal when the Russian war broke out.

Above-water bow tubes were condemned on account of the seas that they took in. As such as exist in armoured vessels are protected by 6-in. armour, they did not improve seaworthiness, the weight in the extreme bow being inconvenient.

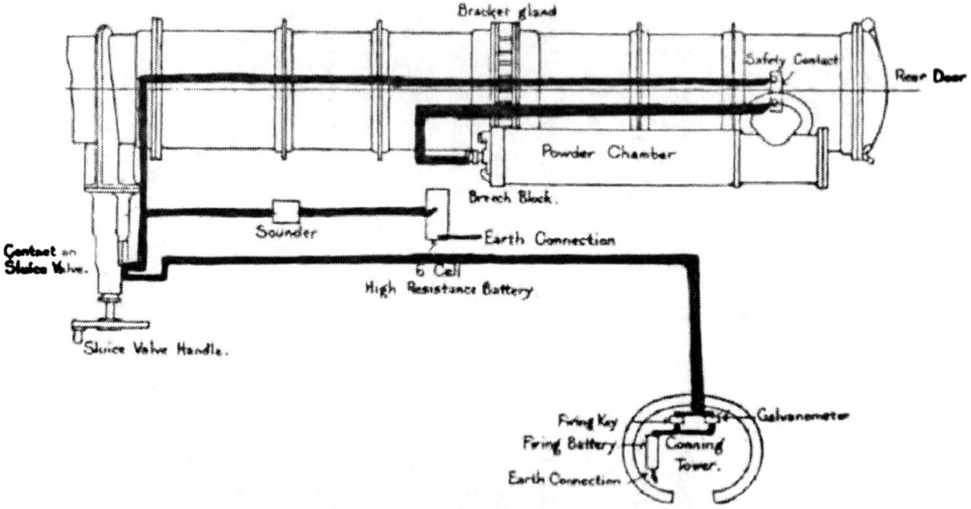

PLAN OF CIRCUITS OF THE ELSWICK TUBE.

CANET 15-CM. (6-IN.) JAPANESE COAST GUN.

4. Armour.

AN armour-plate factory has been established at Kobé, but it is not yet in a position to turn out much except gun-shields.

A characteristic of the Japanese has been their readiness to adopt new processes.

Thus the Fuji and Yashima were designed for compound armour, but the Harvey process coming in while the ships were building, it was at once adopted in preference to compound. So, too, in later ships the improved Harvey, "Harvey-Nickel," was at once used, and in the Iwate and Idzumo belts were shortened a little and speed reduced, so that the Krupp process might be employed for the water-line plates.

In the Mikasa great expense was undertaken solely in order to apply Krupp cemented to curved surfaces instead of the non-cemented and less tough Krupp plates usually so employed. There is some doubt whether this experiment was successful; if Krupp cemented plates are "fiddled with" their special virtue departs. It is also stated, however, that the Mikasa's plates were made on a special process somewhat analogous to the Krupp, but differing from it in certain details, and less liable to injury in bending.

5. Engines and Boilers.

THE engines of Japanese warships are, save in the case of a few small vessels, of British manufacture, and the same as those of British ships.

In boilers, the Belleville type was adopted with the Shikishima, and several older vessels have been re-boilered with it. Almost the first warship to be fitted with this type was the Chiyoda.

With some remarkable exceptions, Japanese naval engineers have not succeeded very conspicuously in securing the very economical coal results which have been obtained with Bellevilles in the British Fleet. A remarkable instance to the contrary was the Idzumo; the Mikasa also did well. The Asahi, when first commissioned, did badly, but, when the art of coal spreading on scientific lines was mastered, suddenly became very economical.

No trouble of any sort has been experienced, and the Japanese have shown themselves singularly adapted to the management of water-tube boilers.

When the Yaeyama was re-boilered, Niclausse generators were fitted to her, but with indifferent success. Consequently, in order to continue experiments on the lines of the British Navy, this type was fitted to the Niitaka and Tsushima, and ordered for one of the new battleships. Apparently the experiment

THE LATEST PATTERN ELSWICK SUBMERGED TUBE.

ARMAMENT AND EQUIPMENT 333

is to be continued to other types, following the example of the British Navy, though the majority of the engineers are averse to such a procedure, both on account of the success obtained with the Belleville and because of the extreme difficulty involved when many types exist, and many of the men sent to a ship are used to some other type of boiler than the one that they are called on to work.

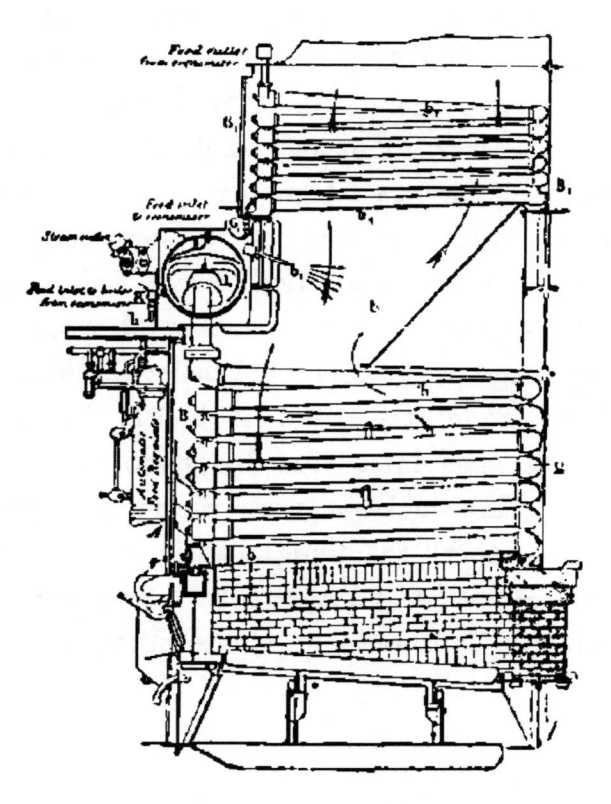

BELLEVILLE BOILER WITH ECONOMISERS.

A water-tube boiler of Japanese design exists—a species of cross between the Belleville and Yarrow, with a little Niclausse thrown in. It does not appear to promise well, and though designed to possess the virtues of each type, seems more likely to embody their weaker points than their strong ones. Such, at least, appears to be the general verdict.

There is also another water-tube boiler of Japanese origin, something like the Thornycroft, which is in the hands of the Temperley Transported Company; but I have not heard of any practical tests of it as yet, its invention being quite recent.

In any case, neither is likely to oust existing types, as most of the valuable points in a boiler are already patented all over the world. The inventors of new types are, therefore, hampered much like inventors of new systems of wireless telegraphy are—some one has been before them. In addition, a water-tube boiler requires some years of practical service before it can be classed as out of the experimental stage. The great advantage possessed by the Belleville, which "in theory" is one of the worst of boilers, lies in the numerous features introduced by years of practical experience. In rough-sea work theory and practice rarely go together; the thing that is ideal on paper is apt at sea to fail unexpectedly. The water-tube boilers fitted in Japanese ships are as follows:—

ARMAMENT AND EQUIPMENT 335

BELLEVILLE.	NICLAUSSE.
Chiyoda (old type).	Niitaka.
Itsukushima.	Yaeyama.
Matsushima (old type).	Tsushima.
Shikishima (old type).	Kashima.
Asahi.	Katori.
Hatsuse.	
Mikasa.	
Yakumo.	
Azuma.	
Iwate.	
Idzumo.	
Takasago.	

The Japanese boiler under experiment is the Miyabara, the invention of the Engineer-in-Chief of the

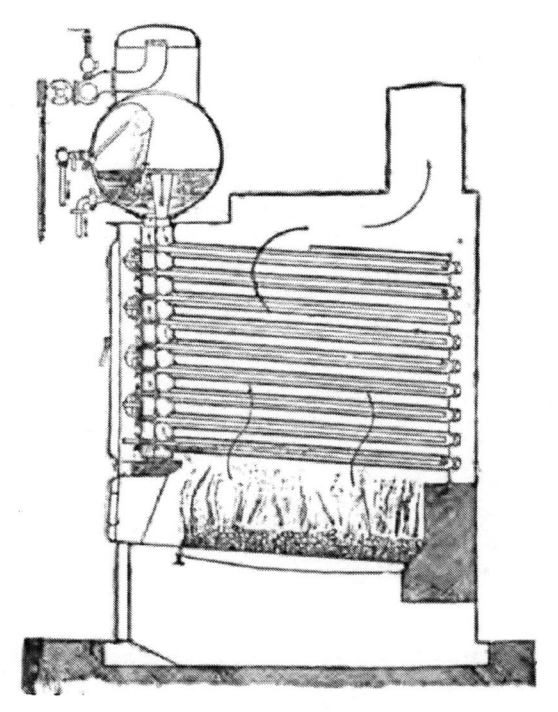

NICLAUSSE BOILER.

R

Japanese Navy. It is to be fitted to the *Otawa*, and probably some other ships. It is also in the *Hashidate*. The inventor recently produced a paper showing its all-round advantages over every other type of water-tube boiler; but this, of course, may be taken *cum grano salis*. However, there is little doubt but that, should it be in any way successful, natural national vanity will lead to its general adoption in preference to European types, just as the $2\frac{1}{2}$-pounder gun has been.

XXIII

OTHER NAVIES AS SEEN BY THE JAPANESE

THE following expressions of opinion are not necessarily entirely representative, but they certainly coincide with the views of a great many of the more travelled officers, and as such will have, no doubt, some considerable interest.

BRITISH.

"British officers are too fond of golf and other games—they do not study enough. They are very stiff at first, but nice when you know them. They are always very clean, spick and span, and well shaved. On board a British warship it is always very impressive —it is the most impressive navy in the world. And it is more ready than many people think."

FRENCH.

"The French is a funny navy, and it is hard to say what is good and what is bad in it, for the thing that looks good may be bad, and the thing that looks bad, good. They have some very clever engineers."

German.

"The German officers all seem 'strong.' To many they seem always overbearing. They hope to be the greatest navy in the world; and plenty of them think that they already are."

Russian.*

"The Russians are brave—very brave. But not many are good, and they are savages. They can be very polite when it suits them; when not—ah! Russian sailors are miserable people who lie in the snow, who have very little money, which they spend in buying cheap fish. They are very dirty. That is all we know of Russian sailors, who are quite like strange people to us. But we have no fear as to the result of a war with the Polar Bear."

United States, America.

"The Americans have a wonderful navy with wonderful ships. Everything American is more wonderful than anything else in the world, so that we do not know what to believe."

Themselves.

Of themselves Japanese officers speak little. But it is not difficult to infer from their talk that they do not in any way feel dissatisfied with themselves. Ship for

---

* Expressed before the Russo-Japanese War.

ship, they are firmly convinced that they are the finest navy in the world; and it cannot be said that up to the moment of writing (June, 1904) they have done anything to cause them to retract this opinion. No body of men could have displayed better qualities than they have from all accounts. It may be added that, in my opinion, every Japanese is also of conviction that Japan is going to be the greatest naval power in the world in the future. With that feeling they entered on the present war. It is a very useful feeling to have.

XXIV

THE WAR WITH RUSSIA

THE war with Russia was the direct outcome of the action of that Power in ousting Japan from Port Arthur. There is little question but that the real object of the Chino-Japanese War was Japan's determination to be the paramount power in the Far East. The action of Russia, France, and Germany in neutralising all that victory gave her completely checkmated Japan, and from that day onward she made little secret of her preparations for a war, the prize of which would be the control of China, and the foundation of a Far Eastern Empire whose ultimate proportions none can foresee.

The political situation between Japan and Russia needs no comment in a purely naval record of events: Japan made ready with a steady determination, where Russia ignored the obvious.

Not till a month or two before the war did Russia recognise that it was inevitable; she then sought refuge in diplomatic delays, which Japan severed by the sudden rupture of negotiations at a moment

VARIAG.

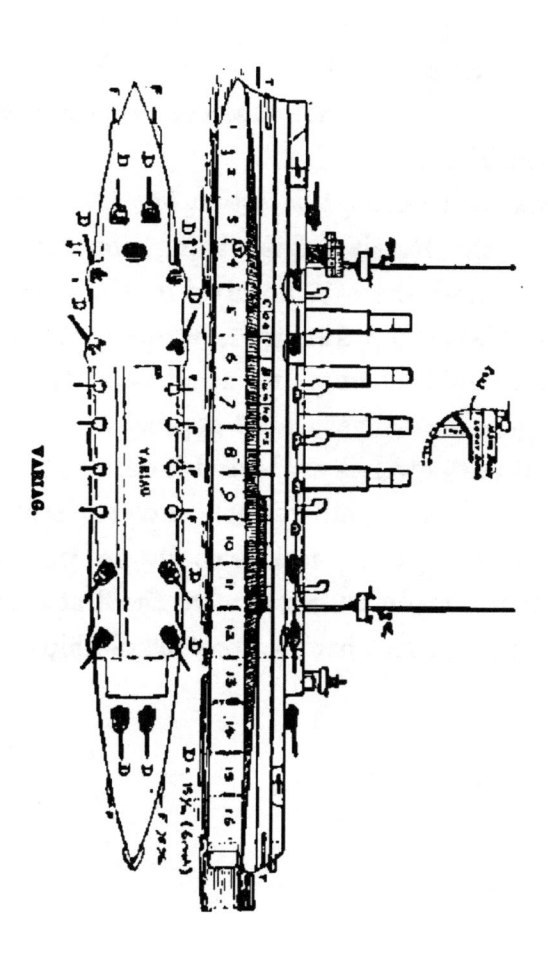

favourable to herself. Much has been written of Japan's "treachery" and Russia's "duplicity," but neither accusation is just.

Following are the Japanese versions of the various incidents of the war, as officially reported:—

They were prefaced by the Chemulpo incident, in which the Asama, Naniwa, Takachiho, Suma, Chiyoda, and Niitaka annihilated the Russian cruiser Variag and the gunboat Korietz.

As a naval incident, this action has little interest or significance, the Russian ships being abnormally over-matched; indeed, there is nothing in the affair worthy of comment save the admirable strategy displayed by the Japanese in thus ensuring absolute victory without taking any risks. A very high appreciation of the real meaning of sea-power is evidenced here.

The rest of the naval war concentrated around Port Arthur. The Japanese task was in no way an easy one, for Russia made no errors after the first stupendous one by which she lost her two best battleships.

[Reproduced by kind permission of the "Graphic."

ADMIRAL TOGO.

FIRST ATTACK ON PORT ARTHUR

ADMIRAL TOGO'S official report of the attack on Port Arthur is dated February 10, 1904, at sea, and is as follows :—

After the combined fleet left Sasebo on the 6th, everything went off as planned.

At midnight, on the 8th, the advance squadron attacked the enemy's advance squadron, the latter being mostly outside the bay.

The Poltava, Askold, and two others were apparently struck by torpedoes.

At noon, on the 9th, the fleet advanced to the offing of Port Arthur Bay, and attacked the enemy for forty minutes, I believe doing considerable damage.

I believe the enemy were greatly demoralised. They stopped fighting at one o'clock, and appeared to retreat to the harbour.

The Japanese fleet suffered but very slight damage, and its fighting strength has not decreased.

Our casualties were four killed and fifty-four wounded. The imperial princes on board suffered no harm.

The conduct of the officers was cool, and not unlike their conduct at manœuvres.

This morning, owing to the heavy south wind, detailed reports from the vessels have not been received, so I merely report the above facts.

Togo.

The ships actually torpedoed were the Tsarevitch, Retvizan, and Pallada, none of which were sunk.

The Japanese fleet consisted of all the modern vessels.

The relative small loss inflicted upon the Russians is explained as follows :—

(1) Several of the Japanese boats followed some scouting Russian boats in error.

(2) The torpedo is an uncertain weapon at the best.

The Japanese boats got in by imitating Russian signals.

In the battle of the 9th very little harm was done on either side. The Novik and several other Russian ships were struck, but the damages were in no case serious. On the Japanese side the Fuji and Iwate received some hits, but these, though extensive, were not of a really serious nature.

SECOND ATTACK

THE official report is as follows:—

On the 13th a division of torpedo-boat destroyers started for Port Arthur during a heavy snowstorm. The boats lost sight of each other and became separated. Only the Hayatori and Asagiri reached Port Arthur. The Asagiri sighted the entrance to the harbour at three o'clock on the morning of the 14th, and was received with a heavy fire by the batteries and scouting torpedo boats. She entered the harbour and discharged a torpedo at a warship from whose funnel smoke was ascending. The Asagiri then emerged safely, returning the fire of the enemy's torpedo-boats.

The same morning, at five o'clock, the Hayatori approached Port Arthur and discerned two Russian ships, which opened fire on her. The destroyer discharged a torpedo, which was seen to explode. The Hayatori also escaped scathless.

It is impossible to state the definite material results, owing to the darkness, but the moral effect was certainly considerable.

Togo.

It has not yet been definitely ascertained whether any Russian ship was sunk; if so, it was only a minor vessel. This attack may be written off as a wasted effort.

ATTACK ON VLADIVOSTOK

THE next incident of note was the attack on Vladivostok, which, again, was barren of results, as the Russians did not attempt to reply.

The official report of the attack on Vladivostok, from Admiral Kamimura, commanding the second squadron, is as follows:—

As pre-arranged, the squadron reached the eastern entrance of Vladivostok on the morning of March 6, after passing through the frozen sea. The enemy's ships were not seen in the outside harbour, and the Japanese vessels approached the batteries on the northeast coast from a point beyond the range of the batteries of the Balzan Promontory and the Bosphorous Strait.

After bombarding the inner harbour for forty minutes from ten minutes to two, the Japanese squadron retired. It is believed that the bombardment effected considerable damage. Soldiers were seen on land, but the Russian batteries did not reply to the Japanese fire.

Black smoke was observed in the eastern entrance about five in the afternoon, and was thought to be from the enemy's ships, but the smoke gradually disappeared. On the morning of the 7th inst. the Japanese squadron reconnoitred America Bay and Strelok Bay, but nothing unusual was seen. The warships again approached the eastern entrance of Vladivostok at noon, but the enemy's ships were not visible, and the batteries did not fire.

The squadron then turned towards Possiet Bay, but seeing nothing of the enemy, retired.

The next operations were more exciting, being officially reported as follows :—

An attack on Port Arthur took place on March 10th, as previously planned.

Our destroyers were formed into two separate flotillas. Both of them reached the outside of the harbour at midnight on the 9th and reconnoitred, but no enemy was seen. At dawn the second flotilla laid special mechanical mines in many places, and succeeded in the task, notwithstanding the intermittent fires from the enemy's forts.

At half-past four a.m. the first flotilla encountered six Russian destroyers at the south of Liaotishan, and a hot action took place for twenty minutes. In its course three of our destroyers—Asashio, Kasumi, and Akatsuki—fought very closely against the enemy's destroyers, almost touching each other, and delivered a hot fire.

The enemy's destroyers were severely injured, either being damaged in engines or suffering from the outbreak of fire, and fled away in great confusion. Our ships also sustained some damage. Casualties on our side are seven petty officers killed and nine men wounded.

The Akatsuki's auxiliary steampipe was destroyed, but all the destroyers of the first flotilla have no difficulty for further fighting or navigation.

The second flotilla, when it was leaving the outside of the harbour at 7 a.m., found two Russian destroyers just coming back into the harbour, and attacked them, intercepting their return course. One of the two escaped, but the other—namely, the Steregutchy—was destroyed and captured by our destroyer Sazanami, which tried to tow it back. However, the leakage was great and the sea very rough, and the towing-rope was broken. Therefore, after the prisoners, four in all, were taken up, the captured ship was left, and she sank at ten minutes past ten a.m.

The damage in the second flotilla is insignificant. Casualties: Two men killed and one officer and three men wounded.

Although the Novik and Bayan came out from the harbour towards the second flotilla, they soon retired into the harbour upon seeing that our cruisers were approaching.

As to the movements of our main squadron and the cruiser squadron, they arrived off Port Arthur at eight a.m. The cruiser squadron at once proceeded towards the front of the mouth of the harbour and supported our destroyer flotilla, as above stated.

The main squadron also approached Liaotishan,

from ten a.m. until twenty minutes to two p.m., and made an indirect bombardment against the harbour. The enemy's forts intermittently returned the fire, but no damage was inflicted upon our ships. A detached squadron of cruisers went to Dalny, and destroyed the enemy's buildings on the San Shan Islands.

The Takasago and Chihaya scouted the western coast of the entrance of Port Arthur, but no enemy was seen.

A Russian destroyer, which had been sunk in Pigeon Bay in the last battle, is found to be the Vnushitelni, of which now the upper parts of the masts and funnels are seen on the surface. All our ships discontinued the battle at two p.m., and retired.

Subsequently an attempt was made to block Port Arthur harbour with sunken ships. It was also hoped to destroy the Retvizan by exploding ships near her, but the attack was completely foiled by the defence.

There was a second bottling expedition of March 27th, which again failed. It led to the death of a valuable officer, Commander Hirose. The official report ran as follows:—

The united squadron again left for Port Arthur on Saturday.

On Sunday morning at half-past three it commenced blockading the harbour entrance. The four steamers to be sunk, escorted by a flotilla of destroyers, advanced to the entrance, facing the enemy's searchlights.

At about two miles from the entrance they were discovered by the enemy, and exposed to fire from the fortress on either shore, and also from the enemy's ships on guard.

Braving these dangers, the four steamers ran into the waterway at the mouth of the harbour. The Chiyo-maru anchored at about half a chain from the shore, to the west of Golden Hill, and blew up. The Fukui-maru, passing to the left of Chiyo-maru, advanced a short distance, and was about to anchor, when she was struck by a torpedo from the enemy's destroyers, and sank. The Yahiko-maru went to the left of the Fukui-maru, and blew up herself.

The Yoneyama-maru reached the harbour entrance, and colliding against the stern of an enemy's destroyer, managed to reach the middle passage by passing between the Chiyo-maru and Fukui-maru. Just at that moment an enemy's torpedo struck and sunk her. The momentum brought her forward to the left shore, and with her bows towards the left side sank sideways.

To have accomplished the work so far under such great disadvantages and dangers must be considered a success and command admiration. It is regrettable, however, that, owing to some space being still left between the Yahiko-maru and Yoneyama-maru, a complete blocking has not been effected.

Those who were engaged in this work are those who had been engaged in the same work before. It was by their special request that only the petty officers and crews were supplanted by new men.

The casualties were as follows:—Commander Hirose and three petty officers killed; Lieut. Shimada mortally wounded; Lieut. Masuki, Engineer Kura, and six petty officers and men slightly wounded. All the rest of the crews were safely picked up by our destroyers.

Commander Hirose and Boatswain Sugino, who were killed, displayed admirable courage. Sugino was just going down to light the magazine on the Fukui-maru, when the ship was struck by the enemy's torpedo, killing him. Commander Hirose, after causing his men to take to the boats, and not finding Sugino, searched through the ship three times. Finding his ship gradually going down, he was compelled to leave her and enter the boat. As the boat was rowing away under the enemy's fire, a shell struck him on the head, and the greater part of his body was blown away, the only remaining part of this brave officer's body being a piece of flesh in the boat.

Commander Hirose was always a model officer, and he leaves a meritorious example and memory which will be everlasting.

For the protection of the steamers and the rescue of their crews, all our flotilla of destroyers did their utmost, in the face of the enemy's severe cannonade. Above all, the destroyers Kotaka and Tsubame penetrated to within a mile of the harbour entrance, where they encountered and engaged an enemy's destroyer, to which they did considerable damage. The Russian destroyer seemed to have had her boiler hit, and sent up a volume of steam, and retreated.

As the officers and men were leaving the harbour after

their work was done, they observed one of the enemy's ships below Golden Hill. She seemed completely disabled.

In spite of the enemy's very hot fire, to which our flotilla was exposed until dawn, no damage whatever was sustained.

The crews on board the Chiyo-maru and Yahi-maru were taken on board the destroyer Tsubame. The crew of the Yoneyama-maru escaped in three boats, and were rescued by the destroyers Misasagi and Karigane. The crew of the Fukui-maru was taken on board the Kasumi.

The following torpedo boats and destroyers took part in the engagement:—

Destroyers.—Shirakumo, Kasumi, Asashio, Akatsuki, Akelbono, Oboro, Inazumi, Ikadzuchi, Usugumo, Sazanami, and Shimonome.

Torpedo boats.—Karigane, Kotaka, Misasagi, Tsubami, Managure, and Hato.

TOGO.

The concluding operation of the first stage of the war was reported as follows by Admiral Togo:—

On the 11th our combined fleet commenced, as previously planned, the eighth attack upon Port Arthur. The fourth and the fifth destroyer flotillas, the fourteenth torpedo flotilla, and the Koryo-maru reached the mouth of Port Arthur at midnight of the 12th, and effected the laying of mines at several points outside the port, defying the enemy's searchlight.

The second destroyer flotilla discovered, at dawn of the 13th, one Russian destroyer trying to enter the harbour, and, after ten minutes' attack, sank her.

Another Russian destroyer was discovered coming from the direction of Liau-tie-shan. We attacked her, but she managed to flee into the harbour.

There were no casualties on our side, except two seamen in the Ikazuchi slightly wounded. There was no time to rescue the enemy's drowning crew, as the Bayan approached.

The third fleet reached outside of Port Arthur at 8 a.m., when the Bayan came out and opened fire. Immediately the Novik, Askold, Diana, Petropavlovsk, Pobieda, and Poltava came out and made offensive attack upon us.

Our third fleet, tardily answering and gradually retiring, enticed the enemy fifteen miles south-east of the port, when our first fleet, being informed through wireless telegraphy from the third fleet, suddenly appeared before the enemy and attacked them.

While the enemy was trying to regain the port, a battleship of the Petropavlovsk type struck mines laid by us in the previous evening, and sank at 10.32 a.m.

Another ship was observed to have lost freedom of movement, but the confusion of enemy's ships prevented us from identifying her. They finally managed to regain the port.

Our third fleet suffered no damage.

The enemy's damage was, besides the above-mentioned, probably slight also.

Our first fleet did not reach firing distance. Our fleets retired at 1 p.m., prepared for another attack.

On the 14th our fleet resailed towards Port Arthur. The second, the fourth, and the fifth destroyer flotillas and the ninth torpedo flotilla joined at 3 a.m., and the third fleet at 7 a.m. No enemy's ship was seen outside the port.

Our first fleet arrived there at 9 a.m., and, discovering three mines laid by the enemy, destroyed them all.

The Kasuga and the Nisshin were despatched to the west of Liau-tie-shan. They made an indirect bombardment for two hours, this being their first action. The new forts at Liau-tie-shan were finally silenced.

Our forces retired at 1.30 p.m.

Togo.

The Russian ship destroyed was Admiral Makaroff's flagship, the Petropavlovsk; the second ship injured was the battleship Pobieda. In the action in which she engaged the third squadron, the Bayan also was damaged, and the effective Russian fleet for the moment reduced to the Peresviet, Sevastopol, Askold, Diana, Novik, and some five destroyers.

Another attempt to block the harbour followed, no less than ten ships being employed. In Japan this attempt was accepted as completely successful; but there are few grounds for believing that it was more than temporarily so.

Too little is yet known of the real facts of the war for many conclusions of value to be drawn; indeed, only one thing is as yet fully clear, and that is the importance of battleships. Russia's failure lay here. Lacking a battleship superiority, she was unable to support her cruisers, and these consequently unable to support the destroyers. As a result, despite the extraordinary activity of the Russian cruiser Bayan, the naval war followed the exact course that any one cognizant of naval affairs could have predicted on February 10, 1904. Only the battleship can confer command of the sea.

Later events to the end of May included the loss of the battleship Hatsuse, by contact with a Russian mine, and the sinking of the cruiser Yoshino, after collision with the Kasuga in a fog.

APPENDICES

THE SINKING OF THE KOW-SHING

Official Report of Captain Togo of the Naniwa

"AT 9.15 a.m., coming close to the Kow-shing, I signalled J. W. (to stop immediately) and twice fired blank shot. The next signal was L. P. (to anchor), which she obeyed. I was at that time very anxious to catch the flying Chinese warship, and I turned a little while in that direction. At that time the Kow-shing signalled D. N. W. R. (may I proceed), which I answered by the signal J. W.

"At 10.40, I sent Lieutenant Hitomi and others as prize officers to her. On seeing all the papers and other things, they found that she was carrying contraband persons. So I ordered her to follow me, which her captain consented to do. When I hoisted the signal L. R. (slip or weigh anchor immediately), she asked me by signal to send a boat for communication. I thought that the captain wished to tell me that he was prevented by the Chinese soldiers from obeying my order. So I ordered Lieutenant Hitomi to go again to her, giving him instructions to bring the Europeans on board the Naniwa, if the Chinese generals were resisting the carrying out of my order. When the lieutenant came alongside, the captain came to the gangway and said that the Chinese generals asked to be allowed to return to Taku, as they did not know that war had broken out. The lieutenant informed me that, when he went there, the Chinese soldiers were in a condition of the greatest confusion and excitement, so that the captain intentionally came down to the gangway and would not let him go on deck. Four hours had been consumed in these fruitless negotiations, and there was no longer room for hesitation, so I signalled M. L. (quit the ship immediately). To this the captain again answered by the signal demanding a boat. At that time I thought it would be rather foolish to send our officers, as the Chinese were in such an excited state. Accordingly I signalled H. J. (boat cannot come). It seemed to me that she was awaiting the arrival of the Chinese fleet; moreover, it was very dangerous to hesitate any longer, so I again hoisted the signal M. L., and at the same time a red flag on the foremast. At 1.10 p.m. I ordered one torpedo and shells to be discharged. The latter hit the engine-room.

"At 1.15 the Kow-shing began to sink from her stern.

"At 1.37 I sent two cutters to rescue the captain, the officers and the rest.

"At 1.46 she sank.

"The spot where she sank is two miles south of the island of Sho-pai-oul."

Captain Galsworthy's Report.

The British steamer Kow-shing, owned by the Indo-China Co., left Shang-hai on July 17th, bound to Taku, under charter to carry Chinese troops from that port to Asan, on the coast of Korea. Arriving at Taku on the 20th, arrangements were made to ship the troops, and on the 23rd 1100 came on board, including two generals, a number of other officers of various ranks, and a German ex-army officer named Hanneken, who came as an ordinary passenger. At 9.50 p.m. on the 23rd the ship proceeded on her voyage to Asan. All went well until the morning of the 25th, when off Shopeiul Island, we passed a man-of-war flying the Japanese naval ensign, with a white flag above it. This vessel proved to be the Chinese warship Tei-yuen. Shortly afterwards we sighted three Japanese men-of-war, the Naniwa, Yoshino, and another (probably the Akitsushiu). The Naniwa at once steamed towards us, flying a signal ordering us to stop. She also fired two blank charges, and signalled us to anchor, which we did at once. The Naniwa then steamed away, apparently to communicate with the other ships. I at once enquired by signal if I might proceed, to which the Naniwa replied, "Heave-to or take the consequences." A boat then came from the Naniwa and an officer came on board. He was received at the gangway, and he asked to see the ship's papers. They were shown him, and his attention particularly called to the fact that she was a British ship. Numerous other questions were asked and answered, the most important one being, "Would the Kow-shing follow the Naniwa?" Being utterly helpless against a man-of-war, I replied that there would be no alternative but to do so, under protest, if ordered. The officer then left the ship, and proceeded to the Naniwa. Shortly after, being still at anchor, I was ordered by signal to cut, slip, or weigh immediately. The Chinese generals learning the meaning of the signals, and finding preparations were being made to follow the Naniwa, objected most emphatically. They were told how useless it would be to resist, as one shot would sink them in a short time. The generals then said they would rather die than obey Japanese orders, and, as they had 1100 men against about 400 on the Naniwa, they would fight sooner than surrender. They were told that if they decided to fight, the foreign officers would leave the ship. The generals then gave orders to the troops on deck to kill us if we obeyed the orders of the Japanese or attempted to leave the ship. With gestures they threatened to cut off our heads, to stab or shoot us; and a lot of men were selected to watch us and carry out the order. A signal was then made requesting the Naniwa to send a boat, in order to communicate the state of affairs. A boat was at once sent, but a crowd of armed Chinese took possession of the gangway, until I prevailed on the generals to send them away. Eventually the officers came alongside, and a message for the commander of the Naniwa was sent, stating that the Chinese refused to allow the Kow-shing to be taken, and insisting upon returning to

Taku. It was again pointed out that she was a British ship, and that she had left port before war had been declared. The boat then returned to the Naniwa, and on her arrival a signal was hoisted ordering the Europeans to leave the ship at once. A reply was given that they were not allowed to leave the ship, and asking for a boat to be sent. Notice was sent to the engineers to be handy on deck in case the Japanese fired. The Naniwa shortly afterwards replied that a boat could not be sent. The Naniwa then hoisted a red flag at the fore, which was apparently a signal for discharging a torpedo, as one was fired at the Kow-shing, but missed her. A broadside of five guns was then fired. At the time I was on the bridge, my officers having left it, and seeing that the soldiers set to watch me had left their station at the foot of the ladder, I rushed to the wheelhouse, and, after obtaining a lifebelt (the last one remaining), I jumped over the ship's side. In doing so I heard a terrific explosion, and upon returning to the surface of the sea I found the atmosphere was thick with smoke and fine coal-powder. I at once struck out for the shore, distant about $1\frac{1}{4}$ miles. There were many Chinese in the water, but I only saw one European, Mr. von Hanneken. As the air cleared, a bullet struck the water close to my ear, and was followed by a shower of bullets. Knowing that shot from the Naniwa could not strike near me, owing to being sheltered by the hull of the Kow-shing, I turned on my back, and saw the Chinese soldiers firing at me from the deck and the 'tween deck ports. As far as possible I protected the back of my head with the lifebelt, and swam as low in the water as I could. Shortly after the Kow-shing went down, stern first. After being in the water some time, I was picked up by the Naniwa's cutter, in a very exhausted condition. The same boat had already rescued one of the quartermasters, who had been wounded in the neck by a rifle bullet. On arriving at the Naniwa we found that the chief officer was the only other person saved by the Japanese, leaving five Europeans connected with the ship, and the passenger, missing. We anchored off Shopeiul about 9 a.m. The firing commenced about 1 p.m., and we were taken aboard the Naniwa about 2.30 p.m. During the evening the Naniwa steamed away, arriving the next morning at the rendezvous of the Japanese Fleet in Korea. We were then transferred to the Yayeyama, together with a Danish electrician, named Muhlenstedt, and about sixty Chinese, who were taken prisoners from the Chinese steamer Tso-kiang, the same day. The Yayeyama then proceeded to Sasebo, arriving on the morning of the 28th. From Sasebo I and Mr. Tamplin, the chief officer, came here in a small tender at noon on Sunday last, having in the mean time been interviewed by Mr. Suyematsu Kencho, President of the Imperial Board of Legislature, who came down from Tokyo for that purpose. The quartermaster remained behind owing to his wound not having properly healed up, whilst Mr. Muhlenstedt is being further detained. During our detention we received every care and attention necessary for our comfort. After arriving here we proceeded to H.M.'s Consulate, and made an affidavit of the entire circumstances. The Naniwa, I may mention, had been damaged on the port quarter from a shot fired from the Tche-yuen in the morning. I can positively say I did not see the Japanese fire on the Chinese in the water. The Chinese killed many of their own people.

LOSS OF THE KOW-SHING

FINDING and Order of a Naval Court, held at H.B.M. Consulate, Nagasaki, on August 7, 1894.

The s.s. Kow-shing was an iron vessel, schooner rigged, of 1355 tons registered tonnage, official number 87000, built at Barrow-in-Furness, and belonging to the port of London. It appears from evidence given before this court that she sailed from Taku on or about the 23rd day of July, 1894, bound for Gasan, in Korea, with no cargo but 1100 Chinese troops on board, that everything went well until the morning of the 25th July, when about 9 a.m. the Naniwa-kan, a Japanese man-of-war, signalled to her to stop and to anchor, with the island of Sho-pei-oul bearing about N. by E., distant $1\frac{1}{4}$ miles. That after communicating with the Kow-shing twice by boat, and ordering the officers to quit the vessel, which they were prevented doing by the Chinese troops, the Naniwa-kan, about 1 p.m., discharged a torpedo at the Kow-shing, and this not striking her the Naniwa-kan fired a broadside of five heavy guns at her and continued firing both heavy and machine guns from deck and tops until she sank, about an hour later. That when firing commenced a number of the crew and Chinese troops jumped overboard, amongst them the master, Thomas Ryder

Galsworthy, the first mate, Lewis Henry Tamplin, and a quartermaster, Lucas Evangelista (a Manilla man), who are the only members of the crew at present known to be saved. The court, having regard to the circumstances above stated, find as follows:—

1. That the ship was sufficiently seaworthy and found well in all necessary respects.

2. That the conduct of the officers and crew before and up to the time of the sinking of the vessel was satisfactory and free from blame.

3. That the cause of the sinking was due to her having been repeatedly struck by heavy cannon shots from the Naniwa-kan, a Japanese man-of-war.

4. That no efforts on the part of the master or crew would have availed to avert the catastrophe.

5. That the court attaches no blame whatever to the master, Thomas Ryder Galsworthy, or any of the officers or crew.

6. The expenses of the Court are merely approved.

Dated at Nagasaki, the 7th day of August, 1894.

JOHN J. QUIN,
H.B.M. Consul, president.

THE ARMISTICE

HIS Majesty the Emperor of Japan having in view of the untoward event which temporarily interrupted the depending negotiations for peace commanded his plenipotentiaries to consent to a temporary armistice,

The undersigned Count Ito Hirobumi, Junii, grand cross of the imperial order of Paullownia, minister president of state, and Viscount Mutsu Munemitsu, Junii, first class of the imperial order of the Sacred Treasure, minister of state for foreign affairs, the plenipotentiaries of His Majesty the Emperor of Japan; and Li Hung-Chang, plenipotentiary of His Majesty the Emperor of China, senior tutor to the Heir Apparent, senior grand secretary of state, minister superintendent of trade for the northern ports of China, viceroy of the province of Chihli and earl of the first rank, have concluded the following treaty of armistice:—

Art. 1. The Imperial governments of Japan and China agree to enforce an armistice between their respective military and naval forces in the provinces of Fêng-tien, Chihli and Shan-tung subject to the provisions contained in the following articles:—

Art. 2. The forces affected by this armistice shall have the right to maintain the positions respectively occupied by them at the time hostilities are actually suspended, but they shall not under any circumstances during the existence of this armistice advance beyond such positions.

Art. 3. The two governments engage during the existence of this treaty not to extend, perfect or advance their attacking works or to reinforce or in anywise to strengthen either for offensive or defensive operations their confronting military line. But this engagement shall not prevent either government from making any new distribution or arrangement of troops not intended to augment or strengthen the armies now actually in the field and engaged in active military operations.

Art. 4. The movement of troops and the transportation of military supplies and all other contraband of war by sea shall be subject to the ordinary rules of war and shall consequently be liable to hostile capture.

Art. 5. This armistice shall be enforced by the imperial governments of Japan and China for the period of 21 days from the date of the signature of this treaty.

In those localities occupied by the troops of the two governments to which there is no telegraphic communication the quickest possible means shall be employed in issuing the orders for the armistice, and the respective commanders of the two countries shall upon the receipt of such orders announce the fact to each other and take steps to enforce the armistice.

Art. 6. This armistice shall terminate, without notice on either side, at mid-day on the 20th day of the 4th month of the 28th year of Meiji corresponding to the 26th day of the 3rd month of the 21st year of Kwang-Hsu. If in the mean time the depending negotiations for peace are broken off, this armistice shall in that case terminate at the same time such negotiations cease.

In witness whereof the plenipotentiaries of Japan and China have hereunto set their hands and affixed their seals.

Done at Shimonosiki, Japan, this 30th day of the 3rd month of the 28th year of Meiji corresponding to the 5th day of the 3rd month of the 21st year of Kwang-Hsu.

    COUNT ITO HIROBUMI (L. S.),
Junii; grand cross of the imperial order of Paullownia; minister president of state; plenipotentiary of His Majesty the Emperor of Japan.

    VISCOUNT MUTSU MUNEMITSU (L. S.),
Junii; first class of the imperial order of the Sacred Treasure; minister of state for foreign affairs; plenipotentiary of His Majesty the Emperor of Japan.

    LI HUNG-CHANG (L. S.),
plenipotentiary of His Majesty the Emperor of China; senior tutor to the Heir

Apparent; senior grand secretary of state; minister superintendent of trade for the northern ports of China; viceroy of the province of Chihli and earl of the first rank.

THE TREATY OF PEACE

(Official translation.)

HIS Majesty the Emperor of Japan and His Majesty the Emperor of China, desiring to restore the blessings of peace to their countries and subjects and to remove all cause for future complications, have named as their plenipotentiaries for the purpose of concluding a treaty of peace, that is to say:

His Majesty the Emperor of Japan, Count Ito Hirobumi, Junii, grand cross of the imperial order of the Paullownia, minister president of state, and Viscount Mutsu Munemitsu, Junii, first class of the imperial order of the Sacred Treasure, minister of state for foreign affairs;

and His Majesty the Emperor of China, Li Hung-chang, senior tutor to the heir apparent, senior grand secretary of state, minister superintendent of trade for the northern ports of China, viceroy of the province of Chihli and earl of the first rank, and Li Ching-Fong, ex-minister of the diplomatic service, of the second official rank;

who, after having exchanged their full powers, which were found to be in good and proper form, have agreed to the following articles:

Art. 1. China recognises definitively the full and complete independence and autonomy of Korea, and in consequence the payment of tribute and the performance of ceremonies and formalities by Korea to China in derogation of such independence and autonomy shall wholly cease for the future.

Art. 2. China cedes to Japan in perpetuity and sovereignty the following territories together with all fortifications, arsenals and public property therein:

(a) The southern portion of the province of Fêng-Tien within the following boundaries:

The line of demarcation begins at the mouth of the River Yalu and ascends that stream to the mouth of the River Anping; from thence the line runs to Funghwang; from thence to Haiching, from thence to Yingkow, forming a line which describes the southern portion of the territory. The places above named are included in the ceded territory. When the line reaches the River Liao at Yingkow it follows the course of that stream to its mouth, where it terminates. The mid-channel of the River Liao shall be taken as the line of demarcation.

The cession also includes all islands appertaining or belonging to the province of Fêng-Tien situated in the eastern portion of the bay of Liaotung and in the northern part of the Yellow Sea.

(b) The Island of Formosa, together with all islands appertaining or belonging to the said Island of Formosa.

(c) The Pescadores Group, that is to say, all islands lying between the 119th and 120th degrees of longitude east of Greenwich and the 23rd and 24th degrees of north latitude.

Art. 3. The alignments of the frontiers described in the preceding article shall be subject to verification and demarcation on the spot, by a joint commission of delimitation consisting of two or more Japanese and two or more Chinese delegates to be appointed immediately after the exchange of the ratifications of this act. In case the boundaries laid down in this act are found to be defective at any point, either on account of topography or in consideration of good administration, it shall also be the duty of the delimitation commission to rectify the same.

The delimitation commission will enter upon its duties as soon as possible, and will bring its labours to a conclusion within the period of one year after appointment.

The alignments laid down in this act shall, however, be maintained until the rectifications of the delimitation commission, if any are made, shall have received the approval of the governments of Japan and China.

Art. 4. China agrees to pay to Japan as a war indemnity the sum of 200,000,000 Kuping Taels. The said sum to be paid in eight instalments. The first instalment of 50,000,000 taels to be paid within six months, and the second instalment of 50,000,000 taels to be paid within twelve months, after the exchange of the ratifications of this act. The remaining sum to be paid in six equal annual instalments, as follows: The first of such equal annual instalments to be paid within two years; the second within three years; the third within four years; the fourth within five years; the fifth within six years, and the sixth within seven years, after the exchange of the ratification of this act. Interest at the rate of 5 per centum per annum shall begin to run on all unpaid portions of the said indemnity from the date the first instalment falls due.

China shall, however, have the right to pay by anticipation at any time any or all of the said instalments. In case the whole amount of the indemnity is paid within three years after the exchange of the ratification of the present act, all interest shall be waived and the interest for two years and a half or for any less period if then already paid shall be included as a part of the principal amount of the indemnity.

Art. 5. The inhabitants of the territories ceded to Japan, who wish to take up their residence outside the ceded districts, shall be at liberty to sell their real property and retire. For this purpose a period of two years from the date of the exchange of the ratifications of the present act shall be granted. At the expiration of that period those of the inhabitants who shall not have left such territories shall, at the option of Japan, be deemed to be Japanese subjects.

Each of the two governments shall, immediately upon the exchange of the ratifications of the present act, send one or more commissioners to Formosa to effect a final transfer of that province; and within the space of two months after the exchange of the ratifications of this act such transfer shall be completed.

Art. 6. All treaties between Japan and China having come to an end in consequence of the war, China engages, immediately upon the exchange of the ratifications of this act, to appoint plenipotentiaries to conclude, with the Japanese plenipotentiaries, a treaty of commerce and navigation and a convention to regulate frontier intercourse and trade. The treaties, conventions and regulations now subsisting between China and European powers shall serve as a basis for the said treaty and convention between Japan and China. From the date of the exchange of the ratifications of this act until the said treaty and convention are brought into actual operation, the Japanese government; its officials; commerce; navigation; frontier intercourse and trade; industries; ships and subjects, shall, in every respect, be accorded by China the most favoured nation treatment.

China makes in addition the following concession, to take effect six months after the date of the present act:

1st.—The following cities, towns and ports, in addition to those already opened, shall be opened to the trade, residence, industries and manufactures of Japanese subjects, under the same conditions and with the same privileges and facilities as exist at the present in cities, towns, and ports of China:

1.—Shashih in the Province of Hupeh.
2.—Chungking in the Province of Szechüan.
3.—Soochow in the Province of Kianghsu.
4.—Hangchow in the Province of Chekiang.

The Japanese government shall have the right to station consuls at any or all of the above-named places.

2nd.—Steam navigation for vessels under the Japanese flag for the conveyance of passengers and cargo shall be extended to the following places:

    1.—On the Upper Yangtsze River, from Ichang to Chungking.

    2.—On the Woosung River and the Canal, from Shanghai to Soochow and Hangchow.

The rules and regulations which now govern the navigation of the inland waters of China by foreign vessels shall, so far as applicable, be enforced in respect of the above-named routes, until new rules and regulations are conjointly agreed to.

3rd.—Japanese subjects purchasing goods or produce in the interior of China shall have the right temporarily to rent or hire warehouses for the storage of the articles so purchased or transported, without the payment of any taxes or exactions whatever.

4th.—Japanese subjects shall be free to engage in all kinds of manufacturing industries in all the open cities, towns and ports of China, and shall be at liberty to import into China all kinds of machinery, paying only the stipulated import duties thereon.

    All articles manufactured by Japanese subjects in China, shall, in respect of inland transit and internal taxes, duties, charges and exactions of all kinds, and also in respect of warehousing and storing facilities in the interior of China, stand upon the same footing and enjoy the same privileges and exemptions as merchandise imported by Japanese subjects into China.

In the event of additional rules and regulations being necessary in connection with these concessions, they shall be embodied in the treaty of commerce and navigation provided for by this article.

Art. 7. Subject to the provisions of the next succeeding article, the evacuation of China by the armies of Japan shall be completely effected within three months after the exchange of the ratifications of the present act.

Art. 8. As a guarantee of the faithful performance of the stipulations of this act, China consents to the temporary occupation of the military forces of Japan of Wei-hai-wei in the Province of Shan-tung.

Upon the payment of the first two instalments of the war indemnity, herein stipulated, this place shall be evacuated by the Japanese forces, provided the Chinese government consents to pledge, under suitable and sufficient arrangements, the customs revenue of China as security for the payment of the principal and interest of the remaining instalments of the said indemnity. In the event no such arrangements are concluded, such evacuation shall only take place upon the payment of the final instalment of the said indemnity.

It is, however, expressly understood that no such evacuation shall take place until after the exchange of the ratifications of the treaty of commerce and navigation.

Art. 9. Immediately upon the exchange of the

ratifications of this act all prisoners of war then held shall be restored, and China undertakes not to ill-treat or punish prisoners of war so restored to her by Japan. China also engages to at once release all Japanese subjects accused of being military spies or charged with any other military offences. China further engages not to punish in any manner, nor to allow to be punished, those Chinese subjects who have in any manner been compromised in their relations with the Japanese army during the war.

Art. 10. All offensive military operations shall cease upon the exchange of the ratifications of this act.

Art. 11. The present act shall be ratified by Their Majesties the Emperor of Japan and the Emperor of China, and ratifications shall be exchanged at Chefoo, on the 8th day of the 5th month of the 28th year of Meiji, corresponding to 14th day of the 4th month of the 21st year of Kuang-Hsü (May 8th, 1895).

In witness whereof, the respective plenipotentiaries have signed the same and have affixed thereto the seal of their arms.

Done at Shimonoseki, in duplicate, this 17th day of the 4th month of the 28th year of Meiji, corresponding to the 23rd day of the 3rd month of 21st year of Kuang-Hsü.

COUNT ITO HIROBUMI [L.L.],
Junii; grand cross of the imperial order of the Paullownia; minister president of state; plenipotentiary of His Majesty the Emperor of Japan.

VISCOUNT MUTSU MUNEMITSU [L.L.],
Junii; first class of the imperial order of the Sacred Treasure; minister of state for foreign affairs; plenipotentiary of His Majesty the Emperor of Japan.

LI HUNG-CHANG [L.L.],
plenipotentiary of His Majesty the Emperor of China, senior tutor to the heir apparent; senior grand secretary of state; minister superintendent of trade for the northern ports of China; viceroy of the province of Chihli and earl of the first rank.

LI CHING-FONG,
plenipotentiary of His Majesty the Emperor of China, ex-minister of the diplomatic service of the second official rank.

CORRESPONDENCE IN CONNECTION WITH THE WEI-HAI-WEI SURRENDER.

"HONOURED SIR,
"An unfortunate turn of events has made us enemies: but as the warfare of to-day does not imply animosity between each and all individuals, we hope our former friendship is still warm enough to assure Your Excellency that these lines, which we address to you with your kind permission, are dictated by a motive higher than that of a mere challenge to surrender. This motive is that of submitting to the calm consideration of a friend a reason for an action which seems to be truly conducive to the good of his country and of himself, although stress of circumstances might temporarily conceal this from him. To whatever cause the successive failures of Chinese arms on both sea and land may be attributed, we think Your Excellency's sound judgement will not fail in assigning them to their true cause, which must be apparent to any unprejudiced observer. In China the literary class is still the governing section, and literary accomplishment is the chief if not the sole way to rank and power now as it was a thousand years ago. We do not venture to deny that this system is excellent in itself, and might well be permanent and sufficient if China

were to stand alone in the world. But national isolation is no longer a possibility. Your Excellency must know what a hard experience the Japanese empire had thirty years ago, and how narrowly she escaped the awful calamity which threatened. To throw away the old principle and to adopt the new, as the sole condition of preserving the integrity of your empire, is as necessary with your government now as it was with ours. The necessity must be attended to, or fall is inevitable sooner or later. That the crisis is being brought about by the Japanese arms is mere chance. It might have been caused by other political difficulties, which are equally destructive. Now at such a juncture is it the part of a truly patriotic man, upon whom the necessity of action devolves, to allow himself to be simply dragged along by force of circumstances? Compared with the re-establishment on a sound working basis of the oldest empire in the world, with its glorious history and its extensive territories, what is the surrender of a fleet or the loss of a whole army? If Your Excellency be truly patriotic and loyal to the cause of your country, we beg you to listen to the words of sympathetic hearts filled with the sense of honour representative of the fighting men of Japan; words which ask you to come and stay in Japan until the time arrives when your services shall be required for the good cause. Not to speak of the numerous instances of final success after temporary humiliation in your own history of the ancient dynasties, let me call your attention to the case of the French Marshal Macmahon, who allowed himself to be detained in the enemy's land till it was expedient that he should return and aid in reforming the government, which instead of dishonouring him raised him to the presidency : or to the case of Osman Pasha whom the unfortunate event of Plevna did not prevent from subsequently filling the post of minister of war and rendering important services in reforming the army. As to the way in which Your Excellency may be received in Japan, let us assure you of the magnanimity of our sovereign. His Majesty not only pardoned his own subjects who fought against the imperial side, but even raised them to important positions according to their personal merits, as in the case of Admiral Enomoto, Privy Councillor Otori, and others. Surely he would be more magnanimous to one who is not his own subject, and whose glorious career is so well known to the world. The great problem with Your Excellency now is whether to submit to the great calamity which must be the inevitable consequence of further adherence to the old principle, or to survive it for the sake of future reform. We know it is the custom of your officials to meet any communication from an opponent with a pride designed to show consciousness of strength or to conceal weakness, but we hope Your Excellency will understand that the present communication is not made without due consideration of the vast interests at stake, but that it is the outcome of the truest sincerity and of feelings which should lead to the realisation of those interests, and we hope you will kindly consider it in that light.

"Should the present communication meet with your approval, the carrying out of its import will, with Your Excellency's permission, be arranged through further communications, and we have the honour to be, etc., etc.

"Signed: COUNT ŌYAMA,
"Signed: ADMIRAL ITO.

"*20th January*, 1895."

THE PROPOSAL TO SURRENDER

"I, TING, commander-in-chief of the Pei-yang squadron, acknowledge having previously received a letter from Vice-Admiral Ito, commander of the port of Sasebo. This letter I have not answered until to-day, owing to the hostilities going on between our fleets. It had been my intention to continue fighting until every one of my men-of-war was sunk and the last sailor killed; but I have reconsidered the matter and now request a truce, hoping thereby to save many lives. I earnestly beseech you to refrain from doing further hurt to the Chinese and Westerners serving in the army and navy of China, as well as to the townspeople of Wei-hai-wei; in return for which I offer to surrender to the empire of Japan all my men-of-war, the forts on Liu-kung-tau and all material of war in and about Wei-hai-wei. If Vice-Admiral Ito will accede to these terms, I desire to have the commander-in-chief of the British warships in the offing as a guarantor of the contract. Requesting an answer to this by to-morrow, I have the honour to remain, etc.

"*Signed:* ADMIRAL TING.

"18th day, 1st month, 21st year of Kwangsbu (12th Feb. 1895)."

"I have the honour to acknowledge the receipt of

your esteemed favour, and to accept the proposal therein contained. Accordingly I shall take over all the men-of-war, the forts and all warlike material from your hands. As to the time when the surrender is to take place, I will consult you again on receiving your reply to this. My idea is, after taking over everything, to escort you and the others referred to in your letter on board one of our warships to some safe place where your convenience may be suited. If I may be permitted to speak quite frankly, I advise you for your own and your country's sake to remain in Japan until the war is over. Should you decide to come to my country you may rest assured that you will be treated with distinguished consideration. But if you desire to return to your native land I shall of course put no obstacle in your path. As for any British guarantee, I think it quite unnecessary, and trust in your honour as an officer and a gallant man. Requesting your reply to this by 10 a.m. to-morrow, I have the honour to remain, etc.

"*Signed*: ADMIRAL ITO.

"*12th February*, 1895."

"I am delighted to learn that you are in the enjoyment of good health. I thank you heartily for your kind reply, and the assurance that the lives of those under me will be spared. You have kindly forwarded me certain gifts, but while I thank you I cannot accept them, our two nations being at war. You write that you desire me to surrender everything into your hands to-morrow. This gives too short a period in which to make the necessary preparations, and I fear that the troops will not be able to evacuate the place by the time specified. I therefore pray you to wait until the 22nd day of the 1st month (Chinese calendar), February 16th. You need not fear that I shall go back from my word.

"*Signed*: ADMIRAL TING.

"18*th day, 1st month* (12*th February*)."

"HIS IMPERIAL MAJESTY'S SHIP MATSUSHIMA,
"*February* 13*th*, 1895.

"To the officers representing the Chinese fleet at Wei-hai-wei.

"I hereby acknowledge the receipt of the letter of Admiral Ting dated the 18th of January of the Chinese year. The report of the death of Admiral Ting last night, communicated verbally by the messenger who brought over the said letter, I received with great personal regret.

"As to postponing taking over the vessels, forts and other materials of war until the 22nd of January of the Chinese year, I am ready to comply with it under a certain condition. This condition is that some responsible Chinese officer should come over to this our flagship Matsushima before 6 o'clock p.m. this day, the 13th of February according to the Japanese year, and we will then make certain arrangements, which have to be definitely fixed, regarding the taking over of the said vessels, forts and other materials of war, as well as the escorting of the Chinese and foreign officers and men out of Wei-hai-wei. In my last letter to the lamented Admiral Ting I stated that as to the hour and other minor conditions I should be glad to make arrangements with him on the morrow; so as he is now dead, these minor conditions have to be arranged with some one who can deal with us in his stead.

"It is my express wish that the said officer who is to come to this our flagship for the above purpose be a Chinese, not a foreign officer, and be it understood that I am willing to receive him with honour.

"J. K. ITO,
  "*Vice-Admiral,*
    "*Commander-in-Chief.*"

THE CONVENTION OF SURRENDER

TOWARDS 7 p.m. of 13th February Tao-tai Niu Chang-Ping, accompanied by Captain Ching, came under a white flag to the Matsushima. He introduced himself as the representative of the naval and military forces at Wei-hai-wei. Admiral Ito then proposed to him several conditions relating to the vessels, forts and materials of war, the escorting of the Chinese and foreign officers and men out of Wei-hai-wei, and so forth. After a consultation of several hours Tao-tai Niu and Captain Ching left the ship, arranging to come back before 2 p.m. on the 14th.

At 2 p.m. on the 14th, Tao-tai Niu, the Chinese plenipotentiary, came again under a white flag, accompanied by Captain Ching, and after further consultation the following terms were agreed upon between the two parties as conditions of capitulation, and the English version of them, which was to serve as the original text, was signed by Admiral Ito and Tao-tai Niu.

Art. I. That a list of the names, functions, and ranks of all the naval and military officers, both Chinese and foreign, required to be transported in safety, should be produced. For foreigners, their nationalities should also be mentioned. As to soldiers, clerks, etc., only their numbers are to be given.

Art. II. That all the naval and military officers, both Chinese and foreign, should pledge themselves by a formal declaration in writing that they will not re-engage themselves in the present war between Japan and China.

Art. III. That all the weapons, powder, and projectiles for use of land forces on the Island of Liu-kung-tau should be collected in fixed places, and these places made known to us. The soldiers of the said land forces shall be landed at Chiu-tau, and from thence they are to be conducted by Japanese guards to the outposts of the Japanese army now occupying the localities around Wei-hai-wei. The landing is to begin from 5 o'clock p.m. on the 14th of February, 1895 (20th January, Chinese calendar), and end before noon on the 15th February, 1895 (21st January of the Chinese calendar).

Art. IV. That Tao-tai Niu, representing the Chinese naval and military forces at Wei-hai-wei as plenipotentiary, should appoint a suitable number of committees, for the delivery of the vessels and forts. These committees are required to send in before noon, February 15th, 1895, a list of the vessels and forts in their charge with the number and kinds of the guns, rifles, and other weapons now contained in these vessels or forts.

Art. V. That the Chinese naval and military officers and men, native and foreign, should be allowed to leave Wei-hai-wei after noon on the 16th of February, 1895 (22nd of January of the Chinese calendar), in the steamship Kwang-Chi, sailing out of the harbour under the condition stipulated in Art. X.

Art. VI. That the Chinese naval and military officers, both native and foreign, should be allowed to take with them their personal movable property only, with the exception of arms, which are to be delivered up even if they be private property. Whenever deemed necessary the things they take away shall be submitted to inspection.

Art. VII. That the permanent residents, *i.e.* the original inhabitants of the Island of Liu-kung-tau, should be persuaded to continue their abode on the island.

Art. VIII. That the landing of the requisite number of the Japanese officers and men, on the Island of Liu-kung-tau, in order to take possession of the forts and materials of war on the island, should commence from 9 o'clock a.m. on the 16th of February, 1895 (22nd of January by Chinese calendar), but that Admiral Ito reserves to himself the right of sending a certain number of the Japanese men-of-war into the harbour, whenever the necessity occurs at any time after the signing of the present stipulations.

The naval officers, both native and foreign, on board the Chinese vessels may remain therein until 9 o'clock a.m. on the 16th February, 1895 (22nd January of Chinese calendar). Those marines, seamen, etc., on board the same vessels who wish to be escorted out of Wei-hai-wei by land should be landed in the same place and escorted in the same way as the soldiers of the land forces, the landing to begin from noon on the 15th of February (21st January of Chinese calendar), that is to say after the landing of the soldiers of the land forces is finished.

Art. IX. That women, children, aged persons and other non-combatants who wish to leave the Island of Liu-kung-tau should be allowed to sail out of either the eastern or western mouth of the harbour in Chinese junks any time after the morning of the 15th of February, 1895 (21st January of the Chinese calendar). These vessels are, however, to be examined by the Japanese naval officers and men in the torpedo boats or the other boats posted at the mouth of the harbour, the examination extending to both persons and baggage.

Art. X. That the coffins of the lamented Admiral Ting and the officers next to him should be allowed to be carried out of the harbour after noon on the 16th of February, 1895 (22nd of January of the Chinese calendar), and before noon on the 23rd of February, 1895 (29th January of the Chinese calendar), in the steamer Kwang-chi, which Admiral Ito refrains from taking possession of and lays at the disposal of Tao-tai Niu as representing the Chinese navy and army at Wei-hai-wei, solely out of respect to the memory of Admiral Ting, who did his duty towards his country.

The said steamer Kwang-chi is to be inspected by the Japanese naval officers on the morning of the 15th February, 1895 (21st January of Chinese calendar), to see that she is not equipped as a war vessel.

Art. XI. That it be always understood that after the present stipulations have been made the Chinese naval and military forces at Wei-hai-wei are to give up all hostile operations against the Japanese naval and military forces, and that the moment such operations are made the present stipulations shall lose effect at once and the Japanese naval and military forces shall resume hostilities.

Signed: ADMIRAL ITO.
Signed: NIU CHANG-PING.

16th February, 28th year of Meiji.
22nd of 1st month, 21st year of Kwangshu.

JAPANESE FLEET IN FEBRUARY, 1904.

(Ships in italics were not ready for sea when the war began.)

BATTLESHIPS.

Approximate unit of battle value.	Rate.	Name.	Launched.	Displacement.	Armour belt.	Principal armament.	Torpedo tubes.	Indicated horse-power.	Nominal speed.
				Tons.	Ins.				Knots.
80	2	Yashima	1896	12,517	18	Four 12-in., ten 6-in., sixteen 12-pdrs.	5	13,687	18
80	2	Fuji	1896	12,649	18	Ditto	5	13,687	18
100	1	Shikishima	1898	15,088	9	Four 12-in., fourteen 6-in., twenty 12-pdrs.	5	14,700	18
100	1	Asahi	1899	15,443	9	Ditto	4	15,207	18
100	1	Mikasa	1900	15,362	9	Ditto	4	15,207	18
100	1	Hatsuse	1899	15,240	9	Ditto	4	14,700	18
125	A1	*Kashima*	Building	16,400	9	Four 12-in., four 10-in., fourteen 6-in., twenty 12-pdrs.	4	(?)	(?)
125	A1	*Katori*	,,	16,400	9		4	(?)	(?)
35	4	Chin-Yen	1882	7,335	14	Four 12-in., four 6-in.	3	6,000	15

394

LIST OF JAPANESE WARSHIPS

Armoured Cruisers.

		Name	Date	Tons	Armour	Armament		Tons	Speed
⎰		Tokiwa	1898	9,855	7	Four 8-in., fourteen 6-in., twelve 12-pdrs.	5	18,248	22
		Asama	1898	9,855	7	Ditto	5	18,248	22
60		Idzumo	1899	9,906	7	Ditto	4	14,700	21
	3	Iwate	—	9,906	7	Ditto	4	14,700	21
		Yakumo	1899	9,800	7	Four 8-in., twelve 6-in., twelve 3-in.	5	15,500	20
		Azuma	1899	9,456	7	Ditto	5	16,600	20
⎱		Nisshin	1903	8,000	6	Four 8-in., fourteen 6-in., ten 12-pdrs.	4	13,500	20
		Kasuga	1903	8,000	6	One 10-in., two 8-in., fourteen 6-in., ten 12-pdrs.	4	13,500	20

Protected Cruisers.

		Name	Date	Tons	Armour	Armament		Tons	Speed
15	6	Akitsushima	1892	3,172	—	Four 6-in., six 4·7-in.	4	8,516	19
20	6	Hashidate	1891	4,278	—	One 12·5-in., eleven 4·7-in.	4	5,400	16
20	6	Itsukushima	1889	4,278	—	Ditto	4	5,400	16
20	6	Matsushima	1890	4,278	—	One 12·5-in., twelve 4·7-in.	4	5,400	16
10	7	Naniwa	1885	3,709	—	Two 10·2-in., six 6-in.	4	7,604	18
10	7	Takachiho	1885	3,709	—	Ditto	4	7,604	18
20	6	Yoshino	1892	4,225	—	Four 6-in., eight 4·7-in.	5	15,967	23
20	6	Chitose	1898	4,836	—	Two 8-in., ten 4·7-in., twelve 3-in.	5	15,714	23
20	6	Kasagi	1898	4,978	—	Ditto	5	17,235	23
20	6	Takasago	1897	4,227	—	Ditto	5	15,967	23
10	7	Idzumi	1883	2,967	—	Two 10-in., six 4·7-in.	—	5,576	17
15	6	Suma	1895	2,700	—	Two 6-in., six 4·7-in.	2	8,500	20
15	6	Akashi	1897	2,800	—	Ditto	2	8,000	20
10	7	Chiyoda	1890	2,439	4½	Ten 4·7-in., fourteen 3-pdrs.	3	5,678	19
10	7	Niitaka	1902	3,400	—	Six 6-in., eight 3-in.	0	9,000	20
10	7	Tsushima	1902	3,400	—	Ditto	0	9,000	20
10	7	*Otawa*	Building	3,400	—	Ditto	0	9,000	20

JAPANESE FLEET (*continued*).

DESTROYERS.[1]

Thornycroft Type.

Name.	Displacement.	Indicated horse-power.	Speed.	Built.
	Tons.		Knots.	
Kagero				
Murakumo				
Ousagoumo	275	5400	30	1898–99
Shinonome				
Shiranōi				
Yuguri				
Asashio				
Shirakuma	385	6000	31	1901
Asagiri (J[2])				
Harusame (J)				

Yarrow Type.

Name.	Displacement.	Indicated horse-power.	Speed.	Built.
Akebono				
Ikadsuchi				
Inanzuma	306	6000	31	1898–99
Oboro				
Sazanami				
Niji[3] (rebuilt) (J)				1903
Akatsuki				
Kasumi	385	6000	31	1901
Hayatori (J)				
Murasame (J)				

TORPEDO BOATS.

First Class.[4]

Name.	Displacement.	Indicated horse-power.	Speed.	Built.
1 Yarrow boat (Kotaka)	190	1400	19	1886
5 „ boats	135	2000	27	1898
1 Krupp boat	128	1015	19	1895
4 Normand boats	150	—	29	1899
1 Schichau boat	130	—	(?)	1900
10 Kobé and Normand boats	110	—	27	1900
15 Kobé and Yarrow boats	150	—	29	1900

Second Class.

Name.	Displacement.	Indicated horse-power.	Speed.	Built.
3 Schichau boats	85	—	23	1891
2 Normand „	80	—	23	1891
20 various boats	56	—	20	—
10 new boats	—	—	23	1901

[1] All have two tubes (18-in.), one 12-pdr. aft, and five 3-pdrs.
[2] J = built in Japan.   [3] The original Niji was wrecked in 1901.
[4] Except the Kotaka and the Krupp boat, which have six tubes (14-in.), all carry three tubes (14-in.).

LIST OF JAPANESE WARSHIPS

JAPANESE FLEET (continued).

Miscellaneous Ships.

Name.	Launched.	Displacement.	Armour belt.	Armament.	Indicated horse-power.	Speed.
		Tons.	Ins.			Knots.
Chihaya	1901	850	—	Two 4·7-in., four 12-pdrs.	6000	21
Tatsuta	1894	875	—	Two 4·7-in.	5500	21
Miyako	1897	1800	—	Ditto	6130	20
Yaeyama	1889	1600	—	Three 4·7-in.	5500	20
Takao	1888	1800	—	Four 6-in., one 4·7-in., one 12-pdr.	2400	15
Akagi	1887	614	—	Four 4·7-in.	700	12
Oshima	1890	640	—	Ditto	1200	16
Atago	1887	640	—	One 8·2-in., one 4·7-in.	700	12
Maya	1887	640	—	Ditto	700	12
Chiokai	1888	640	—	Two 6-in.	700	12
Tsushima	1881	1380	—	Two 10-in., four 4·7-in.	2880	16·4
Musashi	1885	1480	—	Two 6-in., four 4·7-in.	1600	13·5
Yamato	1886	1480	—	Ditto	1600	13·5
Amagi	—	1030	—	Old guns	—	—
Kaimon	—	1360	—	Old guns	—	—
Tenriu	—	1550	—	Old guns	—	—
Fuso	1877	3717	9	Eight 6-in.	3500	13
Hei Yen	1890	2000	8	One 10-in., two 6-in.	2400	11
Six ex-Chinese gunboats	—	—	—	—	—	—

JAPANESE SHIP-NAMES

THE names of a few Japanese ships are singularly beautiful and poetical in their meanings; the majority, however, have little significance. As the meanings of Japanese ship-names are not given in Captain Prince Louis of Battenberg's interesting "Men-of-War Names," a glossary of them is here inserted for reference and information.

All names with the prefix *Chin* (Chinese *Chen*) are Chinese. The names of captured Chinese ships have always been retained by the Japanese, but they have been translated into their own language, *i.e.* as though, when in the past we took the *Téméraire*, we had taken to calling her *The Rash*.

I am indebted to my friends Commander Takarabé and Lieutenant Yamamoto, both of the Imperial Japanese Navy, for the meanings of these ship-names.

Adsuma = a mountain with a poetical history.
Asama = a sacred volcanic island in Japan. The present is the second ship of the name. The first was a pirate frigate that put into a Japanese port to refit and was seized.
Akagi = a mountain in Japan.
Akashi = a beautiful seaside place near Kobé.
Akebono = dawn.
Akitsushima = an old name for Japan (poetical).
Asahi = "the (rising) morning sun."
Amagi = name of a mountain in Japan.

JAPANESE SHIP-NAMES

Atago = name of a mountain in Japan.

Chitose = "long life."

Chiyoda = the name of Shogun's castle and Emperor's palace. The present Chiyoda is the second of the name. (See p. 402.)

Chin Yen = "striking from a long way off." The name is Chinese. This ship was formerly the Chinese Chen Yuen.

Chin Nan = striking south.

Chin To = striking east.

Chin Sei = striking west.

Chin Hoku = striking north.

Chin Chaiu = striking midway.

Chin Pen = striking everywhere near.

Fuso = "Japan."

Fuji = name of the celebrated Japanese mountain, Fuji-Yama. This is the second ship of the name.

Hashidáte = name of a Japanese port.

Hatsuse = a place in Japan celebrated for its maple woods.

Hi-yei = a famous battle mountain in Japan.

Hei-Yen = "pacifying a long way off." This is a captured Chinese ship, Ping Yuen.

Ho-Sho = name of a shore bird.

Inadzuma = "lightning."

Idzumi = a country of Japan.

Ikadzuche = "thunder."

Itsukushima = a Japanese island.

Idzumo = a province of Japan.

Iwate = name of a place in Japan.

Kaimon = "sea gate."

Kasagi = a mountain in Japan.

Katsuragi = a mountain in Japan.

Kagero = "the shimmering mist that rises from the earth on a hot day."

Kotaka = "a hawk."

Kasanga = a mountain in Japan.

Kon-go = a famous battle mountain in Japan.

Mikasa = a mountain.

Maya = a Japanese mountain.

Matsushima = a Japanese island.

Musashi = the province in which Toku is situated.

Miyako = a place in Japan.
Murákumo = "a cloud cluster."
Niji = "rainbow."
Naniwa = a palace of the Emperor's.
Nisshin = "daily progressing."
Oshima = "a large island."
Ousougumo = "thin clouds."
Obero = "Dim."
Rio-jo = "powerful as a dragon." This is a Chinese word.
Shinonome = "daybreak cloud."
Sai Yen = "helping from a long way off."
Sazanami = "the pretty, small waves raised by a zephyr."
Shikishima = an old poetical name for Japan.
Saikio-maru = the merchant steamer Saikio.
Shiranoi = "will-o'-the-wisp."
Suma = a place in Japan close to Akashi.
So-Ko = Chinese.
Takao = a Japanese town.
Tateyama = name of a Japanese mountain.
Takachiho = name of a sacred place in Japan.
Takasago = "Darby and Joan." It is the name of a town associated in poetry with a couple of that nature.
Tátsuta = name of a Japanese mountain.
Tenriu = a river in Japan.
Tsukuba = a mountain in Japan.
Tokiwa = "evergreen."
Tsukushi = a Japanese town.
Yashima = "Japan."
Yaxyama = an island mountain.
Yamato = a Japanese province. Also an old name for Japan (poetical).
Yoshino = a mountain in Japan famous for its beautiful cherry-blossom; hence "cherry-blossom."

SHIPS THAT HAVE BEEN LOST BY SHIPWRECK

TAIEBO No. 1 (small gunboat). Wrecked about 1870.
Unebi (cruiser). Mysteriously lost, with all hands, at sea about 1890. Believed in Japan to have been destroyed by the Chinese.
Tschishima (torpedo cruiser). Foundered on her trial trip in the Inland Sea, 1891. Most of her crew were drowned.
Kohei, ex-Kwang Ping (gunboat). Formerly Chinese. Wrecked off the Pescadores, 1895.
Fuso (ironclad). This ship broke from her cable, and drifted across the ram of the Matsushima during a gale in 1897. She sank, but was subsequently raised and repaired.
Katsuragi (wooden corvette). Wrecked in the later nineties.

WAR LOSSES

Miyako (gunboat). Blown up at Dalny, 1904.
Yoshino (cruiser). Sunk by collision with Kasuga, 1904.
Hatsuse (battleship). Blown up off Port Arthur, 1904.

HISTORICAL SHIP-NAMES

Asama. No. 1, a pirate ship (sailing) captured by the Japanese (p. 195). No. 2, the present armoured cruiser of 9700 tons, launched 1898.

Chiyoda. No. 1, launched in the sixties; a small vessel; now known as Chiyoda-nata. No. 2, launched 1890, of 2450 tons; to replace the Unebi.

Fuji. No. 1, a sailing-ship; always known as Fuji-Yama. No. 2, the present 12,300-ton battleship, launched 1896; always called Fuji only.

Kasuga. No. 1, a paddler of 1270 tons, formerly known as the Kiang Tse; launched in England, 1863; depôt ship at Tsushima. No. 2, purchased from Argentina just before the war with Russia; 8000 tons.

Nisshin. No. 1, a wooden ship, launched in 1869, and now used as a training-ship for boys at Sassebo. No. 2, purchased from Argentina just before the war with Russia; 8000 tons.

A JAPANESE NAVAL "AT HOME"

"CAPTAIN KAWASHIBARA and officers of H.I.J.M.S. Kasagi at home, Monday, March 15th."

The Kasagi herself is an American-built ship.

The peculiarity of this ship lies in the tremendous amount of electricity there is on board her. The ammunition hoists are electric, the lights and bells, of course, are, the engine-room indicators are, and, finally, electric fans are all over the ship. So, too, are telephones.

On the afternoon in question the fair ones of Portsmouth were initiated into all these mysteries, and probably regarded the electric fans as some new and horrible war device. I heard a remark to that effect, anyhow!

Not all the visitors, however, were so inclined to regard everything as a war machine. On Sunday a good many visitors of both sexes found their way to the Kasagi, and peeped into the ward-room, where the officers were wrestling with naval Kriegspiel.

"Race game," said one lady; "how babyish these foreigners are!"

"I don't know, my dear," replied her companion,

apologetically. "Perhaps they gamble on it for high stakes."

"Oh," was the response, "of course that makes a difference!"

For the "At Home" the Kasagi was *en fête*, draped in flags, and generally looking her smartest. Even the engine-room was on show, though I only noticed one visitor venture there—a lady in a light fawn-coloured rig-out, not the best thing to penetrate the mysteries of an engine-room in. Perhaps, however, she contented herself with peeping in.

The main feature of the "At Home" was an entertainment given by the bluejackets. There was quite a long variety programme, with fencing between each "turn." As these encounters are accompanied by wild yells every now and again on the part of the combatants, they are particularly interesting.

There was a conjuring entertainment, which mightily amused the crew, but perhaps puzzled the visitors somewhat as to what it was all about. The best thing of all was a song by a Japanese sailor—a monotonous chant that grew gradually louder, accompanied by various movements with a sword, suggesting that something exciting was about to happen. Then came in English, "That's all; you know!" It was well done, and its flat finale very amusing.

There were dances of various sorts, sack races, egg races, and a few other sports with which we are familiar, interesting here because the performers were Japanese, and also because of their intense zest and evident

A JAPANESE NAVAL "AT HOME"

pleasure. Some English songs by Japanese sailors were one of the interesting bits, too.

Finally, on leaving, each lady guest was presented with a paper chrysanthemum. They had previously been asking the Japanese officers how they managed to get them to bloom in the summer season! The imitations and colouring were perfect. The material for construction: odd bits of paper and—Japanese bluejackets.

INDEX

A

Adams, William, 9
Admiralty, the Japanese, 252
Adsuma, the, 22
Ainus, the, 1
Akagi, the, 68, 119
Akaaki, the, 168
Akatsuki, the, 349
Akitsushima, the, 91, 104, 119, 150
Amagi, the, 39
America, treaty with, 15
Armament and equipment—guns, 313
Armistice with China, 368
Armour, 329
Arturo Prat, the, 53
Asagiri, the, 347
Asaki, the, 181
Asama, the, 195, 342
Asan, battle of, 63, 99, 104, 110
Asashio, the, 349
Askold, the, 345, 355
Atago, the, 68
"At Homes," Japanese, 290, 403
Azuma, the, 195

B

Baltimore, the, 92
Banjo, the, 40
Barr and Stroud, transmitters, 191, 322
     "   "   range-finders, 322
Bayan, the, 203, 350
Belleville boilers, 333
Bertin, M., 36, 72, 74
Boilers, 330
Bravery, Japanese, 283

C

Canet guns, 73, 312, 315, 327
Canopus class, 190
Characteristics, personal, 278
Chemulpo Convention, the, 102
     "   battle of, 342
Chen Yuen, the, 115, 163
Chen-chung, the, 48
Chen-sei, the, 48
Chen-nan, the, 48
Chen-poi, the, 48
Chen-pen, the, 48
Cheng-tung, the, 48
Chihaya, the, 213, 351
Chinese gunboats, 48
Chinese invasion, 6
Chinese war, 99, 101, 368, 372
Chin Yuen, the, 49, 115, 163, 168
Chio Kai, the, 68
Chitose, the, 208
Chiyoda-nata, the, 21
Chiyoda, the, 77, 86, 119, 150, 342
Christians, massacre of, 9
Cleanliness, Japanese, 306
College, naval, 258
Creelman, Mrs., 151
Creusot boats, 68
Cruisers, armoured, 195
     "   protected, 208

D

Destroyers, 215
Diana, the, 355
Dockyards, 237
Dutch establish themselves, 10

E

Elswick battleship, 218
" guns, 73
Engines, 330
Esmeralda, the, 57, 168
Export trade, 249

F

Feudal system, 11
Fei-ting, the, 48
Finance, 256
Fire, danger in action by, 147
Flags, Japanese, 275
Fong, Captain, 105
Formidable, the, 182
Formosa, attack on, 167
France, ships built in, 72, 77
Fu-So, the, 43, 119, 150
Fuji, the, 168 346,
Fuji-Yama, the, 21

G

Galsworthy, Captain, 110, 361, 366
Garibaldi class, 203
Grenfell transmission system, 322
Gunboats, torpedo, 213
Gunnery accessories, 322
Guns, 313
    " Canet, 73, 312, 315, 327
    " Vickers-Maxim, 314, 318
    " Elswick, 73
    " Hebrien, 71

H

Hakodate, port of, 249
    " battle of, 35
Harbours, naval, 242
Hashidate, the, 72, 81, 119, 150
Hatsuse, the, 181
Hayatori, the, 347
Hebrien guns, 71
Hei-chang-ching, the, 48
Hi-Yei, the, 44, 119, 150
Hirose, Commander, 351
Holland, treaty with, 15
Hopkins, Admiral, 36
Ho-sho, the, 39
Ho-wei, the, 48

I

Izumi, the, 58, 168
Idzumo, the, 195
Import trade, 250
Ingles, Captain, R.N., 36, 77
Intelligence Department, 255
Ishikawa, the, 40
Ito, Admiral, 116, 119, 159, 163
Itsukushima, the, 72, 77, 119, 150, 156, 163
Iwate, the, 195, 346

J

Japanese-built ship, the first, 171
Jimmu, Emperor, 2
Jingo, Empress, 2
Jin Jei, the, 47

K

Kabayama, Vice-Admiral Count, 119
Kaimon, the, 54
Kamimura, Admiral, 348
Karigane, the, 354
Kasagi, the, 208, 403
Kashima, the, 218
Kasuga, the, 21, 199, 356
Kasumi, the, 349
Katori, the, 218
Katsuragi, the, 58, 156
Kawashibara, Captain, 403
Keitai Tenno, Emperor, 5
Kiangtse, the, 21
King Yuen, the, 86, 115
Kobé harbour, 246
Kobé, port of, 249
Komei, Emperor, 30
Korea, invasion of, 8
Korietz, the, 342
Kotaka, the, 67, 353
Kou-go, the, 44
Kowshing, sinking of, 63, 99, 110, 359, 366
Kuang Kai, 115
Kuang Ping, 115
Kuper, Admiral, 16
Kuré dockyard, 237
Kuroi, Lieut., 110
Kwang-yi, the, 104

L

Lai Yuen, the, 115, 163
Lao Tung Peninsula, invasion of, 149

Lepanto, type, 64, 78
Li Hung Chang, 113
Loh Feng Lo, 113
Lung-Shan, the, 48

M

Maitzuru dockyard, 241
Makaroff, Admiral, 356
Malacca, the, 21
Masuki, Lieut., 353
Matsushima, the, 72, 119, 150, 163
Maya, the, 68
Mercantile marine, 249
Men, training and entry, 265
Messing, 309
Mikasa, the, 181
Misasagi, the, 354
Miyako, the, 99, 213
Moisshin, the, 29
Mukaijima dock, 242
Mushashi, the, 58
Mutsohito, Emperor, 35

N

Nagasaki harbour, 242
     „   port of, 249
Nahamoto, Admiral, 35
Naniwa, the, 58, 104, 110, 119, 150, 156, 163, 342, 361
Naval college, 258
   „ districts, 252
   „ flags, 275
   „ harbours, 242
   „ titles, 263
Navy, first inception, 43
Navies—British, 337
   „ French, 337
   „ German, 338
   „ Russian, 338
   „ United States, America, 338
   „ Japanese, 338
Niagara, the, 25
Niclausse boiler, 335
Niigata, port of, 249
Niitaka, the, 208, 342
Nippon Yusen Kaisha, 251
Nisshin, the, 39, 199, 356
Novik, the, 346, 350, 355
No. 1 Tebo, the, 26

O

Officers, training and entry of, 251
Ominato harbour, 248

Osaka, port of, 249
Oshima, the, 72, 74

P

Pabieda, the, 355
Pallada, the, 346
Pay, 267
Pensions, 272
Peresviet, the, 356
Personal characteristics—officers, 278
        „   „   men, 303
Petropavlovsk, the, 356
Ping Yuen, the, 85, 115, 168
Politeness, Japanese, 294
Poltava, the, 345, 355
Portuguese, first appearance of, 7
Port Arthur, first attack on, 345
   „   „ second attack on, 347
   „   „ massacre at, 151
Programme, "After the War," 178
     „   the new, 218

R

Retirement, age of, 272
Retvizan, the, 346, 351
Riaden, the, 21
Richardson, murder of Mr., 16
Royal Sovereign, the, 174
Rio Jo, the, 36
Russia, treaty with, 15
   „ war with, 340

S

Sacramento, the, 25
Saigo, the Samaurai chief, 101
Saikio-maru, the, 119
Samaurii caste, 5, 294
Sassebo dockyard, 238
Sazanami, the, 350
Seiki, the, 40
Setsu, the, 29
Shikishima, the, 181, 286
Shimada, Lieut., 352
Shimonoseki, bombardment of, 17
Ship-names, 398
   „   historical, 402
Ships lost by shipwreck, 401
Steamship lines, 251
Steregutchy, the, 350
Stonewall Jackson, the, 22
Submarines, 217
Suma, the, 99, 168, 342

INDEX

T

Takachiho, the, 58, 119, 150, 342
Takahashi Sakuye, Professor, 152
Takao, the, 72, 150
Takasago, the, 208, 351
Tategami dock, 242
Takeshiki harbour, 244
Tateyama, the, 40
Tatsuta, the, 77, 99, 168
Tchao Yong, the, 53, 115, 139
Tche-tien, the, 48
Tche Yuen, the, 63, 104, 115, 168
Tenriu, the, 54
Ting, Admiral, 113, 115, 119, 149, 164, 385, 387, 392
Ting Yuen, the, 49, 113, 115, 163
Titles, naval, 263
Togo, Admiral, 104, 111, 156, 345
Tokio dockyard, 236
Tokiwa, the, 195
Torpedo-boats, 85, 216
Torpedo gunboats, 213
Torpedo-tube, Elswick, 326, 331
Torpedoes, 325
Tracy, Admiral, 22, 36
Trade, export, 249
,,   import, 259
Training—officers, 251
,,   men, 265
Tsarevitch, the, 346
Tschishima, the, 77
Tsubame, the, 353
Tsuboi, Rear-Admiral, 104, 119
Tsukuba, the, 21
Tsukushi, the, 53
Tsushima, the, 208

U

Unebi, the, 77
Uniform, officers', 276
,,   men's, 277
Uniforms in the period about 1865 .. 30
Unyo, the, 26

V

Variag, the, 341, 342
Vickers-Maxim guns, 314, 318
Vladivostok, attack on, 348
Vnushitelni, the, 351
Von Hanneken, 110, 361

W

War with Russia, 340
 ,,   ,,   China, 99, 101, 368, 372
Warships, list of, 394
Wasp, the, 77
Wei-hai-wei, correspondence re surrender, 381
 ,,   proposal to surrender, 385
 ,,   convention of surrender, 389
 ,,   blockade of, 149, 156
Wei Yuen, the, 163

Y

Yakumo, the, 196
Yalu, battle of—Japanese losses, 148
 ,,   ,,   Chinese losses, 148
 ,,   ,,   113
Yamato, the, 58
Yang-wei, the, 53, 139
Yank Wei, the, 115
Yashima, the, 168
Yayeyama, the, 72, 150, 364
Yenomoto, Admiral, 35
Yetajima, Naval College, 258
Yokohama, port of, 249
Yokosuka dockyard, 234
Yoshimo, the, 92, 104, 119, 150, 163

THE END.

PRINTED BY WILLIAM CLOWES AND SONS, LIMITED, LONDON AND BECCLES.